Individuation in Fairy Tales

A C.G. JUNG FOUNDATION BOOK

The C. G. Jung Foundation for Analytical Psychology is dedicated to helping men and women grow in conscious awareness of the psychological realities in themselves and society, find healing and meaning in their lives and greater depth in their relationships, and live in response to their discovered sense of purpose. It welcomes the public to attend its lectures, seminars, films, symposia, and workshops and offers a wide selection of books for sale through its bookstore. The Foundation also publishes *Quadrant,* a semiannual journal, and books on Analytical Psychology and related subjects. For information about Foundation programs or membership, please write to the C. G. Jung Foundation, 28 East 39th Street, New York, NY 10016.

Individuation in Fairy Tales

Revised Edition

Marie-Louise von Franz

Shambhala
Boston & London
1990

Shambhala Publications, Inc.
Horticultural Hall
300 Massachusetts Avenue
Boston, Massachusetts 02115

The text of this book is based on the transcription by
Miss Una Thomas of a series of lectures given by Marie-
Louise von Franz at the C. G. Jung Institute, Zurich,
originally published in 1977. The present edition includes
corrections and additions made by the author.

9 8 7 6 5 4 3 2 1

First Shambhala Edition

Printed in the United States of America on acid-free
paper

Distributed in the United States by Random House
and in Canada by Random house of Canada Ltd.

Library of Congress Cataloging-in-Publication Data
Franz, Marie-Louise von, 1915–
Individuation in fairy tales / Marie-Louise von Franz.
—Rev. ed. p. cm.
"A. C.G. Jung Foundation Book."
Reprint. Originally published: Dallas, Tex.: Spring Publications,
c1977.
ISBN 0-87773-525-5 (alk. paper)
1. Fairy tales—History and criticism.   2. Individuation.
3. Symbolism (Psychology) I. Title.
[GR550.F7 1990]   398.21—dc20   89-43615
CIP

Contents

Preface

This book has originated from a series of lectures given at the C. G. Jung Institute in Zurich. It represents an attempt to bring closer to public understanding what Jung means by the process of individuation. Although it seems to be very difficult for intellectual people to understand it, individuation is a natural, ubiquitous phenomenon which has found innumerable symbolic descriptions in the folk tales of all countries. One can even say that the majority of folk tales deal with one or another aspect of this most meaningful basic life process in man. In order to remain in harmony with the simple storyteller, I have used a direct and colloquial style. The process itself is difficult enough, and one should not further complicate it by sophistication. I have on the contrary tried to bring it "close to home" to all of us, hoping that the reader may be as moved by the stories as I have been.

1

The White Parrot

Individuation is the term with which C. G. Jung describes the psychological process of inner growth and centralization by which the individual finds its own Self. This does not mean to find one's own ego-identity, as is described by many modern psychological schools. By the term *Self,* Jung understands an ultimately unknowable inner center of the total personality and also the totality itself. This center can only be approached but never integrated. Our destiny and our health depend on it. In the various religions and mythologies it is symbolized by the image of the "treasure hard to attain," the mandala and all images of the inner psychic manifestation of the godhead.

In this book, I have chosen to interpret a group of different fairy tales which all circle essentially around the motif of the central treasure represented as a bird or jewel, in order to show the reader some aspects of what is meant by the Self and by the difficult journey we have to undertake in order to find it.

I begin with a Spanish tale called "The White Parrot."[1] Its central motif, a magical white parrot, has been borrowed from the Orient. It is an Iranian tale which in its turn was borrowed in changed form from an Indian one, so you will be able to see not only the interpretation per se, but also how motifs migrate, are changed and built into a new setup. First, we will just naively look at the story, which is not a literary one but was picked up from among the simple people of the Spanish population and was written down in the seventeenth century. It runs as follows.

There was a rich Count who loved a very beautiful but poor
young girl so much that he married her, but afterward, when
he had to go away and take part in a war, he put the Countess,
who was pregnant, under the care of the butler who was to look
after her. But the butler fell in love with her and tried to seduce
her; she refused him, and he was so angry that when she gave
birth to two children he decided to slander her. The twin
children were a boy and a girl and on the forehead of each was a
beautiful star. The butler wrote to the Count saying that he
had thought for a long time that the Countess had had an affair
with a Negro but now it had become quite clear that this was
so because she had given birth to two half-Negro children.

The Count was furious and wrote back saying that the Negro
and the children should be killed and his wife imprisoned. The
butler did not kill the children but put them in a glass box
which he threw into a river, and he imprisoned the Countess.

But it happened that an old man, fishing just then in the
river, saw the glass box and pulled it out in his net and took it
home and found the children wrapped up in a beautiful piece of
silk stuff. He and his wife decided to bring up the children,
but in order to hide the stars on their foreheads they bound
linen bands round them. When the old fisherman and his wife
died, they left all they had to the children.

When the Count returned from the war, without any idea of
what had really happened, the butler felt very uneasy. When he
heard gossip about some marvelous children in the village who
always wore a linen band on their foreheads, he decided that
they should be removed, for he suspected that they might be the
children he wanted killed. He therefore hired a devilish witch,
capable of committing any crime, provided she was well paid,
and ordered her to kill the children. The witch went to see the
little girl when the boy was out and asked her where her
brother was. The girl answered that he had gone out. The
witch then remarked on her wonderful house. The child asked
if she would like to see it and the witch said she would. She
looked all around and said that it was all very beautiful, but that
there was one thing lacking, namely a fountain of silver water,
and if her brother wanted to have that he should just go and
fetch it. He need only go to the spring with a little jug and bring

back some of the silver water, and if he then poured it out in the courtyard they would have the same kind of silver fountain.

The old woman then went away and when the brother returned his little sister told him she wanted this fountain of silver water. The boy said that that was nonsense, and that they did not really need it and that he wouldn't go and fetch it. But the girl cried and worried him about it so much that he finally made up his mind and took a jug and set out to find the silver spring. As he went in the direction indicated by the witch he met an old man who asked him who hated him so much as to send him there? The boy replied that an old woman had told his sister that he should go and fetch the silver water and that was why he had come. The old man agreed that it was true about the silver water, but said that many dangers had to be overcome in fetching the water, for the well was guarded by a lion. Therefore before the boy approached the lion he must watch him very carefully: for when he had his eyes shut the boy must not go near him; but when his eyes were open then he would be asleep, and then the boy could get the water and run away. But he must be very quick because the lion slept very lightly. The boy went, and as the lion had its eyes open just then, he quickly filled his jug with water. When he poured it out in the court-yard a beautiful spray of silver water came up there too and both children were delighted.

The next day the old witch turned up again and asked where the girl's little brother was. The child answered that he was not there, but that the witch should come in and see what a beautiful fountain they had. The old woman came in and bit her lip in a rage when she saw what had happened. She then said that it was all very marvelous but that there was still an oak tree with silver acorns on it, with the cupules of the acorn of gold, and that was what they should have and the girl's little brother must fetch a twig from the oak to be found in such and such a place and plant it in the courtyard and then everything would be perfect.

The same thing happened again and the girl bothered her brother, crying and making scenes so that he said, "Who knows what may happen to me if I go?" but he finally went off to the oak. Again the old man meets him and tells him he is on the road to his own destruction and asks him what he is doing. The boy tells him the whole story and the old man says he should take his horse and ride to the oak; but before alighting from it he should look at the snake which guards the oak and which, when it hides its head, is asleep, so the boy can quickly seize the twig and run away. The boy does this and finds the snake hiding its head, gets a twig and runs away and comes home and plants it in the courtyard, where immediately a beautiful oak tree appears.

When the old witch comes again she bites her lips in a rage, for twice they have escaped, and now she tells the girl that everything is really perfect, except that they should have a beautiful parrot which is quite fantastically valuable and anyone who can catch it will be rich all his life and always be happy and the girl must send her brother to find it. When the brother comes home the girl again starts worrying him, saying that she wants this white parrot. The boy says that her whims will cost him dearly in the end, but she says that this will be the last time. The boy makes her promise this and then he goes off to find the white parrot.

On the way the old man meets him and tells him that if he goes in that direction he will come to a beautiful garden, with a lot of birds on the trees but he must not go near any of them, and that after a while a beautiful white parrot will come and sit on a round stone which will turn on its own axis, and the parrot will say, "Does no one there want to catch me? Is there nobody there who will seize me? If nobody likes me, then they should leave me alone." It will turn around in a circle several times until it is tired and then will put its head under its wing and then it can be taken, but the boy must be very, very careful not to touch it a minute before, but must wait until it has gone sound asleep with its head under its wing. Otherwise, if he takes it a minute too soon, it will look up and then the boy will be petrified. He will find a lot of people there who have already suffered that fate.

The boy goes and finds everything just as the old man had described and a round stone with a circle of petrified people around it. After a while the white parrot appears and is more beautiful than anyone can imagine. It sits on the round stone and asks, "Does no one want to catch me? Is there nobody there who will seize me? If nobody likes me, then they should leave me alone." And then it puts its head under its wing. The boy is terribly afraid of touching it, but is just a bit too eager and is one second too soon and the parrot sees him and flies away and the boy is turned into stone.

When the girl sees that the boy does not return she begins to be afraid that something has happened to him and blames herself, and when the old witch comes the next day she is in tears. But the old woman hides her satisfaction and says she should not worry, that the boy will come back, he has just been delighted with all the beautiful things he has seen in the garden, which is why he has forgotten for a while to return. The best thing the girl can do is to go herself and see what has happened and fetch him back. Perhaps he has forgotten the way. So the old witch persuades the girl who so badly wants to know what has happened to her brother to go and look for him. She takes the same direction as she had seen the boy take and she too meets the old man who asks who hates her enough to send her there. The girl tells him that she is looking for her brother who has been sent to find the white parrot and has never returned. The old man tells her that her brother has been turned into stone because he has not obeyed. She must not be sad, for she can rescue him, but she must do exactly what he says and tells her the same thing that he told her brother, and says that she must now be *really* very careful not to take the parrot too soon, but really wait until it is asleep and then take tight hold of it. She goes and waits until the parrot is asleep and then seizes it, and at that moment all the stone statues begin to come to life again, her little brother and a lot of men among whom was also the father of the children, the Count, for he at some time had tried to get the parrot and had been petrified.

They are all delighted with the little sister who has redeemed them and the children invite them all to a big dinner party at which the brother explains that they do not know who their parents were but that they had been found by a fisherman in a glass case. Then the Count wants to see the piece of silk in which they had been wrapped and when he looks at it he sees that his own coat of arms is embroidered in the silk, and he becomes more and more suspicious that the children may be his and he is very thoughtful and will not eat any more but stares at his plate.

5

Then suddenly the parrot, who always sits on the little girl's shoulder, remarks to the Count that he is very thoughtful and that if he wants to know the truth about the things he is thinking of, he should have his wife fetched from the prison and she will tell him who the children are.

The Count goes home and fetches the Countess out of the prison and hears exactly what happened and she tells him that he can recognize his children by the stars on their foreheads. The Countess recognizes the children as soon as she sees them, takes away the bands from around their foreheads, and shows them to the Count. Then the Count is convinced of the wickedness of the butler and says he is to be killed, but the old witch, who had heard what was happening, escapes before they can get her. Afterward the Count and Countess lived happily with their children and were never separated from the white parrot.

It is always a good idea to count the figures before starting the interpretation of a story. In the beginning of this story, there is a quaternio composed of the Count and the Countess and the two children; but that group is cut apart by the intrigues of the butler, who later associates with the witch. For some reason he has inhibitions and does not kill the children but throws them into the water and afterward hires a witch to kill them. Thus the children are removed and the Countess put in prison. Then the star children, after being thrown into the water, are fished up by the old fisherman and his wife. The situation now is that at the court there are only three people left: the Count, the butler, and the witch in the background, while in the unconscious there is a new quaternio: the star children and the fisherman and his wife. Then the two latter die.

One sees, however, that there is always a tendency to build a four around the two figures of the children, who seem to attract completeness. In the first case, the butler is in the background, but later he hires the witch who is the acting figure and performs the splitting actions. Then comes the white parrot, an absolutely new figure, and it reunites the original quaternio. Thus in the end there are again Count

and Countess and the two star children, but now centered by
the parrot, and it is specially pointed out in the last sentence
of the story that they are never separated from it. That seems
to be the guarantee that this time the quaternio will not be
split again because, as will later be proved by the amplifications on the parrot, it knows everything. So we can be pretty
sure that this last quaternio is a solid group of four people,
because the spirit of truth and all-knowingness, personified
in the parrot, can protect them from now on. The butler is
destroyed, and the witch awaits further opportunities for
making mischief elsewhere but does not intend to do it in
this connection any longer. She was hired, anyhow, which
means that she herself was not really interested in destroying
this family, but only did it for money, while the butler had
an emotional motive for his destructive activity.

So one sees a movement of a complete configuration of four
figures destroyed, restored in the unconscious, destroyed
again, and then restored again in the conscious human area.

We will first look at the story from a rational angle. The tale
is a literary composition, the first part of which is about a
woman who gives birth to the children while her husband is
away and is then slandered by somebody and the husband
writes that she is to be destroyed and thrown into prison, and
so on. The first theme is to be found in innumerable European stories. It comes from medieval legends where saintly
women were slandered in this way. In most medieval parallels, the innocent woman who gives birth to miraculous
children and is then slandered and thrown into prison is
generally persecuted directly by a witch, or some evil female
figure, while here there is this strange complication that first
the butler comes in, who is then replaced by the witch.

The motif of the parrot, who tells the truth and is a kind
of spirit of truth, is not European but has immigrated into
Spain from India and into our story via a Persian collection
which we will discuss later.

The motifs of the silver well and the golden oak come from

alchemical sources and must have come into this story through some alchemical parable, probably one of Bernardus Trevisanus' of the sixteenth century; but that is a guess, and it might be from some other source, since it is a very widespread alchemical motif. Spain is one of the countries into which alchemy was introduced through the Arabs in its earliest stages, as far back as the ninth and tenth centuries. Some of the earliest Arabic treatises on alchemy were translated into Latin in Spain.

In this case, one can more or less find the elements from which the story has been built up. But you will see that if we interpret it as if it were a dream, or a symbolic story, it is entirely coherent and makes complete sense, in spite of being composed of a clutter of different elements. This is something which has always created a great deal of controversy about fairy tales, because literary historians always have the feeling that if they have proved that one part comes from one country and another from somewhere else, that then it is not an original tale but an accumulation of stories without much meaning. However, I hope to be able to show that even a story put together from different known elements is still coherent and conveys a meaning which is specifically compensatory to the conscious attitude in the country in which it is told. So the fact that motifs migrate, and that such a story is like an unconscious product which compensates a specific conscious situation, is ultimately not a contradiction. But it will become clearer if we simply first interpret the story.

The first setup is not at the King's court as so often happens, but in the castle of a count. In fairy tales generally the essential events take place either in the lowest strata of the population, among the poor people, or with soldiers who have deserted, or cripples, or people who have nothing to eat and who are driven by their poverty to take refuge in the woods. Either such people as these are the heroes of the story, or, generally, it is people of royal blood, or barons, or counts, etc., of the upper layer of the population.

The King usually represents the dominant of collective

consciousness. He symbolizes the central content of collective consciousness and, as this element is of vital importance for a cultural setup and for a human group or a nation, naturally it is also constantly exposed to the transforming influence of the collective unconscious.

A rich count would not be quite the same thing because he is not so representative of the dominant attitude but, one could say, is only one of such sets. In general, he would, therefore, represent not so much the central dominant conscious attitude of a group, but rather the model or style of general "good behavior." In a country where there is an aristocratic order of society, the simple people look up to the counts and the like as people who ought to serve as their model of behavior—model figures on which they could pattern themselves. In England the ideal of the gentleman should be kept alive by those who claim to be gentlemen. In Spain there is the Spanish grandee with all his fussy rules of behavior and of honor toward women, and so on, which form a kind of national idea of the nobleman, the model for behavior: Don Quixote, for instance. This Count, therefore, represents such an ideal, but he does something quite unusual; he does not, as is customary, marry for money or to replenish the gold on his arms, he does not marry a rich American, but a poor girl of the country.

The Count thus proves himself capable of following an individual feeling and not only social and conventional considerations. He can follow the dictates of his heart instead of collective rules. That is probably why he is rewarded by having those miraculous star children and that is also probably why, in the final quaternio group, he is not thrown out but is still there with his wife and his two miraculous children, showing that the Count does not need renewal or removal as the old King, there is nothing wrong about him, in contrast to the many fairy tales where the old King at the end of the story is removed or deposed and replaced by the son. Here the central setup is all right and is therefore not changed, which is probably due to the fact that this Count has a right and normal human and feeling relationship to the feminine principle.

It is an outside war which separates the Count from his family and brings in the butler. But here we must put a question mark, for something must be wrong in this first complete family setup, because this Count must at least not have a very good human instinct to have such a butler and to entrust his wife and everything else to him while he himself is away. He must have been lacking in some human judgment and in general, psychologically, we know that it is the people who do not know enough about their own shadow and their own dark side who are most likely to fall victims to evil influences.

If one knows about all the evil possibilities within oneself then one develops a kind of second sight or capacity for getting a whiff of the same thing in other people. A jealous woman who has realized her own jealousy will always recognize jealousy in the eyes of another woman. The only way, therefore, not to walk through the world like an innocent well-brought-up fool, protected by father and mother from the evils of this world and therefore cheated and lied to and stolen from at every corner, is to go down into the depths of one's own evil, which enables one usually to develop the instinctual recognition of corresponding elements in other people.

Thus, whatever we could say about this perfect Count at the beginning, he certainly is an innocent fool, first because he has such a butler and second, because when the butler writes him slandering his wife, he believes him at once. He does not even think of first writing to his wife telling her that he has heard horrible things about her and what has she to say about it, but right away walks into the trap. So there you can say that he seems to be a noble gentleman, a model figure of social and cultural human behavior, which would be all right, except for an amazing lack of instinctive awareness of the true situation. One can see, therefore, why at the end of the story he is safe through the fact that he now has a parrot which has all the knowledge he lacks. So if you look at what happens you see that everything is all right, except that people are out of contact with reality and do not know about things and what is going on. They are fools estranged from the world and in the end they have a demonic and a rather dubious wicked creature, for this parrot is not as beautifully white as his feather garment indicates, but from now on it will save them trouble. Its integration is essential, and the whole story moves toward this goal.

Christ, as you know, admonished his disciples to be as wise as serpents, and that is something which is generally forgotten: as the English say, the rain it raineth every day, upon the just and unjust fellow, but mainly on the just, because the unjust takes the just's umbrella!

If you think of the Spanish civilization and of the fact that Spain is the place which gave birth to Don Quixote and the famous story about him, then you will realize that this problem of the perfect, innocent cavalier who is not up to the problems of reality is really a Spanish problem, or at least a problem of the Spanish aristocracy.

The butler is perhaps not quite as devilish or bad as he at first appears because he simply falls in love with the lonely and very beautiful Countess, which is only human, all too human. But his passion carries him away and all his evil deeds afterward result from this first wrong step which he takes when he falls in love and tries to seduce the Countess, and are all born out of his rage because she refused him. He is not directly a murderer, as we shall see later on. He does not dare kill the children himself. He seems to be slowly drawn into his evil deeds. First he is carried away by erotic passion and then has to cover that up and so, more and more, gets into the dark side. He has a passionate nature which leads to all kinds of difficulties. This too, we know, is a problem in the more southern Latin countries of Europe, where erotic passion is very strong and can sweep away a man's conscious ideals of behavior very easily. The uninte-grated shadow of sexual passion in the men in the ruling position is what opens the door to the dark influence of the dark side of the mother archetype.

We know that in all the southern Latin European countries the archetype of the Great Mother is even much more alive today than in our realm and plays a great role in the background of the culture and unconscious of modern people of these countries. They are still more under her dominion, for she was the dominant archetype of Mediterranean civilization for long before Christianity. In civilizations with a more matriarchal tinge, the animal impulsiveness of men is indulged in and cultivated more than in patriarchal societies.

In most patriarchal societies, which are generally also those which have an ideal of loyalty and of a spiritual goal, there are usually initiations and rules which tend to domesticate and overcome the animal and sex impulsiveness of man with military self-discipline, because these impulses offset every spiritual order and military organization and all those institutions conceived by the male Logos. In civilizations where the feminine element is more dominant, the military self-discipline ideal is generally less dominant, and therefore there is less suppression of this side. But it becomes a problem in another way, because it creates the kind of trouble which we have in this story and which, for instance, shows why Spaniards are the last people in Europe who still need bullfights to express symbolically the overcoming of sexual impulsiveness by self-discipline.

As C. G. Jung once explained, we in northern Europe no longer need bullfights. If anything, our men should revive the bulls and feed them very thoroughly on good grassy meadows and be very kind to them, because we live, as Jung once mockingly said, in the age of easy chairs, when men are even too lazy to play a guitar beneath a girl's window! But in Spain bullfighting has not been abolished and the great symbolic achievement in the art of self-discipline which the toreador needs in order to be able to accomplish his task of overcoming the bull still seems to be meaningful. In the south of France, the bulls are no longer killed, though they still have bullfights. In Spain the practice seems to be becoming wobbly; it is not quite definite whether they intend to continue with it or not. A situation seems to have been reached where it no longer has any symbolic meaning, and then all the other criticisms that it is a nasty bloody affair and so on prevail against the enthusiasm for the symbolic actions which hitherto seem to have carried people away.

Here in this story we see how alive this problem still is in Spain, for this butler falls in love at once with the Countess and then is carried away into all sorts of evil deeds because she has not accepted him. Typically enough, he brings in the beautiful shadow projection, namely that the Countess has had an affair with a Negro and has given birth to partly colored children, the Negro being the usual symbol onto whom one projects the black side in oneself. The butler invents a Negro who has never existed to throw all the guilt upon him. Finding a shadow figure represented by a Negro is typical for Spanish fairy tales because of the strong invasion of Arabic and Moorish civilizations in the Middle Ages, and it happened to the Spaniards, as has happened to other white societies, that they projected all their primitive and dark shadow side onto these "Negroes."

The Count, in his innocence, or let's rather call it right away his stupidity, believes the butler and orders him to kill the Negro and children and to imprison his wife. The butler does not dare to kill the children, but puts them into a glass case and throws them into a river. Beginning with the stories of Sargon, Moses, and Ramses III, this myth of the miraculous child who is not killed but thrown in a glass or wooden case into the river has been retold in innumerable stories all over the world. Think of the Perseus myth, for instance, and of innumerable fairy tales, for example "The Three Golden Hairs of the Devil" in the Grimm fairy tales. A very thorough collection of the motif can be found in Joseph Campbell's book *The Hero with a Thousand Faces,*[2] where you will find many parallels to this story. The children are sometimes thrown in a basket or in a glass case or in a coffin, or just into the water. They are exposed to the elements.

Psychologically, it is interesting to see how those people who intend to remove the children act in a strange—we would say neurotic—double way: they intend to destory the children, but at the same time do something to save them. Their left hand does not know what their right hand does and acts a bit better than the right hand intends. It is as though they just could not quite make up their minds to destroy the child whom they really want removed.

Killing corresponds psychologically to total repression. Very often in dreams people dream of killing a person or an animal; or there are those terrible dream motifs, which I think practically all people have dreamed at some time, that something dead comes alive, or a corpse suddenly opens its eyes or moves, and so on. One can assume that this content, characterized as being dead, has been as much out of the conscious area of this personality and field of awareness as a dead person is from this life. One could call it completely repressed, in the sense that it can no longer manifest itself even indirectly through neurotic symptoms or anything in the area of consciousness. All civilizations, as you know, dread *revenants*, the coming back of the dead, of ghosts; and so the *revenants* are a most widespread psychological motif, and these totally repressed factors sometimes come back from their tombs and bother people again.

The butler does not succeed in accomplishing his plan. He puts the children in a glass case—but there is still another strange thing: why not put them into a wooden box, which would be cheaper and easier to get hold of? And there would be much less danger of the children being fished out again. But, naturally, if he puts them in a glass case, so that anybody can see from a distance of twenty yards that there are children in it, he really invites someone to fish the thing out of the water again. So there is again this strange kind of double action: he wants to kill the children and does not quite want to do so. He puts them into a glass case so that one can see what is there. You see that he is not totally evil, for with his left hand he plays against himself.

A glass case is a typical fairy-tale motif. You know of one famous one, namely where Snow White lies in a glass coffin and the dwarfs take her away in it. So we have to ask why a *glass* case, especially as we may guess that this story probably originated in about the fifteenth or sixteenth century, when glass was still very rare and valuable.

In some alchemical writings, glass was compared to a miraculous substance. It was "immaterial" because you could see through it as if it were not matter, and like crystal, it was a symbol of "spiritual matter." But glass has also the great advantage that it can insulate, and keep warmth inside a room. Thus alchemists and chemists ascribed the most miraculous qualities to glass, and it still is one of the best insulating materials there is, which is why it is so useful to us. But glass cuts you off, as far as your animal activity is concerned; it separates you from something which you cannot take hold of to give you warmth, you cannot contact through it, in the original sense of *tangere,* but you can see through it. Mentally you are not cut off. You can look at everything through glass practically undisturbed, for you can see as well as though it were not there.

So glass is a material which does not cut one off intellectually from other things, but it cuts off the animal contact. That is why it is often used by people as a simile when they feel cut off emotionally from their surroundings. People very often say, "It feels as if there were a glass wall between him and me," or "between me and my surroundings." That means: "I see perfectly well what is going on, I can talk to people, but the animal and feeling contact, the warmth contact is cut off by a glass wall"—which is why one hears often of people who walk about as though they had a glass wall around them: you cannot get near them. You can have an intellectual discussion with them, but you cannot imagine having a really warm contact with them, for the glass wall comes up.

Here these children are put in this situation of being insulated against contact with the human area and thrown into the water. To be thrown into the water is like being handed over to Fate—one might be carried away anywhere, carried away and destroyed, or carried away and rescued; one is confided to the flow of life. Here again is the strange attitude of the butler, for he could have *buried* them in the glass case! But like Pilate, he washes his hands of the whole thing! He says, "All right, I will throw them into the water and then I have no more responsibility as to what happens to them." Naturally the stream of life supports the childen and brings them into the right hands which rescue them.

We have so far interpreted this story without discussing what the children mean. It is easier to understand what a figure means when one can see more about its role within the story. Now the very fact that these children are thrown into the water in a glass case puts them into a parallel with all the many mythological and religious heroes of the different civilizations. Though in the first part of the story they do not achieve many heroic deeds, we can assume that they must represent something parallel to the heroes of other myths who are generally also <u>born in a marvelous way</u> and are then <u>exposed in a similar manner</u>.

Also, both children bear a star on their foreheads, another typical sign of the hero. Most, or many, mythological heroes have specific marks from their birth which show that they will be the carriers of a specific and unusual fate. Some have a moon on their foreheads, or a hidden mark somewhere on their bodies, or they even have a disfiguration, as for instance Oedipus, or they may have a slight fault which marks them as an unusual figure. If we stay with the motif of the star, we can say that it always points to a very special or chosen individual fate. For instance, the Swiss saint Niklaus von der Flüe, when he was still in his mother's womb, according to the legend, saw a star and in later life he always spoke of this, saying that he knew therefore that he should bring some

16

Ba soul

light into the darkness of his age. He understood this vision quite well.

In Egypt, the king, and in later times also ordinary people, had different souls. One was the *Ka* soul, which is more the inherited vitality, sexual potency, and intelligence. The other, the *Ba* soul, is the immortal part, the preconscious individuality and also what survives after death. The *Ba* is represented in hieroglyphs either by the sign of a bird or as a star. So the star here again represents the immortal and specific individual nucleus of the personality. As Helmuth Jacobsohn points out in his comment on the discussion of "The World-Weary Man with his *Ba*,"[3] the *Ba* soul is not quite identical with what we would now call the Self, because it also contains many elements which we would attribute to the conscious personality. This is due to the fact that, if we go four thousand years back (which we need to do to understand this writing), we see that many things which nowadays we attribute to the ego personality and our ego consciousness were at that time still part of what we now call the Self.

In Roman times, every male Roman had a *genius* and every female Roman a *juno,* a kind of protective demon. A *genius* was represented as a brilliant youth, with a horn of plenty filled with fruit, and dancing, and every Roman on his birthday sacrificed to his *genius* for his own welfare. The *genius* was what made you feel well and healthy and able to stand a lot of drinking without getting drunk. It made you potent as a man and vital altogether, but it also gave you brilliant and good ideas. If, for instance, you were in a fix and suddenly had an idea how to get out of it you would not be conceited, as we are, congratulating ourselves on being such bright people, but would thank your *genius* for putting that seed of a good idea into your head. In later times the *genius* was also called a man's "star."

There one can see that in Roman times much of what we now tend to look upon as part of the conscious personality was still attributed to the unconscious nucleus. Our ego has evolved more and more and has assimilated many elements which in former times human beings still felt to be an autonomous part of their unconscious personality. We therefore always have to be very careful not to apply such terms as *Ego* and *the Self,* etc., inconsiderately and without reflection onto historically old material. We must always remember that the situation then was completely different. We cannot simply apply our concepts to those times, but only *cum grano salis* and with certain restrictions and additions. Therefore you can say that the star, or the *Ba* soul, which is represented by a star in Egypt, represents what we call the Self and also a part of what we would now call the conscious individuality of a person.

In the Middle Ages the symbol of the star represented outstanding personalities. Christ, for instance, was called the Morning Star more often even than the Sun, but also higher ecclesiastical personalities were called stars which surround the Sun (Christ). In many texts stars are interpreted in this way, showing that the old Egyptian idea of the outstanding and leading personality still survived in the new cultural form. As is known, the Roman emperors were transformed into stars when they died, and when an emperor was dying all the Roman astronomers searched the heavens for the new star which would represent the star soul of the Emperor who had appeared now in this or that constellation at the moment when he left the earth.

The star has still another strange quality. In astrology, the constellations of the stars (not a single star but the constellations) were used to define the essence of a personality. A horoscope is a setup of stars in a specific position, and that was thought of as expressing the essence of an individual personality and was read in this way.

This way of thinking is to be found also in China, where the moment in time and the place, or the point in the space-time continuum where a human being appears on earth, was looked upon as being simultaneously the expression of the individual essence of that personality. There was a famous Chinese sage about whose birth there were two legends. This

18

hero was born into a certain famous family and all the diviners were assembled to find out which ancestor was reborn in him. According to the one story, one diviner named an ancestor, and as everybody knew this to be right, it was prescribed that he should wear the number 8, that hares and not chickens should always be sacrificed to him, etc. There was a whole etiquette connected with this special number. According to another, completely parallel story, the diviner does not find the number and name but finds the exact site in the space-time continuum where the individual was born, and that expresses his being as well. The whole etiquette of his birth, his name, and everything else depends on that. Thus in Chinese thought the moment where a human being enters the world is symbolic of its essence.

Jung tried to illustrate this by saying that if we really are wine connoisseurs, then we can taste the wine and say, "1952, from the north—or south—slope of such and such a place." But not only wine carries the quality of the time and place where it came into existence; we too, so to speak, carry something of that in us which partly expresses our being, and because the stars were looked on as the indicators of time and space configurations, they are also the indicators of the individual essence of a human being. One cannot separate this idea of the special human being who is announced by a star, or marked by one, from the astrological thought which naturally prevailed in those former times. The Star of Bethlehem fits in here also.

These two children in our story are thus marked as something supernatural. In his paper on the "Divine Child,"[4] Jung has shown that the mythological child motif is a symbol of the Self, i.e., one of the many images which illustrate the mystical, divine core of the human being. But here it is important to stress the specific nature of a symbol of the Self because, as you know, a golden ball, a star, a crystal, a tree, and a round object are all also symbols of the Self. Therefore it always seems to me to be essential to ask: what does it mean when the Self is represented as a child, in contrast, for instance, to an inanimate object, or a helpful animal, or anything else? Why just a child? Why is that particular symbol chosen by the unconscious?

In the symbol of the child is implied the element of youthfulness. A whole future is ahead, there is a new start in life, something which has still the plenitude of a beginning situation with all its rich inexhaustible possibilities. The child generally still possesses that spirit of truthfulness which we tend to lose through the influence of education. It still says: "Granny, you are old, when are you going to die?" and such uninhibited things, and it therefore also expresses absolute spontaneity and genuineness of the personality, which accounts for the proverb that children and fools speak the truth. They are still simply themselves, completely genuine, at least when quite young, and therefore within an adult the symbol of the child hints at that mysterious capacity of which one is sometimes aware and where one never knows whether one is right or wrong.

You know how sometimes you are in a situation where everything is awkward and suddenly something pops out of your mouth, or wants to do so, and you do not know whether you are now an *enfant terrible,* or your shadow wants to mess up the situation, or whether you must at all costs swallow the idea, or you must say the thing! Then you can only take the risk and speak, and perhaps that saves the situation and everything falls into place. It was the redeeming thing! Quivering with fear you discover that you have said the redeeming word! You can only say that it was not your idea but that something just popped out of you, you suddenly felt like saying that, you didn't know why. But then there is the terrible thing, namely that the symbol of the child does represent not only this capacity of the Self for hitting the nail on the head, for the naive truth which puts everything right, but it can just as well be an infantile shadow—and you never know whether it is your infantile shadow, or wanting to behave like an *enfant terrible,* or whether the Self wants you to say a genuine word and to bring truth out of you. That is the awkward spot you always get into when the symbol, or the archetype, of the child wells up in you and wants to interfere with the situation.

There is a famous Zen koan about a Zen Buddhist monastery where the monks quarrelled about the possession of a cat. There were two groups of monks, say the kitchen monks versus the others, and both sides wanted to claim possession of the cat. They got quite out of themselves, and instead of thinking of their meditation and finding the "Buddha Mind," they all quarrelled about the cat. So the Abbot thought that must stop and assembled all the monks. He took the cat and a sword and said that somebody should say or do something to save the cat, or else he would kill it. Nobody did anything, so he simply killed the animal, and in this way removed the disturbing complex. Later, his favorite pupil, who had been to the village to buy something, came back, and the Abbot asked him what he would have done. This pupil took off his sandals and put them on his head, and the Abbot exclaimed: "You would have saved the cat!"

That is only one of the many, many Buddhist koans which you can read, and as always the object is to express this action of the child Self. It is genuine spontaneity, the ability to do the right thing. In a Western way, if you think about it symbolically, its meaning is very simple. Shoes represent the standpoint: you must simply reverse your standpoint and then the cat does not matter any longer and is no longer a problem, for you give up your ego claim. If all those monks had given up their ego claim the cat would not have mattered any more. It was only in the "illusion mind" of their ego that possession of this cat really existed, so it needed only reversal of the standpoint and the cat would have been saved. But this pupil does not express this in words, but by the most immediate and genuine gesture which the Abbot at once understood.

That is the child, the absolutely spontaneous capacity in one to save a situation. For example: in a discussion you see things going wrong and feel that something could be done if only you could get hold of the right idea; but the more you concentrate on it with your ego the more you block it out! Generally if you want to be the one to say the right word and do the right thing you are lost. But if, by the grace of God, you are in Tao, or in the right position, then the child in you will say or do the right thing.

In a recent book,[5] Laurens van der Post describes a situation in which he had been in a Japanese concentration camp. There was a terrific conflict going on and they foresaw a lot of terrible executions. Suddenly one of the prisoners beside van der Post, a man who had been tortured before and was very sick, said to him, with his eyes shining, that he was going to do the saving thing. The others had no idea what he meant to do, and in the worst moment he suddenly walked out of the row of prisoners lined up in the courtyard, marched up to the governor of the camp—which was such an impertinence that everyone was too amazed to stop him—and kissed him! Seen from a Japanese point of view, that was such a dastardly insult, and such a shocking thing seen from a Western angle, that everyone was shocked out of their wits. The whole discussion was dropped, the prisoners went back to their cells, and the Japanese officers returned to their place. The man paid for it with his life but he had saved the whole situation, and the Japanese officer later saved a lock of the man's hair to offer it to the shrine of his own ancestors at home, showing the deep respect he felt for someone who had had the genius to do such a foolish, or childish, or crazy but saving thing in a crucial moment.

That was such an inspiration of the divine child. It was something you could never have figured out. If you had made up your mind to do something foolish to change the axis, or pivot, of the human situation, you could never have thought of such a thing. But in an *abaissement du niveau mental,* where the man was already very sick, he became inspired by the unconscious and got that idea, which he meant as a gesture of love, as a gesture of reconciliation. It didn't work that way, but in spite of not being understood it worked right, and saved the lives of a number of people.

That is why there are so many myths where the divine child walks among tigers and lions. Tigers and lions are negative, destructive emotions. Generally, when destructive human situations come up, it is because destructive emotion is piled up, and then nobody can move out of them. But then there is the myth of the child who puts his hand on the lion, or strokes a snake. That is because something is not caught in the negative emotion. Something is still genuine and spontaneous, and therefore can act in a saving way. There are again and again human situations where only such an act can save one. We all have that in us, and we sometimes know that if only that thing would come up, we would be safe, or would again find the right way; and that is why the child is a symbol of the Self. But in dream interpretation the problem always is that the child is just as often a symbol of the infantile shadow, and that is something which should sometimes even be sacrificially slaughtered, or should be very severely disciplined.

In our story we have no doubts, because through those star marks the children are clearly characterized as an aspect of the Self and not of the infantile part of the personality or something childish. Therefore we can here take them as this kernel of spontaneity, the kernel of being alive, of being genuine and having the saving, right ideas. This is what the child represents here, and, naturally, also the renewal of life.

In this story the children are a brother and a sister. The divine child in elaborate mythology and in alchemical writings is sometimes characterized as a hermaphrodite. But that would never come in a fairy tale, where such "perverse" figures do not appear. Instead of a hermaphrodite as a symbol to characterize the union of all opposites, including the opposites of male and female, in myths and fairy tales there is very often a couple, a little brother and a sister, who together form the hermaphroditic totality of the Self. They represent wholeness in its male-female aspect. In spite of this, we cannot simply take them as the male-female, double aspect of one thing, because in a later phase of our story they are split, and actually at the end the little sister, under the influence of the witch, acts very destructively against the brother. She chases him three times into death, but then rescues him, because the fourth time she goes herself and seizes the parrot, so she first nearly kills her brother and then saves his life. She therefore has a very ambiguous relationship to the male figure, who just heroically does what he is told to do but then is a bit stupid, probably like his father, and therefore makes a mistake. The girl is cleverer, but also closer to evil because she listens to the insinuations of the witch.

We must therefore look at this pair of children in a more differentiated way and say that, taken as a whole, they are the symbol of the renewal of life, a new personality, but that the female side seems closer to darkness and to the principle of evil which is a bit too much rejected in the ruling attitude. In the Count's house we know that evil is not taken seriously enough, and in the girl is an element capable of contacting the dark side, and even of rescuing the whole situation in the end. If it had not been for the little sister our story would have gone completely wrong. We might see in this a general feature of Christian mythology, where from the beginning, with Eve and the snake in Paradise, it was thought that the feminine element was closer to the dark side of life, closer to evil, and more open to evil inspirations.

At least since the spread of the myth of the Virgin Mary, however, the feminine is also called the rescuing symbol. Thus, in many hymns about the Virgin Mary it is said that she put right what her sister Eve did wrong, or, for instance, that Eve brought death and sin into the world while Mary rescued us from death and sin by giving birth to the Savior. Therefore, at least in our civilization, the feminine element is in one way closer to the dark side and evil in general, but is looked on as being sometimes also the redeeming thing. For instance, the Virgin Mary is responsible for the fact that God became man, so if you think that this is a deterioration—

it is not so thought of, but you could think of it in that way—
then you can say that just because she pulled God down into
the human realms she brought salvation. So the feminine
element is, for better or for worse, looked on as being closer
to darkness, closer to the human element, closer to the less
spiritual, less absolute.

In the Middle Ages the Virgin Mary was looked on as
being specially friendly to sinners, taking them under her big
cloak. When God is a bit too severe and wants to condemn
them, she just puts her cloak over them and says "Oh well,
they are just my children." She protects them in this way
from the evil revengeful side of God. Mary is human, so she
can understand a bit better if we misbehave. She is not so far
away and can look at things from a more relative standpoint,
and that is why she puts in a good word for us. She says to
God, "Well, you cannot be strict with those anthropoids
down there on earth!" That is the typical idea of the feminine
element as reconciling the divine with the human, and the
spiritual with the earthly, good and evil.

Women like to think more in exceptions, they do not
believe in absolute rules. If they make a rule or believe in
rules, then it is the animus. In themselves they always feel
that what they think is right, and never mind whether there
is a rule about it or not. That is the more natural tendency.
The following story by Anatole France characterizes this
feminine nature.[6] There was once a very short-sighted saint
who went to an island where he wished to convert the people,
and, to his great delight, they all streamed down to the shore
in their best clothes—cutaways and white shirts—and he
thought they were really eager to be baptized. But he was a
bit shy and would not go near them, so from his boat and at
a safe distance—he had probably forgotten his spectacles—
he baptized the whole lot of them, but, unfortunately, they
were penguins! So in Heaven there was a terrible row because
everybody who has received baptism has an immortal soul
and must therefore be admitted into Heaven, and now they
had, according to their own male rules, to admit the pen-

guins! But that was of course against another rule, for animals were not allowed on an equal level in Heaven, so what could be done? They called in all the specialists on canonical law and all the saints and God the Father and everybody else, and they discussed the question for hours with all its pros and cons, but could not find a solution. God finally had an idea and said they could ask Saint Catherine of Siena. When she was told the whole story she just shook her head and said, *"Mais c'est bien simple, donnez-leur une âme, mais une petite!"* "That's very simple, give them a soul, but just a small one!" That is the feminine way of thinking and how one solves impossible problems!

By counting the figures in the beginning, we saw that a quaternio broke up, re-formed, and finally was consolidated in the end. The action of the tale has also a fourfold rhythm. We can set up four "stations" to show a space pattern, as well as a time pattern. In the first "station," there is the lion where the water of life can be fetched for the well which afterward is in the courtyard. Then, in the second "station," there is the snake under the tree, with the silver and gold acorns. Then there is the parrot, which is in both the third and fourth "stations" because it brought first destruction to the boy and then life and solution for the girl; so it has a double function and acts twice as a "station" on the way. The children go twice, first the boy goes and gets destroyed and then the girl goes and puts everything right. From then on the witch disappears and the leading factor, or what carries on the action, is the parrot, for it tells the Count to take his wife out of prison and try to find out what is the matter with the children; it is now the leader which whispers guidance into people's ears, with the result that the original quaternio is restored (Count, Countess, and the two children). This time it is centered and led by the parrot for the last sentence of our fairy tale, which points to the real result of the story: they were never again separated from the parrot. This time the quaternio is safe and cannot easily be split apart like the first one because the parrot, which is a kind of spirit of truth, will now look after them.

In this pattern there is first the human quaternio which is split apart by the butler; then again a human quaternio (the fisherman and his wife and the two children) is split apart by death and the butler, through the witch. The third is a nature quaternio, with the lion, the snake, and the parrot in its double function. In this there are no human beings, it is a natural mandala and that has a lot to do with alchemical symbolism. So it could be said that the two human quaternios are pushed downward until they meet the nature mandala, the inhuman one, and then they are restored, but with a bit of nature, an animal spirit in it. Before they only had the evil shadow spirit of the butler to guide them, but now they are guided by the white parrot.

Then the children are thrown in the water and live with the fisher folk, which would not be in the limelight of collective consciousness, for there they are in a lower layer of the population, in the dark, so to speak, and close to nature. That phase is completely hidden, it is the hidden mystery which nobody knows about and it needs a dangerous journey to get there, and then they return into the limelight of collective consciousness, but bringing with them this new element in the form of the parrot.

That is the structural rhythm of the story. If you draw it you can practically see the meaning. It seems as if the model of perfect behavior was too much estranged from nature and this whole series of events leads to a relative and partial integration of nature. I say relative and partial, and you have to take that for the moment without knowing why, because later on I go to the Iranian or Persian model story in which you will see that things go much deeper, and there integration is much more complete. This is only a kind of surface scratching, they do not get quite down to the depths and they therefore do not bring up the whole thing, they only bring up a part.

There is always a kind of spirit of action which carries the story on. In the first quaternio it is represented by the shadow, an evil man; in the second, by the witch, and then in the last steps, it is the parrot, so there is a kind of transformation of the guiding factor. Then comes the witch with the counteraction of the wise old man. You could say that at first the guiding factor is completely evil, and then there is one which counteracts itself, a negative with a positive factor. The one says go and do this, in order that the children may be destroyed and the other says what to do in order that they might be saved. The libido which pushes the action slowly assumes another character: first it is seemingly purely negative, then ambivalent, and then positive. So there is a very subtle structure in our seemingly naive story.

The end result is relatively static because the parrot is very, very clever and is the spirit of truth; one has the feeling that if another butler comes and tries to put through some mischief the parrot will prevent it at once. So one feels that the last group of four people is safer, for now they have a kind of spirit of life experience and wisdom with them which probably will protect them to a certain extent.

Actually, if one looks at fairy tales more closely, no fairy-tale end is a solution forever. It is only as if a positive solution is reached *for the moment,* but one has the feeling that if life were to go on, trouble might start again. It is like an eternal melody, it ends on a suspended note, and you wait for the next melody to begin. This is what led Oriental storytellers to tell a long string of such stories in a series one after the other, and that is because it is purely in the unconscious; it is not completely realized. To quote Goethe: "*Gestaltung, Umgestaltung, des ew'gen Sinnes ewige Untcrhaltung,*" "transformation and again transformation, the eternal entertainment of the eternal spirit."

One could say that a static structure would only be found in a human being who integrates it, but here there is only its archetypal model; it is only a *relatively* static structure compared to a completely unstable one. But the feeling that this quaternity might still fall apart is right, for another story might begin! It might begin, for instance, that there was a Count and a Countess and two children and they had a beloved parrot and the Count was afraid that the parrot would be stolen so he put it in a golden cage and put the key under his wife's pillow, but then an evil man of the woods comes and steals the parrot, and then the hero comes, etc. So if you are an Oriental storyteller you can easily hang on a new rhythm.

That, in a way, is what fairy tales are. In our countries there are only partial combinations of chains; for instance, stories in which the hero seizes a fish, or a mermaid, or a bird-girl, and by robbing her of her animal skin forces her to marry him. Then, after a while, she finds the skin again or he makes a mistake by ill-treating her or beating her, or he calls her a fish, the one thing he should not have done, and she disappears again. Many stories end like that, and there are some which simply from there hang on the story of a quest, or the husband who made a mistake is left alone and dies of melancholy, or kills himself, or remains queer for the rest of his life, and wanders eight years to the end of the world and then he finds his wife again.

There may actually be two stories in which the quest type and the mermaid or bird-bride type of story have been put together. So we also have such formations, but they are not as long as the Indian and other Oriental formations. But the tendency always just to spin on a yarn from where it left off comes out in our type of story too, because in a way the deeper layers of the unconscious are a kind of everlasting wave movement which goes on underneath. The storyteller gets caught, as it were, in that rhythm and tends to do the same thing.

In the Orient, the storyteller generally goes on telling all day long and people come and listen for a while and then leave some money and go. But there are lazy people who sit through the whole day, so he can make an everlasting story, just adding on another bit, and with that he really follows a certain rhythm of life. We assume that probably that kind of movement of the unconscious pattern of dreams probably goes on in the daytime. We do not dream only in the night but probably even during the day have a kind of subterranean dream process, though we are not aware of it. We assume that this is so because sometimes in the daytime people make a mistake when talking and mention someone they knew twenty years ago and have forgotten, and they say, "How funny that I should mention Aunt So-and-So," and then that same night they dream about the aunt. So it looks as though this aunt was already constellated in the daytime dream for they had made that mistake when talking, but the dream could not come up, except in such a *lapsus linguae,* until the night. There are also people who can just look inside and observe their "dreams" in daytime. Very intuitive people can bring up a hypnagogic condition any time they like and just look inside and see what is going on in the unconscious, but many people cannot do that.

In the interpretation of what the two star-marked children mean, we saw that it was the girl who brings the solution. In this dangerous stage of the story, the boy succumbs to the witch's trick and the girl saves the situation—she seizes the parrot and brings it in again. So we cannot take the children only as the symbol of the Self, as a hermaphroditic symbol and union of the opposites; there is a slight accent showing that the feminine element is more positive, or at least more up to the situation, than the masculine element. If we see now from the general structure that the problem is to bring in the spirit of nature, this is in tune with the old idea that the feminine element is closer to the nature spirit and therefore acts here as a saving factor. That is why the story by Anatole France is important, because it shows that the feminine mind is capable of thinking in exceptions; it is less caught in its own red tape and its own rules and therefore in a way is closer to nature. Jung always pointed out that in the mind of women there is what he called the natural mind, a kind of recklessness but also a matter-of-factness which the mind of men lacks, and which, if it is integrated, can sometimes be of great use. I know, for instance, that once a man who had been in analysis with Jung for a long time said, "I feel more or less all right, not much is happening, but somehow I feel as though something is not quite right with me; but I can't put my finger on it." Jung said, "I do not know either, but go to a woman and ask her, women generally see such things which we men do not."

In this story the male element, the butler, first brings destruction, but later, when the destructive element becomes feminine, the girl listens and she brings it in and out. She acts like Eve and Mary in one. In the Middle Ages, Eve was known as the woman who brought in death, and Mary as the woman who redeemed us from death. The girl acts as both in one figure, bringing in the destruction and then leading out of it again. The result in this story is the integration of this supernatural wise parrot.

One could therefore say that the children represent a symbol of the Self in its *statu nascendi*, being constellated and activated only in the unconscious, not yet in any way integrated or realized in consciousness. There is a slight accent on the feminine aspect as the more active and the more important of the two. The little boy and his sister as the double hero of a story occur frequently: for instance, the little brother and sister in "Hansel and Gretel," where again it is first Hansel who has a certain positive function.[7] When the parents push them out into the woods, he takes the pebbles and drops them on the path and they find their way home. But later Hansel is the stupid one and gets caught by the witch, and would have been eaten by her if Gretel hadn't had the good idea of pushing her into the stove and so redeeming herself and her brother. So there too the accent is on the girl and the witch-like, rather evil, mind of Gretel. The way she behaves with the witch is not very elegant, but it is quite appropriate and it saves the situation.

Here there is a similar constellation, which we must understand in a compensatory way. Probably here in the dominating conscious attitude there is too much accent on masculine values, and therefore compensatory feminine values are stressed; the natural mind of women and their seeming wickedness—or, let's say, their irrational approach—is represented as the important factor.

In general, if a symbol appears in a double form it means that what it symbolizes is approaching the threshold of consciousness. In number symbolism the number 2 is always described as the different one, or the otherness. From the series of natural numbers that follow 1, you can say, retrospectively, that 2 is a number but not really a number yet. There is a quarrel about this, for the Chinese say that 2 is not a number while the Pythagoreans say that it is *not yet quite* a number, but the beginning of one. Most number symbolism systems only let the symbolic numbers begin with three, because with 2 you have only the difference or the otherness to the one, where there is one thing and against it another thing, *to heteron* or *thateron* in Platonic language, and therefore two stands for "otherness." One can say that it is the absolute *conditio sine qua non* of discriminating consciousness to be able to state oneness and otherness. If I cannot distinguish between one object and another or between an object and a subject, but am still in a total feeling of oneness, then I am in a relatively unconscious state; I am in the all-encompassing oneness of life but I am not conscious.[8]

Consciousness cannot be separated from the capacity for discrimination; discrimination means to see and be able to state the difference between things. If a content is completely in the unconscious, then it probably is even its own opposite, it is everything. Let us assume, for instance, that you have a vague, disagreeable feeling that something is stirring in your unconscious. You have not dreamt or fantasied about anything yet, you just feel that your energy is piling up a bit. You can only state that this is the unconscious which is stirring, or chasing you, but you cannot yet say what it is. As soon as it appears as a dream image, or as an unconscious impulse, or as a *tic nerveux,* or whatever you like (for it can come up in a thousand forms), then you can say that this is that and can separate it, at least relatively, from the rest of your unconscious psyche. You state its otherness, its differ-ence, from the whole vague thing which we call the uncon-scious psyche. This is probably why contents, when they are completely unconscious, are, so to speak, contaminated with the whole of the unconscious—only when they have a certain intensity do they become differentiated, approach the thresh-old, and become other than the rest of the unconscious. When we talk about the unconscious we use a concept which characterizes it as a kind of complete continuum, like a magnetic field in physics. William James already compared the unconscious to a "field." Then a content comes up and the moment it touches the threshold of consciousness it is cut into two parts, into a one and the other. The one is the aspect which I can state, while the other remains in the unconscious, and that is why, generally, when you have dream images of a complete double, you dream about a person doubled, or of two dogs, two cats, two trees or two similar houses, and so on. So we can only conclude that now something is approaching the threshold of consciousness, is beginning to fall apart into that which will be grasped by consciousness while the other will fade away into the layer below. The next stage will be that the second content pushes up a bit more and forms an opposite, a shadow, which becomes definite as well. When the content is really over the threshold, then the otherness enters the field of conscious-ness too. Then there are the many, many mythological and dream motifs of opposite things: the good and the bad dog, a black and a white bird, and so on, of which one is character-ized as being closer to consciousness and is therefore called bright, good, etc., and one is more removed from conscious-ness and generally characterized more negatively.

So doubleness means touching the threshold of conscious-ness, being still a little ambiguous, consciousness not yet knowing how to say what is what, partly still mixed up with the continuum of other unconscious contents. Here we could probably assume that the girl would be the shadow part, because that part is closer to the realm of the whole unconscious and, as has been pointed out, because she is open to the insinuations and evil whispering of the witch, closer to the dark side below. All this is very much in the state of unrealized life processes and not very much integrated in any cultural realization.

When a symbol of the Self appears as a child it means that it appears in the spontaneity of the human being and in life processes, but without much *theoria,* without much *Weltanschauung* or spiritual capacity in collective consciousness to integrate it yet or to name it. It is more an event than something understood, a possibility, but not yet a realized fact.

Let us look back at the events of the story: the Count married beneath him socially when he married a poor girl, so already there is expressed a certain need or tendency to renew his life by vivifying it from the layers below. Because he has taken this positive step, his wife gives birth to those star children. That means that now even deeper contents, a new form of life, constellates. But whenever something positive constellates in the unconscious there is a danger of a stiffening of consciousness against it.

Sometimes people come into analysis and say they want to be cured of this and that and want this and that, but sometimes—they may mention it or they may not—they have somewhere in a drawer something about which they have made up their minds that "that is all right and therefore does not need to be discussed in the analysis, that wherever analysis leads, this is the one thing which need not be brought in, and does not need to be discussed." And then they have an uncanny feeling and each time the dream associations would lead to this drawer they quickly break off associating and bring something else in, so that you have to wait quite a while until you can catch them *in flagranti* when they make a mistake and do not at once see the connection.

And then they have to be told to come on and open up that drawer, but they say that they thought that was quite unimportant! If there is such a reaction you can be quite sure that that stuff is highly explosive, otherwise such precautions would not be needed. It is a not-yet-integrated hot complex.

Behind the birth of those children there is a terrific possibility of new psychological events and realizations which accounts for this reaction of the stiffening of consciousness. The tendency to cut in half, to cut it away, comes from the action of the butler which I have already interpreted and which is really dictated by his greed in wanting to marry the Countess himself. There is a double possibility of a negative, shadowy reaction of consciousness in such cases. Either it is the drawer technique, which is to cut out and put away the new content, or the shadow wants to assimilate the new thing in accordance with his own desires.

This would be a shadowy assimilation of the thing, assimilating it for ego purposes. Again and again people approach the unconscious for very well-defined utilitarian purposes. One could even say that wanting to be better off, or wanting to be cured, is in a way still an egotistical approach. It is still just wanting to get the help of the unconscious. Wanting to be healthy is to a certain extent a legitimate ego wish and therefore generally the unconscious cooperates with it, because it is legitimate to want to be normal, but sometimes if the person only wants that from the unconscious, after a while negative dreams come up showing that it wants to guide the person further and not just cure the symptom, something much more than that is wanted by the unconscious; or the person is cured of the symptoms, but then their unconscious presents a bill! This and that and the other thing must be done, and if the person does not obey the symptom will recur.

It is as if people then really had to go out on the path of individuation for its own sake and not only just to be better off, or to sleep better, or become potent again, or whatever it may be. The bill has to be paid, for once the water of the unconscious has been tapped it runs on and cannot be turned off again. Every utilitarian approach to the unconscious, or just wanting to make use of it, has destructive effects, just as, we are now beginning to realize, it has in outer nature. For if we only exploit our forests, animals, and the minerals in the earth, then we disturb the biological balance and either we or later generations have to pay a very big bill. Nature seems to want to keep its own balance and set its own purposes and have its own biological whole and does not want to be exploited by one-sided utilitarian calculations.

This butler, therefore, would correspond to a kind of greedy, one-sided, egotistical attitude which interferes and bursts apart the first quaternio where the Count is not up to the situation. The valuable part, the two children, is put into the glass case and thrown into the flow of life in the unconscious, but the fisherman and his wife fish the children up and reconstitute a quaternio in a hidden place. That it is a fisherman is obvious: he by profession takes contents out of the water and is therefore the archetype of the savior or the wise man, who can bring up life from the depths. You need only to think of Christ, the fisher of men, or of the fisher King in the story of the Grail. In fairy tales very often this great archetypal image appears only modestly in an inconspicuous form such as this fisherman and his wife, but if you think of the archetypal background, you will understand that they are the original father and mother, father spirit and mother nature adopting the repressed contents, this possibility of individuation.

However, if this were to remain the way it is now, nothing more would happen, the children would live here happily, for being modest and not themselves in any way ambitious they would stay forever with their parents and later probably learn the occupation of fishing and go on in this hidden way. Therefore another event is needed to push the story on. The fisherman and his wife die, which means that those positive but relatively inconspicuous archetypal figures which give protection to the Self disappear again into the unconscious and the butler again interferes with the story by sending a witch.

Now brother and sister live alone, and this calls for the interference of the witch and the wise old man. The witch comes when the little boy is away and says "Oh, your house is charming and very nice, but you know you ought to have a spring of the water of life in the courtyard and then things would be perfect." And so she calls up the girl's greed and the boy is sent to find the water from this spring, but it is guarded by a lion which has the strange quality that when it has its eyes open it sleeps and when it has its eyes shut it is awake, and therefore the water has to be taken when it has its eyes open and the little boy succeeds this first time.

To interpret the witch is not difficult because, in general in fairy tales, she represents the dark side of the great earth goddess. In our countries, the cult of earth goddesses has practically vanished and the positive aspects of the mother archetype in Catholic countries have been integrated into the figure of the Virgin Mary, while the negative and destructive, the death side, has been repressed into the unconscious. In Protestant countries the whole archetype of the mother in both its aspects has been completely eliminated from religious life. Therefore the archetype of the earth mother and mother nature in her different aspects plays such an enormous role in all European fairy tales. The witch also plays a role in other fairy tales, where she always simply represents the destructive side of the archetypal feminine principle, the principle of death, of disease, of disintegration, or one could also call it the evil of unconsciousness in a certain form, that which resists consciousness: intrigue, greed, being driven, and all those impulses which you can find out about if you just see what witches do in different tales. They generally intrigue, poison, kill, or eat people, or they slander them so that they quarrel with each other. Those are the main activities of mythological witches, and of human witches as well.

The witch is counterbalanced by the wise old man who tells the boy what she is after and helps him along. One could say that the battle really goes on between the wise old man and the witch, for the children are not up to the situation at all. Because they have lost their fisherman parents they get other parents now, half evil and half good, the witch and the wise old man, who in a way replace the benevolent fisherfolk parents. But they are in conflict and try to create conflict between the brother and sister. So there was a harmonious family in the unconscious, and then comes the disharmony, for the old man crosses out the witch's plans and she tries to set the girl against the boy. Even the boy, when for the third time his sister sends him out, says, "You will kill me with your whims." Here, for the first time, the two children are not in harmony any longer, and the boy feels threatened by the girl and does not want to go at once, but the girl makes a scene and cries. The unconscious seems to tend toward disharmony in order that the Self may again be brought up into consciousness.

Sometimes when one analyzes people who have themselves analyzed for a long time and therefore are fairly in balance and capable of keeping in balance with themselves and their own unconscious processes, they come with dreams of a most horrible conflict. The analysand comes, and one says, "How are you?" and gets the answer, "I am all right!" "What has happened?" "Not much, I couldn't say much, I am working and at home things are all right too." "What have you dreamt?" And, out of the blue, there are most terrible dreams, all about war and an awful fight!

The other day such a person brought me a most horrible dream: he and his wife and someone else had all committed suicide by taking sleeping tablets! I said: "Where on earth is that?" "I don't know, I tried to think myself and couldn't find out!" In such a case you can only wait, for it means that the unconscious wants a conflict, it wants to burst apart the relatively harmonious setup in order that a higher level may be reached. This analysand, for instance, has not completely

38

filled out his frame. One feels definitely that he could be more than he is. He lives a less important and less full life, one with a smaller horizon than he is capable of living. Under those circumstances the unconscious bursts the harmony arrived at in order that it may be restored on a higher level, and then there are those mysterious sudden flare-ups of an unconscious conflict in dreams. But it never stays in the dreams, for after a while something happens outside, or in the consciousness of the person, which corresponds to inner conflict. I only want to point out that the catastrophic dream often comes first, it is clearly not the result of a conscious conflict, or conscious wrong behavior, but the conflict is a really spontaneous creation of the unconscious, it itself creates conflict to tear apart a too-small unit in order to enlarge it.

That happens often when people have drawn a mandala, a symbol of complete harmony. One would think that the inner growth would go on from there. Most often, however, the mandala falls apart again and the inner growth re-begins, seemingly from zero. It is not an additive process, but has a more complicated rhythm, and very often if a great progress of consciousness is intended, the unconscious first undoes everything so that when one is engaged on this path and is disturbed again and again, one feels as if one had not realized anything, for everything appears to be lost again. One just wonders whether one ever realized anything, or had ever been conscious or in harmony. One feels as if one were once more in the same state as when one's analysis first began! But that is quite normal and besides, this depressed condition is not real; it only looks like that, it is a phase where the harmony is broken up in order that a more differentiated center may be built up again.

In our fairy tale also the harmonious structure is broken apart; a terrific tension between the wise old man and the witch is constituted and carried into the behavior of the boy and the girl, who for the first time are against each other, the girl listening to the witch's insinuations.

Next comes the motif of the well where the boy has to take a jug and fetch some of the water of life. It is magic water, for he only needs to pour a little onto the courtyard at his home to have the same spring there; it is obviously the magical water of life which alone is capable of producing such a miracle. We could go on forever amplifying this spring, the miraculous water of life, because this is an international mythological motif found practically everywhere. But the fact that this well produces silver water points to a more specific area of amplification, namely the symbolism of alchemy. Only in alchemy does one definitely find this motif of the water, which is generally of silver or gold, and this points to the fact that our story has probably come from alchemical sources.

In general, in the very earliest texts we have of the first century, or, for instance, in the so-called visions of Zosimos,[9] which belong to the end of the third century A.D. (though some motifs go even further back), alchemists very often try to explain parables and similes in order to illustrate their insight into the material processes, and Zosimos tells dreams he had about it. The motifs of these parables, which were partly constructed and partly authentic dreams of early alchemists, traveled back into general folklore mythology. In alchemy there was an endeavor to exemplify or explain mysterious processes by the use of folklore similes, and vice versa, folklore again borrowed alchemical parables and similes and assimilated them into their stories.

In our story the spring is not a well or a spring of silver *and* gold, as it is in many other stories and normally was in alchemy. In alchemy, Mercurius, the mysterious figure of the *prima materia,* is generally a mysterious liquid, the elixir of life, the eternal water which usually generates silver and gold; it either produces silver and gold or sometimes also from the beginning consists of silver and gold. Here only the silver is stressed, which lays the accent on the feminine element because, in alchemical tradition, gold is ascribed to the sun and silver to the moon. Silver represents the feminine and the corruptible metal. It very easily turns black and has to be constantly cleaned, in contrast to gold, and therefore represents something ever-changing, like the moon, which constantly turns black and has to be made to shine again in Heaven. So the moon rules over all corruptible nature, according to Aristotle; it rules over the menstruation of women and all the changes in nature. Above its sphere begins nature's incorruptible and divine sphere, ruled over by the sun and the firmament. Moisture, death, the feminine, the diseases of women, the corruption of metals—all that belongs in the area over which the moon rules and silver is its specific metal. It is the bride of gold, the corruptible female, which has to be transformed before becoming gold itself.

So if the witch calls the attention of the girl to the fact that the silver water is lacking, she is quite right, because we know from the very beginning of the story that somehow the feminine element is not emphasized enough and that the integration of nature and the feminine element is what is lacking. So the witch, though her aim is destruction really, as so often, works for good, because this silver well represents the feminine aspect of the flow of unconscious energy.

In general, one can say that the water of life, or what is symbolized by it, is what man has always sought. We had it in paradise, but lost it. Symbolically it expresses this psychological experience which one could describe as the feeling that life is flowing in a meaningful way. Sometimes when you ask somebody how they are, they say, "Oh, a lot is happening, not all agreeable, but I can say that I am in the flow of life, I am all right." There are ups and downs, but you feel, to use a more technical modern simile, that your plane is riding approximately on the radar beam. You are where you belong, and then you have this absolutely marvel- ous feeling of being alive. Even the vicissitudes and difficulties of fate and human life can be accepted if one has basically this contact with the flow of libido in the unconscious, which is why we make all this effort about dream interpretation, because only by it can we tell where the flow of unconscious libido is moving and try to adapt our conscious movement to it, for then we feel alive. Then, even if not much happens in our lives, or we have a boring job to do, or all sorts of frustrations, we feel inwardly alive.

How important this feeling is you can perhaps best realize if you have ever analyzed a millionaire or any person who had everything he wanted on the outside and was capable of getting it. They can have the car, the clothes, or the house they like, they can go anywhere and, within the limitations of health, can have everything, yet if they haven't the flow of life, what is the use of it all! Generally people project the flow of life into outer objects, they think that if they had a different wife and more money, or something like that, then they would have it, but that is a pure projection which you can see best if someone has all that, for then you realize that that is not it! What people really seek, even if they project it sometimes onto outer objects, is the feeling of being alive. That is the highest thing one can reach, during this life at least, and therefore it has always been a simile for any kind of religious mystical experience, because that conveys this feeling most. Or you can say that if you have this experience of life, it *is* in a way a religious mystical experience! Medieval mystics, for instance, would tell you that the inner experience of God was the well of life, and the Zen Buddhists say that when they find *samadhi* it is like drinking a cup of cool water after thirsting in the desert.

In all civilizations and in all cultural setups you find this as a simile of the experience of complete satisfaction and a complete plenitude of life experience, and here it is the same thing. That is what is still lacking in our tale, but it is specifically the silver water that is this experience, with a feminine tinge. It is vitality, but in the realm of the moon, not in the realm of higher spiritual experience. Because here it is silver water, it means that the experience of life sought is not a medieval spiritual experience but rather a vitality which comes from this earthly, corruptible area of human life, to speak alchemical language. Silver is sometimes ascribed also to Venus—though she owns copper in most texts—and therefore to the feminine principle in general.

The silver well is guarded by a lion, and as the silver water refers to alchemical symbolism, it is wiser to amplify the lion also from this area. It plays a tremendous role in all alchemical texts, and it probably entered the field of alchemical language through the role it had in the Egyptian funeral ritual. The Sphinx is actually the portrait of an Egyptian king in his lion shape, because the king, when resurrected and in his postmortal shape, is very often represented as a lion, which in the whole complicated ritual of death in Egypt is an ancient symbol of resurrection. Sometimes, the Egyptians represented this mystery as a double lion: one symbolizing the sun setting in the West and the other looking to the East and symbolizing the rising sun. The lion refers to the mystical moment where the sun touches the midnight point under the earth and therefore turns from the death-bringing setting sun to the rising sun, for the Egyptians associated the setting sun with age and death. The double lion represented this mystical moment of transition between death and resurrection, the turning point of the sun toward the East as an aspect of resurrected life at the moment of midnight, because the way of the sun god over the upper horizon and below the earth represented the transformation of the psychic energy toward consciousness and again back into the unconscious.

Probably also from Egyptian sources, the lion was still looked on in medieval symbolism as being an agent of resurrection. The story that when the lioness gives birth to her cubs they are dead until the male lion comes and roars over them and brings them to life is repeated in all medieval bestiaries. It is probably a late repercussion of this old Egyptian mythology of the lion as the agent of resurrection, and has to do with the mystery of the sun and of life with its rhythmical change between consciousness and unconsciousness.

The Egyptians, when they embalmed their corpses, put

them on a marble table with a lion head facing in opposite
directions at either end. One can see such marble tables like
beds at the Cairo Museum with a lion head at each end and
generally with the feet made of lion's paws. On such a marble
table, called the death bed and the bed of resurrection, with
little holes in it so that the liquids might flow away, they put
the corpse when they performed this rather complicated
ritual of embalming. When the corpse of the king was lying
on this bed he was lying in the deepest underworld, and
while the priest was taking out the brain and the entrails and
washing the corpse in natrium chloride, his soul was, so to
speak, dwelling in the underworld, and when the process of
mummification was finished he would resurrect again.

So the lion is the guardian of the underworld, the guardian
of this mysterious subterranean process which transforms
death into life. As the symbolism of Western alchemy comes
mainly from Egypt and as alchemy started in the Hellenized
late Egyptian period, the alchemists used it again because
they thought that transforming their matter and changing it
into gold was a kind of analogy to the transformation of the
mortal body of the king into his immortal shape as a mummy.
The idea was a primitive sort of analogy: just as the Anubis
priest takes the mortal remains of the Egyptian king, his
corpse, and by a chemical operation changes him into an
immortal being, so must we take the mortal metals of silver
and copper, which are corruptible and decay and corrode,
and by a chemical operation change them into incorruptible
matter, namely into gold. That is a complete analogy in
thinking, and they even talked about their chemical operations as a *taricheusis,* which means mummification. They say
you must *taricheuein,* mummify, the metals to transform
them into gold.

In other words, the process of individuation was in Egypt
projected into postmortal processes happening in the corpse
and by the alchemists into their chemical operations of
transforming the metals. In this the lion always plays the role
of the paradoxical agent, which stands between death and

life, between morning and evening; it rules over both aspects and brings forth the renewal. In later alchemical texts, when the old king is dissolved in order to be renewed, he very often is either eaten by a lion or transforms himself into a lion. In a complicated story by Canon Ripley, for instance, the queen gives rebirth to the king, and while he dwells again in her womb she has to eat the flesh of the lion, in order to give the right diet to the embryo in her womb till the king is reborn as the new King of Kings.

Jung has interpreted this lion motif in the chapter "Rex" of his *Mysterium Coniunctionis*.[10] He writes that in order to be renewed, the king first has to be transformed into his chthonic nature. So we can conclude that the lion represents the chthonic nature, the earth aspect of the king. When he dies he goes into the earth, into the realm of the lion and is there transformed. Because the king represents the dominant of collective consciousness, it means that, in order to be renewed, every dominant of collective consciousness, every central image of the Self which dominates in a cultural setup, has to fall back from time to time into the unconscious and be renewed there, While the king is dead, in primitive tribes, for instance, there is a complete cultural blackout. In certain tribes, during the interregnum, while one chief is dead and his successor not yet elected, everybody may steal and kill. This means that all the cultural rules of decent human behavior are overthrown. For three days, there is a complete blackout of consciousness: greed, murder, and all crime, every darkness, may dominate for a set period. A very mitigated form still exists in the medieval and antique rituals for a Carnival king, where on one day in the year it is not the king who rules, but some fool or condemned criminal who gets the crown and may, for this one day, rule the whole town and have all the parties and women and everything else he likes before he is executed. This represents the chthonic side, the shadow of the king, which rules during the interregnum.

Still more mitigated traces exist in the award of amnesties

for past crimes on the nomination of a new ruler. The prisons are opened that the past may be annihilated and a new beginning made. That is the mildest form of those much wilder rituals of the past where during a set period of time complete destructive darkness was allowed, all those things which normally the laws of the chief and the tribe keep down and taboo. We could say that the darkest side of the unconscious is allowed to manifest directly in that moment where not only the king is dead but, for the primitive tribe, it could be said that God was dead. Their god is dead because the king is an incarnation of the deity of the tribe, of the spiritual principle. It is the moment of complete disorientation, a moment which in an individual's life would practically correspond to a psychotic dissociation, a complete blackout of consciousness. We have had quite a bit lately of these cultural blackouts of consciousness, and unfortunately might get still a bit more, because we are living in a time when the old king has died and is renewing himself in the depths. During such a blackout the lion rules, one of the dominant images of the shadow of the king.

Negatively, the lion represents the principle of power, and there again the modern analogy is clear; for wherever a civilizatory or cultural setup has no uniting religious goal, there are political power fights among the dictators and cliques which dictate the whole fate of a civilization. In a small group that would mean that if people are not linked by a common spiritual goal, by the teamwork required by some common higher interest, then they start fighting about who is to be president and who cashier and all the rest of it. If there is not a still more powerful symbol to unite the people, there is a disrupting influence together with prestige and vanity fights. That is why, for example, the little groups of early Christians, who had a real spiritual bond and even originally called themselves Brother or Sister in Christ, those little cliques of slaves or traders, absolutely inconspicuous people, overcame the whole power setup of the Roman Empire. Seventy years after Christ's death Pliny said of them,

"I tortured a few slaves but could not find anything more than a ridiculous superstition!" Why? Because the Roman Empire had no more spiritual religious life to hold it together and therefore had to decay in the continuous power fights of the small and big fishes among them. Those cliques which had the new god on their side represented the king who had renewed himself at that moment; they overcame because they were the only people capable of working on something beyond themselves, or of keeping peace among each other for some higher goal. If one is not bound by a common goal one just cannot stand other people, for they get on one's nerves too much.

We are in a similar situation once more, for the death of the old king and the time when the lion dominates, representing power and prestige drives, is an eternally recurring archetypal situation in human life—which is why there are lions under thrones or people call themselves "lion of Judah," for they represent the power principle.

The lion is not only negative, for he has two heads. According to the Egyptians he looks toward death but also toward renewal; he is the ancient symbol of resurrection. He represents the summer heat, the summer solstice in astrology, light and passion, and renewal. In *Mysterium Coniunctionis,* Jung stresses not only the power aspect but also the sex drive, which the lion sometimes represents. It could be said that he represents any kind of very hot passionate drive, whether power or sex. Jung brings many examples, especially the green lion in alchemy which is associated with Venus, representing the sex impulse, sexual desire and its passion, and this is the lion's more positive aspect. But whenever the lion appears we know that the personality is confronted with strong, passionate impulses, desires, passions, and affects which are stronger than the ego.

A lion can also represent rage. I remember that a woman who was in a tearing rage against another member of the family, dreamt that she had to keep her door shut against the lion, who wanted constantly to break into the room. There it was neither power nor sex, but simply terrific animal affect. As king of the animals he represents a very powerful drive of that kind. If a human being has lost his religious steering point, he disintegrates and becomes partly the prey of affects such as sex and power and other drives and desires. That is the interregnum, the time when the dominating ideal or symbol is dead and snakes and lions are around. It is the moment where the personality is flooded by greed. Yet a lion is something highly alive, and in the case of a sick human being, one is sometimes terribly glad if he exhibits some ambition or sex drive or affect, because that is where life is.

Often behind very lame, passive states of melancholy, such a lion is roaring around. People just sit; they take pills, and nothing means anything any more. You offer them this or that and they just turn their heads in disgust, in deep depression, and you can make quite a good guess that—not always, but very often—they madly want something and cannot admit it even to themselves. They think it crazy and therefore put it aside and then, naturally, everything else is nothing. From the dreams one generally can find out what they so madly want and then, suddenly, the deep melancholy turns into being absolutely run over by greed.

That is why it is very dangerous to release such a deep depression, for sometimes that is the moment of suicide. When the affect and the greed for life come out and cannot be fulfilled at once, such people may kill themselves. Before, the greed was not even admitted; but when it is admitted and is then frustrated—when the lion does not at once get what it wants—then the person may kill himself. So it is very dangerous to let such a lion out of his black cage, the mummufication stage. Nevertheless, if you can overcome that crisis, then you have all the life which was lacking before. There is a strong life drive, and you have something to work upon; there is a lively personality which wants something and goes for it with passion. Then it is only a question of how to integrate the lion so that he does not destroy everything, and the taming of the lion would be the next step in the transformation. That is why the alchemist said, "When the lion turns up you have to take a sword and cut off his paws," because he wants to grab and claw everything; he has to be tamed and subdued.

That is what the lion represents, more or less, psychologically. It could be said that wherever the well of life lies, there the lion is also, for wherever there is a pearl there is a monster lying on it, wherever there is a treasure there is a snake wound around it, and wherever there is the water of life there is a lion guarding it. You cannot get near the Self and the meaning of life without being on the razor's edge of falling into greed, into darkness, and into the shadowy aspect of the personality. One does not even know if it is not necessary sometimes to fall into it, because otherwise it cannot be assimilated. Because of this people do not like analysts, for frequently through analysis the good-goody boy or the tame little girl at home becomes absolutely impossible. Why? Because they become temporarily lions and snakes. They want things and grab things and they make scenes and do all sorts of evil and then other people say, "And that's the result of sending them into analysis!" But life cannot go further before first going downward. There is no new king before he has lain in the lion bed and disintegrated for a day. People who have greedy desires and do not admit them to themselves, and try to behave conventionally and correctly instead, are just something to write off.

So the lion has to be released and then is destructive, and his paws have to be cut off. The lion is the terrible thing and the thing which has to be met all the way. But here—and I therefore put a question mark at this motif and through this whole fairy tale—here the boy has to *steal* the water of life from the lion while he is asleep with his eyes open. Then he quickly has to take it away so that the lion has not time to wake up. The boy himself does not confront the lion. We will not judge whether that is good or bad, we will only judge when, through the earlier Persian parallel, we see how to value this story.

And now comes this puzzling motif of why the lion sleeps with its eyes open and is awake when it has its eyes shut. When the passionate, greedy nature has its eyes open, it looks at the outer object. When my lion has its eyes open and it is a power lion, it looks for some important position somewhere, and when it is a sex lion then I want some partner somewhere, or want something else; when my lion has its eyes open and looks at an outer object, then it represents what we call blind passion! Passion is blind, greed is blind, and generally if one gives in to it one falls headlong into some kind of nasty trap. That's why, for instance, Jung said that only one terrible thing can happen to a woman, namely that her power plot might win out. If it is frustrated it is all right, but if she gets what she wants then she is lost, and you could say the same for men. If a man wants to be top dog, let him have it! That is about the worst you can do to him, because the lion which looks toward outer objects is really asleep, i.e., deeply unconscious and, in a way, completely blind.

Yet every passion has a symbolic aspect. You see that best if you look at people who are crazy about money. They are rarely greedy for actual money, but money means something symbolic to them. They project into it the plenitude of life, or power, or freedom. "If I had money then I would not have to submit to social obligations." Or they project security into money—where it is not—and that is why they are so passionate about it. The same thing may hold for sexual passion, for an object once obtained is discarded. It wasn't it! One only thought it was. But there was something symbolic there, as in the Don Juan type of neurosis where it is always the mother the man is chasing, or a perfect woman. But when he has once slept with her, he finds that the mystery he was looking for was not there—and he leaves her again and begins again, because he is really looking for something symbolic.

Therefore you can say that when passion shuts its eyes, then it becomes conscious, which means that when you can see the inner object within a passionate drive, can look within

50

at the real object and what it is driving at in its symbolic
meaning, then you have the real gold. Passion is awake but is
turned inside, and toward the outer it looks as if asleep.
When you leave off wanting outer things, that fades away
and becomes quiet. Now, the boy in our story does not
himself confront the lion, but takes the water of life away
when the lion seems asleep, and that means when the lion
has his eyes open, he is in a state of blind greed, and does
not notice that his greatest value is being stolen.

To separate the flow of life from the greed factor would be
a parallel to realizing that what the human being is looking
for is not the desired object but the water of life: the real
objective is to be alive in a meaningful way. Greed is something blind which might just as well be left out of the picture.
The boy sneaks past the lion and leaves it and when it wakes
up—well, the boy has the water, it is too late!

That is perhaps the feminine way of behaving; a hero
would instead have overcome the lion, as for instance Hera-
cles had to do. Here there is only the idea of not confronting
oneself. I think on account of this slightly evasive trick of not
fighting the lion, but just tricking it, the witch can come
back again. It is a bit too cheap to do it this way, by just
sidetracking passion.

There are people who in a certain stage of their analysis
get a wild, passionate transference to the analyst and then
cannot quite bring it up because they do not want to be hit
over the head. If they turn up as a lion they will naturally be
hit over the head, so, as they don't like to be tortured, they
keep their lion nicely in their pockets and never show it.
That means they never confess their passionate transference.
Women do it with the help of the animus. They say, "Oh, I
know he is not in love with me, so I know I have to be
reasonable"; "My analyst is married"; or God knows what! So
they never let the lion out, and then they say (and one cannot
deny it): "I know also that the main goal of my analytical
process is not a love affair with the analyst, I know that from
the symbolism of my dreams, so why should I get into this?"

They try to get the water of life and just leave the lion out of the picture, and they succeed—to a certain extent.

That can be done quite successfully if the real inner main goal of life is not there; then you can just leave it, so to speak, aside. But in spite of it, one has skipped a process of suffering. If one confronts the lion, even knowing ahead that he will have to be killed in the end, one goes through certain things which are otherwise missed. Because to be tortured by one's passion is meaningful, but it is not pleasant, and that is why certain people try to sidetrack it, by knowing ahead what the outcome will be. But by this they escape a certain cooking heat which, had it been put under them, would have cooked them better; so they remain a bit raw.

To return to our story: the boy sidetracks the lion by taking the water when it has its eyes open. He thus succeeds in creating the silver well in the courtyard of the house where he lives with his little sister. But the old witch comes again and discovers that she has not succeeded in killing him. So she again puts the poison of desire into the little sister's mind and tells her of the oak whose acorns are of silver in cupules of gold. This acorn is a symbol which unites the opposites of silver and gold, the sun and moon metals. If the boy only breaks off a little branch or twig from the oak tree and puts it in the courtyard, there will be another beautiful oak tree there. Again the boy sets out, and again the wise old man comes and says that the boy should take the horse and go to the oak. But he must be sure to look at the snake which guards it, and only when it hides its head and sleeps can he break off a branch. The boy does this and succeeds in getting the oak, and then comes the third episode with the parrot.

As we were induced to look at alchemical symbolism in the motif of the silver water, we can find more alchemical symbolism about the oak, and even a connection between it and the silver well in the second part of Jung's *Mysterium*

Coniunctionis ("The Paradoxa"). "Jung discusses here various alchemical and other commentaries regarding a very mysterious (fictitious?) inscription on a supposedly antique tombstone of a certain Lucius Agatho which was found in the Renaissance. Various scholars tried to reconstruct the mysterious inscription of a tomb and in doing so projected their own wildest fantasies onto it. One of them, Malvasius, fantasized that Aelia, the woman of the couple in the tomb, was an ungodly spirit who was "enclosed and affixed in a Junonian oak."

The tomb was dedicated to a Mr. Quintus Verconius Agathoni. The interpreters overlooked the point by shortening Quinto to Qu and read it instead as Querconius Agathoni, and then *quercus,* an oak, was projected into that name. Another alchemist, in order to amplify the man's name, brought in an Italian poem of the time of a sun and moon oak which represents the elementary world. It runs:

> In a garden adorned with marvelous flowers,
> Grew a red and a white rose,
> In the center grew a great oak,
> From which sprang four suns.

In a Latin variation it is said that the oak not only has four suns as flowers, but also the sun and moon proceed from it as flowers.

As Jung points out, this is probably a vague reminiscence of a famous oak of the antique philosopher Pherecydes, who interpreted the whole world as being an oak tree over which a coat was spread on which all things were embroidered, so that our world is really that embroidery which is thrown over the world oak.

Another important text about the connection between the well and the oak is to be found in a parable written by the famous Bernardus Trevisanus (Count of the March and Trevis, who lived from 1406 to 1490).

> He tells the parable of an adept who finds a clear spring set about with the finest stone and "secured to the trunk

of an oak-tree," the whole surrounded by a wall. This is
the King's bath in which he seeks renewal. An old man,
Hermes, the mystagogue, explains how the King had this
bath built: he placed it in an old oak, "cloven in the
midst." The fountain was surrounded by a thick wall,
and "first it was enclosed in hard, bright stone, then in a
hollow oak."[12]

In this parable, as Jung points out, there is no Queen.
Probably the oak therefore replaces the Queen, and if this is
so it is particularly interesting that it is hollow and split, and
has this vessel or well in it. It thus represents the mother in
a double form, for the tree represents the mother principle
and the source of life. The bath of the King is, so to speak, a
maternal womb in which he renews himself. Jung then goes
on to quote other alchemical texts which are probably more
or less influenced by this classic and famous parable of the
Count of Trevis.

I think that probably this parable has also directly influenced our story. We saw before that the missing feminine
element, the mother element, seems to be the problem in our
story and that both the well and the oak seem to represent
mother symbols from which renewal comes. In contrast to
the silver will, which contains only the feminine element,
the oak contains both, because the acorns are of silver and
gold and unite the opposites of sun and moon, the male and
female.

Thus, going to the deeper center of the unconscious, the
symbol which the brother has to bring back becomes more
and more essential and important. Also there is a guardian of
this mysterious world oak, which represents the matrix and
place of renewal in the unconscious, a snake, in contrast to
the lion at the silver well. The twig with the acorn on it has
to be stolen when the snake hides its head. This is not as
paradoxical as with the lion, for it is normal for the snake to
be asleep when it hides its head. In the third phase it is the
same, when the parrot puts its head under its wing, the
obvious position for sleep.

It seems puzzling that the containing feminine cup of the acorn is golden, while the more phallic acorn itself is made from the feminine metal, silver. Gold always signifies the highest value, so this might mean that the feminine cup is the thing of highest value. In any case, the acorn is thus characterized as a union of opposites.

Taking the twig when the snake is not looking repeats the motif of sidetracking the central thing, in contrast to some of the alchemical parallels where a dragon guards the oak and where the hero has to kill the dragon. Here the dragon or snake, which are one and the same thing mythologically, has not to be overcome but must be outwitted at the moment when it sleeps. So again the confrontation with the deeper elements and the spirit of the unconscious is avoided and only the fruit of the unconscious is taken.

This refers to a certain superficiality, probably to be seen in connection with the fact that the hero and the heroine of the story are children, and therefore the whole story runs on an infantile line; the hero is a symbol of the renewal of the personality but still *in statu nascendi,* on an infantile level, and there is no real confrontation with the deeper layers of the unconscious. It is the wise old man who gives the advice that this superficial way is the way out of the trouble, so we may not criticize it but must accept it as right. It corresponds to a certain attitude of wisdom, not to take on a conflict when one is not up to it.

The same thing occurs frequently in an analytical situation, for it is no use stirring deeper layers of the unconscious if consciousness is not up to it. In such cases there is generally a natural instinctive tendency to sidetrack or avoid the confrontation, something with which the analyst should certainly not interfere. If the analysand is inclined to evade certain basic problems, one must consider the possibility that he cannot confront this deeper layer; and therefore to sidetrack the essential problem is wisdom.

We know from Jung's works into what deep waters alchemical symbolism leads. It is neither more nor less than a kind of secret, compensatory religious tendency which relates to the official Christian doctrine, as dreams relate to consciousness, in a partly complementary and partly compensatory way. Therefore if the problem of the lion and the snake were taken up, it would mean that the problem of a non-Christian, pagan religious attitude was taken seriously into account. This was not constellated in Spain at the time of our story. In the original (Persian) source of our story the problem of a church doctrine does not exist, but the story has been altered and adapted to the situation of the nation in which it is being told.

It could also be said that the relative smoothness and undramatic course of this story tells us something about the national psychological situation in which it came into being, namely that the main source of religious experience is contained in the Catholic doctrine and the Catholic church, and therefore the underlying pagan tendencies are relatively depotentiated, which is why the more basic layers of the unconscious are not touched upon in our text.

Still the witch is not satisfied, and again she puts the poison of desire into the little girl's head and says, "Well, you should still have a parrot, and I know of a very valuable one and whoever catches it will be rich all his life and your brother should get that now." This time the little brother definitely has a premonition of something, he senses that this task will be too difficult for him and he really tries not to go. He even attacks his little sister and says, "You will kill me with your whims if you continue in this way," but the sister insists. So he goes to find the parrot, and again the old man meets him and tells him how to do it. "You will come," he says, "to a beautiful garden with a lot of trees and birds, and after a while a beautiful white parrot will come and will sit on a round stone"—here there is again the stone of the Trevisanus parable which covers a well—"and it will turn in a circle and will say, 'Does no one there want to catch me? Is there nobody there who will seize me? If nobody likes me, they should leave me alone, if nobody likes me they should leave me alone.' And then it will put its head under its wing and you can seize it, but you must not be too quick, because if you take it before it is completely asleep then it will escape, and you will be petrified and stay there like all those who went there before."

Everything happens as the old man foretold, but the little brother is a bit nervous. As soon as the parrot begins to hide its head under its wing, he is so afraid of not getting it that he is a bit too eager, and puts his hand out too quickly. The parrot flies away and the little brother is petrified and does not return.

The symbol of the parrot is so important that we will amplify it later. For the moment I only want to say that the parrot, in certain Arabic stories, is a kind of Hermes-Mercurius figure, a psychopompos, who speaks the truth (though in a rather ambiguous way) and therefore brings all sorts of dramatic stories to a positive end.

There is a famous book which exists in a Persian and Turkish version called the *Tuti-Nameh, The Book of the Parrot.*[13] It is a collection of Oriental novels similar to the Arabian Nights. In "The Thousand and One Nights," the King wants to kill Scheherezade. In order to delay her own death, she tells him another story every night, till the King is so attached to her that when she ends after a thousand and one nights, he is no longer determined to kill her.

The *Tuti-Nameh* is the story of a young merchant who is passionately in love with his young wife and they are very happy together, but then he goes to the marketplace and there is offered a parrot. He says he cannot pay a thousand gold coins for such a stupid bird, but the owner says that his bird even knows the Koran by heart. To this the merchant asks what is the use of a bird who does not understand the meaning of the words quoting the Koran, and even if he repeats the prayer verses, that does not mean that anyone who hears what he says should pray! Why should he give a thousand gold coins for such a parrot? The parrot's answers are always in poetry, and now "he begins to boil like the sea and to sing like the nightingale," and he says, "I praise you, Sâid, what you say is not nonsense, but is correct, but it applies to other birds and animals—not to me. My heart is filled to the brim with pearls of wisdom and with precious stones of the knowledge of the truth, even the future is known to me and even the supernatural is understood by my intelligence. Whoever follows my advice moves on a path of happiness." And then he says that he wants the merchant to buy him because he does not want to fall into the hands of a fool who will not know his value and will torture him. Then Sâid says, "Well, I begin to be very much inclined to buy you, but you see my whole fortune consists of only a thousand gold coins." "Such talk," says the parrot, "becomes a man of your insight and intelligence, but I have a suggestion to make. There is a kind of spice which can now be bought very cheaply on the market, but in three days' time merchants will come from all around and there will be a tremendous increase in its price, so if you buy now you will make a lot of money." Sâid accepts this advice and makes another five thousand gold coins and so is able to buy the parrot. He even buys it a wife and they live together as a quaternio: Sâid and his wife, and the parrot and its wife.

Then one day the parrot stresses the advantage of a voyage overseas and the young man Sâid is so impressed that he decides to go and tells his wife of his intention. She cries and complains; Sâid, in order to comfort her, tells her how profitable it will be, but she answers that formerly he would not have left her for a second. However, Sâid succeeds in comforting her and sets forth. When he has gone the wife, called Mâhi-Scheker, often goes to the parrot's cage and complains. But after a year she falls in love with a beautiful young man in the neighborhood and after some slight moral conflict decides to go off and meet him. But, as she feels a little bit uneasy and remembers that her husband had told her that if ever she made a connection with another young man, she should at least ask the parrot's advice, she goes to the parrot's wife, feeling more akin to the other female, and tells her of her plan. But the parrot's wife says, "Oh, good gracious, but that is immoral, you must not do that, you must be faithful to your husband!" This makes the merchant's wife so furious that she takes the bird and wrings its neck and kills it. But this has put her in such a rage that she has no desire to meet the young man and waits for the next evening, when she again dresses up, but again she feels slight qualms of conscience and this time goes to the parrot itself and tells it her plans, and it thinks, "Oh dear, now I am in a fix! If I tell her that she should not go she will kill me as she did my wife yesterday and, on the other hand, I must prevent her from going!" So he says, "Oh, you are absolutely right," and he makes her a whole stream of poetical compliments and another stream of compliments about her future lover and approves strongly of the whole thing but says that he must think it all over carefully. And so he calms her and spends the night trying to think what he can do. Again next evening Mâhi-Scheker dresses up and goes to the parrot, and again he flatters her, saying that though Sâid bought it, it was she who fed it, but she must be careful that it does not happen to her as it happened to So-and-So! "Oh, what was that?" asks Mâhi-Scheker. "Oh, but that is too long a story, I can't tell you now, the night is too far advanced and through lying awake thinking all last night I can hardly keep my eyes open," says the parrot. So she goes to rest but the next evening, all dressed up and bejeweled, she goes to the parrot and he tells her a long story in the Oriental way and the morning comes and it is again too late, she has missed the night!

And so, like Scheherezade in "The Thousand and One Nights," the parrot tells a different beautiful story each night and in this way prevents Mâhi-Scheker from committing adultery till the very day when her own husband returns. Then the parrot tells the whole story and there is a general reconciliation and, as a favor for having saved the situation, about which naturally the wife is also glad, the parrot only asks to be set free and be allowed to fly about at will. So they live happily together forever after, and the parrot visits them in a friendly way from time to time. And the story ends with a moral exhortation that these stories should be taken very seriously and meditated upon.

There is much more to this parrot, but we see here that it functions as a kind of slightly paradoxical, slightly ambiguous spirit, but with positive intentions. In this version of the *Tuti-Nameh* it can really be compared to the famous figure of Khidr, Allah's first angel, who, in the eighteenth sura of the Koran, also functions in this strange way, namely with a kind of paradoxical higher morale.[13] If one looks at Khidr naively, as Moses does in the eighteenth sura of the Koran, his deeds seem immoral but really mean pursuing a higher form of fulfilling the will of God and a higher form of ethical realization. The parrot, in a way, behaves ambiguously because it seemingly approves of the love affair and, in a very dishonest way, flatters Mâhi-Scheker with all sorts of praise and poems and thus outwits her for her own good.

There are Turkish fairy tales, on the other hand, in which the parrot is definitely destructive. For instance, a woman loves a young man, in the positive sense of the word, and the story runs that she should have him, but it is the parrot who betrays her to the enemy. So the parrot is a very ambiguous figure, mainly positive, but sometimes also described as a slanderer and destroyer. It has something of this mercurial, ambiguous quality here, in the way it turns in a circle and says, "Does no one there want to catch me? Is there nobody there who will seize me? If nobody likes me they should leave me alone." It does not impose itself, it is the spirit of nature: if you can seize it, all right; but it has that evasiveness which the alchemists always complain about in their Mercurius which they seek, for that same thing escapes human grasp.

The witch does not see this aspect of the parrot, she only says that whoever catches it will be rich for his whole life, and we see from the *Tuti-Nameh* that the parrot is quite capable of very concrete business tricks and understands stock market problems! It is up to date in this area of life as well and can give very good advice, though this is not the main purpose. In the *Tuti-Nameh* story it really makes use of the merchant's greed for money so that the merchant may buy it, and then starts quite a different way of advising him, and not just about money. The witch sees only the material advantage; she personifies this eternal human tendency to exploit nature and, insofar as the unconscious is also pure nature, to exploit it in an utilitarian way as well. This is correctly put into the mouth of a witch because, in its final aspect, it is utterly destructive, just as is the exploitation of nature.

One sees this poison frequently in people who, for example, read Jung's work in an infantile way and realize that getting on with the unconscious obviously makes one feel better. Then they obey their dreams with the side intention of thus becoming the top dog in society, the most attractive man for all women, and goodness knows what else they may desire; then they suddenly get furious when they realize that this does not come off. This kind of infantile plot of wanting to exploit the unconscious and set goals for purely conscious reasons has sneaked into their relationship with the unconscious. The process of individuation is becoming *oneself*, not becoming happy in a kindergarten.

The parrot must be seized when it puts its head under its wing, and here there is a different motif: the object itself has to be seized when asleep, while with the water and the twig the guardian of the object had to be asleep. This is connected with the fact that the parrot is apparently very evasive; it sleeps very lightly, and if you don't get it at the moment when it is unconscious it will fly away, as it does in our story. (In the original Persian version it is just like that, for there the parrot is not asleep but always evades the arrows shot at it.) So the main motif is the parrot's evasiveness, and it is this which makes the little brother nervous and eager and hasty in wanting to get at it.

The evasiveness of the spirit of truth in nature is beautifully described at the beginning of the *Odyssey* when Menelaus tells Telemachus (who is searching for his father, Ulysses) how he himself had been stranded on the Island of Pharos. He had had to contact Proteus, the King of the Sea, in order to get away. Proteus counts his herds at midday and then lies down to sleep. At this moment, Menelaus and his companions have to jump and seize him, to get the truth out of him and find out which god has cut Menelaus' voyage short, and how to get home. As soon as Proteus is seized, he changes first into a lion, then into a snake, a panther, and a great boar, then into water, and then into a tree. He changes his shape again and again and it is said in the *Odyssey* that Menelaus and his three companions have to hold him fast and not let him go until he again takes on his own shape as Proteus, the old Sea King. Then Proteus says, "Now, my son, what do you want?" The old Sea King is called *nemertes* in Greek, which means "never deceiving," "the truthful," but in spite of the fact that he never deceives and always speaks the truth he goes through all that phantasmagoria and has to be pinned down for a long time until at last he tells the truth.

This is the same problem of the evasiveness of the spirit of the unconscious, and anybody who has had some experience in dealing with his own unconscious knows how cryptic it sometimes can be. That is what is so annoying, especially when we are in a conflict and want advice, for instead of telling you nicely what you ought to do when you would do it like a good child—you are quite ready to be a good child and do it—the dreams seem really to mock you! They say, "You can do this or that"! They seem to give you advice, but with question marks about it, and you discuss it a whole hour with your analyst, saying that you really do not know what the dream means: it could mean this, or just the opposite! So it tricks you; and the more you are driven and in a hasty driven mood, the worse it gets. Generally, if one can stand the agony of no decision and go on watching the dreams without making any hasty movement, the situation clarifies and one eventually gets a dream which clearly illustrates the point, or in consciousness one gets a feeling of what to do. Then one can decide without a dream, one has a strong feeling as to what one is going to do and will stick to that, no matter what the unconscious thinks about it; the solution out of the agony of doubt, the solution as a third thing comes into existence. But a certain backbone and inner strength of personality is needed to stand the agony. Haste is of the devil, as the alchemists say, and all hastiness or nervous wanting of a quick decision is a symptom of psychological weakness and childishness. Panic is the one really catastrophic thing in dealing with the unconscious.

But the evasiveness of its nature spirit always throws us into such a situation, and this is what the parrot does too. Anyone who can catch hold of it can take it, and if he cannot then he had better leave it alone. Also, in situations of conflict the unconscious sometimes does not refer to the conflict. A man who does not know whether he should divorce or not is plagued day and night, running up and down the ladder of doubt, but the dreams talk of something completely different, just as if the whole conscious conflict did not exist. It would be the right thing to be able to switch and listen to the unconscious, but sometimes consciousness is so caught in its own view of things and its own ideas of conflicts having to be decided one way or another that the unconscious is not heard; and then, metaphorically speaking, the latter simply shrugs its shoulders and says, "If nobody likes me, they need not take me," as the parrot does. The unconscious, like this parrot, does not have a missionary attitude either, though at bottom it seems to be benevolent.

The parrot has to be asleep to be snatched and taken, just as the snake and the lion had to be asleep (though with open eyes) in order to get the precious objects they guarded. Here the alertness of the parrot has to be outwitted, and that is different from the original *Tuti-Nameh* story, where the parrot *is* rather like a missionary; for there it really intends to help Sâid, though that will also be to its own advantage. It wants to be free and not to fall into the hands of a fool, and in the Persian story it is again as absolutely evasive as in our story. So there are different variations if you amplify the motif of the parrot, but here we will stick to our version, where it has to be asleep. This obviously shows that the clash with what we could call the unconsciousness, the alert vitality of the parrot, has to be avoided again, as does the clash with the serpent which hides its head.

In alchemy the snake is generally represented in the form of a snake which bites its own tail, the famous ouroboros, and this is looked on as a union of the opposites, of the head and the tail. Sometimes the tail is interpreted as a phallic thing, because it enters the snake's mouth, and the head as a feminine end. So it contains the opposites of male and female. More often, the head part of the Ouroboros snake in alchemy is the meaningful, positive element in the *prima materia*, its spiritual element, and the tail is its destructive, poisonous element. There are several old Greek texts which say to take only the head when you work on this and to leave the tail alone, while other texts say that the whole snake has to be cooked, for it is the *prima materia*. But if there is anything dubious, it is the tail and not the head. This naturally refers to the age-old conflict of Western civilization, between the so-called spiritual and the so-called physical, or material, aspects of the psychic processes and the unconscious. Wherever there is an influence of spiritualization, there comes again this preference for the head against the snake's tail and mention of the tail as the thing to be thrown away—as the *terra damnata*, as the Latin alchemists later call it, the condemned earth which has to be thrown away and not integrated into the alchemical opus. In other texts the head and the tail both belong in the opus and are more characterized as the phallic and the receptive, the material and the spiritual ends of one and the same thing.

I say so-called mental and so-called physical because at present we have a split view of the world in our conscious theoretical standpoint. I doubt that this is more than a conscious splitting of one phenomenon. So for the sake of clarification, I speak of it as *so-called*. As Jung intimates in his writings, we are probably dealing with one and the same phenomenon which, when observed from within, looks psychic, and when observed statistically from the outside manifests itself as physical.

I have never found the snake's head to be negative in alchemical symbolism, so it is a very unusual motif here that the snake must hide its head when it is not dangerous. From a more primitive, natural standpoint, it is quite clear that by hiding its head there is a chance that the snake will not see the little boy and therefore will not bite him. However, this is not quite correct, because snakes are very shortsighted and have a very poor sense of smell. They have other ways of knowing when an enemy is approaching. They seem to sense it from the vibrations of the surrounding earth and such things (just how has not yet been discovered), but the concentration of sense perception in the head of the snake is definitely very limited. They seem to have a diffused capacity of sense perception spread over their whole body. Toads have a similar capacity, for if you destroy a toad's eyes it can still dimly see through its moist skin, and only if the skin is dried is it blind. So, on those lower layers of animal life there is a certain amount of diffused sense perception in some way, but so far we have no details as to how it functions. But probably if a snake hides its head, to speak naively, then it does not look, just like a bird which hides its head under its wing does not see, and then it can be taken. But here again there is a slight avoidance of meeting the snake face to face, just like the avoidance of meeting the parrot.

The confrontation with the spirit of the unconscious does not happen directly anywhere in this story, so there remains a certain amount of an exploiting conscious attitude, of taking the advantage wherever possible. But this time it is not successful, and now the witch really begins to triumph. She sends the little sister to see what has happened to her little brother, hoping that now with a final act she can destroy both of them. But the little sister is more fortunate than her brother—she really waits until the parrot is fast asleep and succeeds in seizing the bird.

The end of the story needs not much comment, and from now on you can interpret it yourself: the parrot is the spirit of truth, it brings out the truth, good is rewarded and evil is punished, the old family quaternio is restored and is now centered by this parrot, which probably will give them riches and good advice to the end of their lives, or at least we will hope so.

But we have not yet finished with the parrot. We have also not yet interpreted the petrification which occurs if one tries to snatch the parrot too soon. We will go into this more deeply in the next story. "The Bath Bâdgerd," but can make a beginning here.

The following is an extract from a poem in the *Tuti-Nameh* which describes the parrot. The *Tuti-Nameh* begins "In the name of Allah," and with this poem:

> In innumerable ways will I praise the Lord,
> The exalted, the all-wise Lord,
> Who, by the gift of speech, has distinguished man
> above all living things.
> Whose pleasure it was to raise His head saying:
> I have given them honor.
> Many thousand times would I also bless
> The Lord of prophecy, the shining star, the precious stone.
> In the jewel box of speech,
> The pride and delight of all earthly beings.
>
> Muhammad the elected,
> The talking bird,
> Who was conscious that he spoke not of his own inclination.
> The singing nightingale whose mouth
> Proclaimed only pure revelation.
> Who on straight paths leads to redemption
> Those who hold to the rope of his laws.

So Muhammad himself is called "the talking bird," and the talking bird is naturally the parrot, and in the text verse he is "the singing nightingale," another bird who reveals pure truth and who never speaks of his own desire—we would say he never speaks from his ego—but is a tool to announce the divine truth of Allah. So Muhammad, according to this introductory poem, is identified with the parrot because that is the bird which speaks the absolute truth.

In another place in the story it is said that the parrot is "the well of speech, the threshold of strange, wonderful thoughts." That is said of the parrot just in a kind of aside in the middle of the text, and the parrot has said itself that it is full of pearls of wisdom and precious stones and the knowledge of the truth; its heart is filled to the brim, and it knows the future and supernatural things. It is a symbol for the mysterious truth which the unconscious speaks. That means that it is a "threshold" phenomenon, it conveys the wondrous thoughts of the unconscious in its speech. It is probably the paradoxical nature of the fact that it is a bird which speaks in human language which makes it a very fitting symbol. It conveys the fact that it is something non-human (for we assume that we do not at all understand what a bird thinks or does), and yet in spite of this it can sometimes talk in language understandable by humans. And, last but not least, it is also a symbol of Muhammad.

Muhammad leads people on the rope of the law of the Koran, out of the labyrinth of this world to eternal bliss. One cannot help responding a little bit like Sâid, who felt, when he first met the parrot, that even if such a creature did read the verses of the Koran, there was no meaning in it, for it did not understand them itself! It just "parrots" the verses of the Koran and so, even if it calls people to prayer, one would not have to obey, one could just shrug one's shoulders and say, "Oh, but that is the parrot, it is not a human being speaking!" If we then consider that in certain other Turkish stories the parrot becomes a demonic destroyer, and further, that in this version it is guilty of having petrified innumerable people, we may perhaps be allowed to put a question mark against our parrot, and wonder if it does not also express this dangerous tendency to repeat original religious truths in a mechanical way, and by so doing, keep people unconscious and become a destructive spirit.

This again exemplifies the terrific incompatibility of the conscious and unconscious psyche in the human being, which confronts us and becomes a most urgent conflict. For instance, when the greatest truths, religious problems, are in question, how much should one repeat once-revealed truths and make them a conscious law, a conscious saying, and a conscious opinion, and become a parrot, mechanically repeating such truths? For they are truths, and you cannot therefore just say that you want them changed! What would be the use of saying, for example, having once realized that two and two make four, "Oh well, I don't mind, I am bored with people saying that two and two make four, let's rather say that two and two make five! Just for fun and for a change!" We know quite well that this is impossible. If something is true then it is always true, and everybody has to admit it, or else it is just ridiculous. On the other hand, for people who feel that the religious truth (for instance of the Koran, or of Buddha's teaching) is *the* truth, then there is only one possibility: to repeat it from then on, like a mathematical truth. But then you have the parrot! You glide off into being like that bird which speaks the words, at least so Sâid thinks, without knowing what it is saying—the bird being, so to speak, a mechanical contraption. You could just as well nowadays take a tape recorder for a parrot, and then always repeat the same truth. All book religions which rely on a once-and-forever revealed truth are immediately threatened by the negative aspect of the parrot symbol, namely by petrification.

Now we understand the spirit of petrification, because whoever falls a victim to this parroting spirit, now taken in the negative sense of the word, is psychologically petrified, and no more development is possible. And not only the human being but the whole of civilization is petrified, as we know quite well from history. Then you have all the habitual liturgical and other religious mechanisms which are devoid of any inner meaning or inner experience, which petrify the whole of society and the individual and his development. Naturally one can say, "Yes, but that is only for those people who do not know how to 'grasp' the parrot," and that is quite right. Through all this layer of mechanical tradition one can still comprehend and understand the original meaning and its original vital essence, and then petrification does not take place. If one can still read such a revealed text or religious experience with the eyes of the soul, then it still conveys life and the original meaning, and then the effect of petrification does not occur. But that depends on getting the parrot at the right moment, getting it when it is in a situation where it cannot escape you. If one is careless, then the original meaning escapes one, one gets sidetracked by words. Anyone who has studied theology, or analyzed theologians, those of all civilizations, will know to what I am alluding. It is a question of getting caught in meaningless words and phrases and in a kind of intellectual play with formal discussions, but the real gist of the original meaning and experience is not there any longer.

This is the dangerous side of the parrot, which is not emphasized in our story, but to which there is an illusion in the introductory poem in the *Tuti-Nameh,* where it is said that Muhammad is that bird which leads those to redemption on straight paths who hold to the rope of his laws. That means that you are just like a camel or a sheep, lined up on a rope which Muhammad pulls, and if you march in a row you will arrive at the goal. You needn't think, you needn't find your way, you needn't make any individual or personal effort, but just keep within that railing or barrier and that leads you straight to Paradise, or, as our fairy tale implies, to petrification! There you see that fairy tales are related to collective consciousness as the dream is related to an individual's consciousness: there is a slight compensatory function which points to certain dangers which are not indicated openly in collective consciousness.

In the Islamic world there is a split between the Sunnite

and the Shi'ite movement. The latter has always endeavored to be on the compensatory side of the unconscious and thus counteract the petrification of the Sunnite movement, the orthodox school which kept to the literal interpretation of the Koran and to its rules. Within the Shi'ite confession alchemical symbolism flourished. Eighty percent of the great Arabian alchemists belonged to the Shi'ites, and not to the Sunnite confession, which for us is very revealing because alchemical symbolism, and alchemy in general, was not only, as Jung points out, a subterranean compensatory movement in Christian Europe, but had exactly the same function within the Arabic civilization. There too it belonged to the subterranean, more mystical complementary movements which counteracted the petrification of collective consciousness in a very similar way as it afterward did in the Middle Ages for us. Particularly in Persia, Shi'ite and Ismailian sects flourished, as did alchemy. It was the country where there was the greatest development of alchemy, and one sees this mirrored even in such simple material as fairy tales. With this goes a relationship with nature and the beginnings of natural science, which always belong in this area of thought.

2

The Bath Bâdgerd

We come now to a Persian fairy tale which, to my mind, has directly influenced our Spanish story of "The White Parrot." It is entitled "The Secret of the Bath Bâdgerd."[15] The word "Bâdgerd" means "the castle of nothingness," so if you translate the title it means: "The Secret of the Bath called the Castle of Nothingness." The hero of this story is called Hâtim at-Tâi, "Tâi" being the tribal name. He belongs to the tribe of the Tâim and his personal name is Hâtim. The story is part of a well-known novel in which Hâtim at-Tâi seems to have been a historical figure, but some parts of the novel have also become a folklore story, which shows once more that sometimes in these countries novels become stories about simple folk.

Hâtim at-Tâi seems to have been a poet of the sixth or seventh century A.D. His poems, the "Kisse i Hâtim at-Tâi," were translated in 1830 by Forbes, in Calcutta. He was tremendously generous, and therefore in literature he became the ideal of generosity. He gave away all his fortune to the poor, and it is said that on his tomb there is an enormous stone bowl which is interpreted as representing the bowl from which every day he fed the poor of his whole land. Everybody was invited and fed by him, and anybody could stay at his court and live there. But there is something much more interesting about Hâtim at-Tâi's tomb, namely that around this stone bowl, the emblem of his generosity, was a mandala composed of eight women at the four corners, their hair unbound as women in the Orient wear it when mourning, with the stone bowl in the center. This bowl evokes alchemical associations, and actually our story is full of alchemical symbolism. Hâtim at-Tâi might have been one of those princes who promoted the study of alchemy, as did many rulers in those centuries.

In the *Encyclopedia of Islam* it is said that even nowadays there are still folk stories to the effect that this tomb is to be found somewhere, and there are descriptions of it as a kind of numinous place like the castle of the Grail. Like the Grail, it has to be found on some mysterious quest, and innumerable ghost and miracle stories are told about it. Nobody has yet found or discovered it. Thus the tomb of Hâtim at-Tâi is a real analogy to the Grail. It plays the same role in Persian folklore as the latter plays in our Celtic and Germanic folklore, the Grail too being a tomb and a vessel, carried and guarded by women. There have even been theories that the tomb motif is connected with the Grail motif in our countries, and that the latter was imported from the Orient. The tomb seems to be the only legacy of the historical Hâtim at-Tâi, and because of its highly symbolic character, it impresses the fantasy of the Persian and Iraqi people to this day.

Here is the fairy tale which they tell about Hâtim at-Tâi, "The Secret of the Bath Bâdgerd":

> In the service of the Queen Husn Bânû, Hâtim at-Tâi took as the seventh of many tasks (he is one of those cavaliers who just take on tasks for his King or Queen) the exploration of the Bath Bâdgerd, the Castle of Nothingness. He went out into the desert, and before the gates of the town he met an old man who invited him to his house and asked him where he was going, and Hâtim answered that he was going to explore the Bath Bâdgerd. The old man was silent for a long time and then said, "Young man, what enemy sent you to the Bath Bâdgerd? Nobody knows where it is; I have only found out that no one who ever tried to explore it ever came back. In the town of Qâ'tan is a King of the name of Hârith, and he has put a police cordon around the city so that everybody who tries to find the Bath Bâdgerd may be taken to him; nobody knows why he does

that, or whether he kills the people or lets them go." But Hâtim says that he has to go and that God must protect him, and he will not be put off this task. The old man therefore blesses him and again says, "Go back, this bath is a bewitched place, and nobody knows where it is, nobody has ever come back," and so on. But since Hâtim persists, the old man starts him on his way and then says that he should go to the right, and then he will come to a mountain at the foot of which there are many cypress trees, beyond which there is a desert where he must turn to the left—the way to the right is less difficult but more dangerous.

So Hâtim goes on and sees that near the village people sit together and dance and are having a sort of party and a lot of food, so he joins them and asks why they are so happy. They tell him that in the desert there is a powerful dragon, and when he takes on human shape all the young girls of the town are brought to him and there is a big festival and the dragon selects the girl he likes best. Now they are celebrating this festival, but not because they feel like it. They are forced to have it, and God only knows which girl the dragon will now take away from them. They are really in absolute despair, though pretending to be very happy. Hâtim then says, "So this happy festival is really a very sad day for you," and they agree that that is so, but he says that he will stay with them and see what he can do. Then he is placed beside the King of this country, who explains that the dragon is a kind of djin of a very destructive nature. Hâtim asks that the people be told to do exactly what he bids them. When the dragon has chosen one of their daughters they must tell him that there is a very noble young man who has ordered that the girl should not be given up without his permission and if, in his rage at this, the djin can destroy the whole kingdom within one year, he, the young man, can turn it into a desert in one second.

Everything happens like this, and when the dragon comes as a djin and is shown all the girls, they tell him of the young man who says that the girl should not be given to him, and the djin says, "Well, let the young man come here!" When Hâtim comes the djin says, "Young man, I have never seen you in this town before. Why do you mislead these people who have obeyed me before?" Hâtim replies that he does not want to interfere at all, but in the country from which he comes, the bridegroom has to go through a few ceremonies before he marries his bride. The djin asks what these ceremonies are, and Hâtim says that he has with him a talisman which he inherited from his forefathers, and this is put into the water from which the future bridegrooms drinks. Hâtim thereupon puts the talisman into the water from which the djin drinks—but naturally this is a trick, because the talisman takes away the djin's power. The second ceremony, Hâtim says, is that the bridegroom gets into a big barrel which is then closed, and he has to work his way out. If he can do this, it is all right and he will get the bride, and if not, he must give the young man two thousand diamonds for the bride. Of course the djin laughs and thinks he still has his magic strength, and so he gets into the barrel, from which naturally he cannot get out, and they set fire to it. He calls for help but is burned painfully to death, after which Hâtim has the barrel buried deep in the earth. He tells the people that now they can have their real festival because their misery has come to an end. The King gives him a lot of gold and silver, but in accordance with his generous nature he distributes it all to the poor, and after three days he goes on his way.

Afterward he climbs a mountain and then comes to an immense desert through which he wanders for days, sometimes drinking fresh spring water and sometimes brackish water. But then he comes to a bifurcation in the road and hesitates as to which to take, whether left or right, and he gets mixed up and thinks the old man advised him to go to the left, so he goes to the left. But after a while he becomes uncertain and then remembers that the old man had said he should go to the right. So he thinks he must go back, but gets lost in a lot of thorn bushes, and then becomes very unhappy and says the old man was right, this way is full of horror, and the thorns will certainly bring him into great difficulty.

I am not just being muddleheaded here; there is an annotation to the story saying that everyone is very confused in this part, for the storyteller also got mixed up in the thorny bushes. From the reproaches which he gets later, it looks as though Hâtim still stays on the wrong path, the one he was warned against. However, eventually, after many days he manages to get out, and then he sees animals racing toward him. They look like mongrel foxes and jackals and panthers, and Hâtim, terrified,

runs away as fast as he can but doesn't know how to escape
them. As he is standing shivering and hesitating, the old man
suddenly appears again and says, "Young man, you should listen
to the words of older and more experienced men and should not
despise their advice. Now take your talisman against those
animals and see the power of Allah." So Hâtim throws the
talisman, and the old man disappears and the earth becomes
first yellow, then black and then green and finally red, and
when the red appears, the animals become completely wild and
tear each other to pieces. Hâtim wonders about this sudden
enmity and what turned the animals against each other instead
of against him, but he thanks God and picks up his talisman
and goes on.

Farther on he comes to a forest of bronze, which is full of
metal splinters which pierce his shoes, and his feet get all cut.
So he bandages them and limps on. Then come giant scorpions
with eyes that glitter like wolves' eyes, but again the old man
appears and shows him how he can throw his talisman on the
ground; again the earth takes on all those colors, and when the
red appears the scorpions attack each other with such ferocity
that not one is left alive.

In time Hâtim comes to the town of Qâ'tan, and there he
puts two precious diamonds, two precious rubies, and two pearls
into his pockets and goes to the King's palace, where he says
that he is a merchant and comes from Schâhâbâd. He says he
want to see King Hârith, and he gives the King all these
precious stones so that the latter becomes very friendly and
invites him to sit near his throne and to stay with him for
a time. After a while the King even asks Hâtim to stay with him
forever, but Hâtim always gives him more precious stones, first
the pearls and afterward the diamonds, so that the King is
always propitated. But Hâtim always intimates that he still has a
wish. The King thinks naturally that it is his daughter and
finally offers her, but Hâtim says, "No, it is not even that
I want to marry your daughter," and he is so wily in the
conversation that King Hârith promises to fulfill his wish if he
can. Only after Hârith has promised that he will give him
anything or fulfill any wish he may express, does Hâtim say that
his wish is to see the Bath Bâdgerd and the King must let him
go there.

When the King hears this he sits silently and bows his head, and Hâtim says, "O King, why are you so sad?" The King replies, "Young man, many thoughts come into my mind; the first is that I have vowed never to let anyone go to the Bath Bâdgerd and the second thought is that nobody who ever went there has ever returned, and it would be a shame to let such a noble and handsome young man go there; and finally, if I do not let you go I shall be breaking the promise which I made you, so I do not know what to do!" Hâtim then answers, "O King, if God wills, I shall return alive and see you again, so just let me go!" The King then gets up and embraces him and agrees to let him go and says he will help him and show him the way. So Hâtim leaves the King and goes happily on his way, talking to the companions whom the King has sent with him. Soon he sees a strange domelike object which looks like the top of a mountain, and he asks the people with him what it is. They tell him it is the gate to the Bath Bâdgerd and that in seven days they will reach it.

At the end of this time they meet an immense army, and Hâtim asks what this means. His comrades tell him that Sâmân Idrak, the guardian of the bath, has this army here because he refuses entrance to everybody who had not been given a permit by the King of Qât'an, the place where Hâtim was before. So Hâtim shows his permit and is let in, but Sâmân Idrak, the owner of this army and guardian of the bath, says, "Young man, are you so tired of life that you don't want to listen to what I say? There is still time. If you turn back you will save your life, but if you go on you will regret your obstinance and pay for it with your life!" But when Sâmân Idrak sees that nothing would deter Hâtim from his enterprise, he leads him to the bath and Hâtim looks at the immense door which reaches right to the clouds, such an enormous door as he has never seen in his whole life. On it is an inscription in the Syrian language which says: "This enchanted place, built in the time of King Gayomard, will long remain as a sign, and whoever falls under its spell will never escape from it again, but amazement and horror will be his lot. He will hunger and thirst. It is true that he will be able to eat of the fruits of the garden as long as he still lives, and will see what there is to be seen in this place, but he will have great difficulties ever getting out again."

When Hâtim reads this he thinks to himself that the inscription really told him the secret of the bath, so why should he go further? He is about to turn back when he realizes that he has not yet discovered the *real* secret, so he says that what has to happen must happen and he must go on. Then he says goodbye to all his companions and after a few steps is within the door. Looking back to see if his companions are following him, he can see neither door nor people, only an endless desert stretching as far as the eye can see. Then, for the first time, he fully realizes what the name Bath Bâdgerd, Castle of Nothingness, means, and he realizes that now, having passed the door, he is going toward his death, and he says to himself, "Well, Hâtim, in this desert you will bury your bones." Then he looks all around, but everywhere there is nothing but the same desert. So he just goes on at random.

After many days he sees a human figure coming toward him, and when he is closer he sees that it is a young man who carries a mirror under his arm. The man greets Hâtim and shows him the mirror, and Hâtim takes it and looks at himself and asks whether one can use the bath and if the young man is the barber. (In those Oriental baths there is always a barber, for people generally get shaved at the same time, and such barbers always carry a mirror with them.) Then Hâtim asks where the bath is and the man answers that it is a bit farther on. Hâtim asks whether it is the Bath Bâdgerd, and the man says, "Yes, just that," and Hâtim is pleased and asks the man why he left the bath. The man replies that it is a part of his duties always to meet foreign people who come there and to take them to the bath and serve them and get his tip. "If you wish," he says, "you can follow me to the bath, and I hope I may have some of your superfluous money." "All right," says Hâtim, "I have been on a long journey and would like to have a bath."

So they continue and after about a mile there appears in front of them an immense cupola which seems to reach up to Heaven, and Hâtim asks what building that is, and is told that it is the Bath Bâdgerd. When they reach it the barber goes ahead and tells Hâtim to follow and the latter obeys. But when he wants to shut the door behind him he sees that is is already walled in with a stone wall, and Hâtim thinks that he will never get out of this bath again! The barber then leads him to the bath and tells

him he can get in and he will bring some warm water. But
Hâtim says he cannot get into the bath with all his clothes on,
he needs a loincloth. So the barber brings him one, and he
undresses and puts it on and gets into the bath. The barber
brings a bowl of warm water and pours it over his head. Twice
he returns with warm water, but while Hâtim is pouring the
third bowl of warm water over his head, there is a tremendous
thundering noise and the whole bath becomes dark and for a
while Hâtim stands there in utter darkness, completely confused. Slowly the darkness lifts, and barber and bath have both
disappeared; only the cupola remains, but it is like a great
vaulted rock, and the whole place is filled with water which is
almost up to his calves. Terrified, Hâtim wonders what kind
of uncanny magic this is—meanwhile the water rises up to his
knees, and he wades around and tries to find a door but cannot
find one anywhere, and soon the water is up to his waist.
Horrified, he looks around but finds no exit, and then the water
is up to his chin! All the time Hâtim is thinking that this is why
the people who came to the bath never came out again, for they
just got drowned, and you, Hâtim, will also meet your death in
these floods, it is impossible to escape them! "Well," he thinks,
"if man is confronted with death, he should turn his eyes to the
all-merciful God," and then he prays, "Oh Lord, I have given
all my strength in your service and I have only one life, but even
if I had a thousand lives I would submit them to your will. Thy
will be done." He tries thus to comfort himself, but the water
comes higher and higher and so he has to swim, and he swims
around the bath and the water rises right up until Hâtim's head
reaches the cupola over the middle of the bath. Tired out with
swimming, he tries to catch hold of that and rest for a moment,
but the moment he touches this round stone there is a tremendous clap of thunder, and suddenly he is standing out in the
desert, where, as far as can be seen, there is nothing but
endless wasteland. "Well," he thinks, "if I escaped the flood,
then I might even escape all the rest of this uncanny magic with
a whole skin."

For three days and nights he walks on, and then he catches
sight of a tall building. Hoping to find someone living there, he
goes toward it and sees that there is a big garden surrounding
the building. The gate is open, but when he goes through it the

garden suddenly disappears, and when he turns around to go
out again there is no trace of a gate, everything is uncanny.
"Oh," he thinks, "what new torture is this? Haven't I yet got
out of this magic circle?" Meanwhile the garden reappears, and
since he is forced to stay in it, he walks around in it. There
are trees covered with fruit and all kinds of flowers in beautiful
colors. He is hungry, so he picks a lot of fruit, but no matter
how much he eats he is never satisfied. He eats about a thousand pounds but remains just as hungry. But he has taken
courage again and goes on comforted. When he gets closer to
the castle he sees many stone statues standing around like idols,
or gods. He wonders what they mean but nobody is there to
disclose the secret.

While he is standing there sunk in thought a parrot calls out
from inside the castle, saying, "Young man, why do you stand
there? How did you get here, and why have you already finished
with life?" Hâtim looks up and listens to the voice, and then he
notices the entrance to the castle, over which is the following
inscription: "O you servant of God, you will probably never leave
this Bath Bâdgerd alive! This place was enchanted by Gayomard, who, one day when he went out hunting, found a diamond
which shone like the radiant sun and the gleaming moon. He
picked it up and, filled with amazement, showed it to his court
and to learned men, asking if they had ever seen such a stone,
and nobody had. So Gayomard said that he would keep it in a
place where nobody could ever find it, and to protect it he
brought about all this magic and built the Bath Bâdgerd. Even
the parrot sitting in its cage is under its spell! O servant of God,
within the castle on a golden throne are a bow and arrow, and
if you want to escape from here you must take these and with
them kill the parrot, and if you hit him the spell will be broken
and if you miss him you will become a stone statue."

When Hâtim has read this he looks at the stone statues and
says sadly, "Ah, that is how those statues came into existence,
and you too, Hâtim, will end your days in this witch's cauldron.
Yet man proposes and God disposes!" Thinking in this way, he
goes into the castle, takes the bow and arrow which lie on the
golden throne, and shoots at the parrot, but the parrot flies up
to the roof and the arrow misses and Hâtim's legs become stone
up to his knees. The parrot then flies back to its place and says

mockingly, "Go your way, young man, this is no place for
you!" With his bow and arrow in his hand, Hâtim then tries
with his stone legs to jump towards the parrot so as to be closer
next time, but he has to stop a hundred feet away from the bird,
for his feet are so heavy that he cannot get nearer. Then the
tears come into his eyes as he thinks, "How awful to have to live
here days and nights in such a miserable state! Shoot again,
Hâtim, at least to get petrified like the others!"

He shoots a second time, misses again, and is petrified up to
his navel. The parrot has again flown up to the roof and says as
before, "Do go your way, young man, this is no place for you!"
Hâtim again gives a jump, holding his bow and arrow, but again
has to stop a hundred feet away from the parrot. Then, crying,
he says, "May nobody miss the goal of his life as I have done!"
He still has one arrow left, so commending himself to the
protection of God, he aims at the parrot and, crying "God is
great!" shuts his eyes and shoots. Against all his expectations,
the arrow hits the parrot. A cloud of dust rises up and thunder
fills the air and the earth becomes dark. Confused by all the
noise, Hâtim thinks he has turned into a statue. But when the
thunder ceases and he opens his eyes again, the garden, the
cage, the golden throne, and the bow and arrow have disappeared, and instead lies before him an enormous beautiful
diamond. And Hâtim goes to it and picks it up. His legs are no
longer petrified and all the statues have become alive. Hâtim
tells them everything that has happened, and they all thank him
and offer to serve him as his slaves. Hâtim tells them to follow
him to Qât'an. Nobody knows where that is, but luck is with
them and they find the right way, and after several days, find
the door by which they had entered the Bath Bâdgerd. On the
other side of the gate they find Sâmân Idrak, the guardian of
the bath, and Hâtim tells him of all his experiences. And
Sâmân Idrak takes them to his home and then sets them on
their way. Upon arrival at Qât'an, Hâtim seeks out King Hârith
and tells him everything and shows him the diamond which he
says he must take to Queen Husn Bânû. Then he begs him to
give the men with him money and horses so that each may reach
his own country. This is done, and Hâtim and King Hârith say
goodbye and Hâtim returns to Schâhâbâd.

Queen Husn Bânû's people recognize Hâtim and bring him to

the palace, where the Queen receives him and listens to his story and looks at the diamond. After the Queen's wedding with Prince Munîr has been celebrated, Hâtim returns to Yemen, his own country, where he later inherits the throne from his father and lives in happiness all the days of his life.

Before entering into the interpretation of this Persian story, we have to return to the end of the Spanish version because only now can we look more closely at the parrot.

We saw before that the miraculous parrot is the motif of Oriental fairy tales in a book called the *Tuti-Nameh, The Book of the Parrot,* where a parrot tells all the stories in order to prevent the heroine from committing adultery. The translator of the *Tuti-Nameh* tells us that the original was an Indian story called "Cuka Saptati, The Seventy Stories of the Parrot." So the homeland of this motif is actually India. In India this was a very popular collection of stories, mostly of a light erotic character, as are most of those in the *Tuti-Nameh.* Then in the beginning of the fourteenth century the book was translated into the Persian language by a famous author called Nashebi, who shortened, changed, and embellished it, and shaped it into a Persian novel, so that only certain fragments still indicate its Indian origin. Later it was also translated into the Arabic language. At that time there was the old Turkish version, which no longer exists; a new Turkish translation was made in the seventeenth century. There exists an English translation of the Turkish version by Gladwin (Calcutta, 1801).

We need not go deeper into this collection of parrot stories, even the Indian ones, because it is only the motif of the *parrot* which has walked through all those times and places, while the content around it has completely changed. What we see is that the parrot functions in the original Indian country as the *vetala* does in the famous story of *The King and the Corpse,* which Heinrich Zimmer has brilliantly commented upon.[16] In that tale, a *vetala,* generally translated as "demon," gets into one of the corpses at the place of burial. When the King receives the order to take the corpse down from the tree on

which it is hanging, the *vetala* makes himself heavier and
heavier, and all the night long tells the King a story and then
snaps back to its tree, so that the next morning the King
finds the corpse again hanging there. He patiently goes back
and unhooks it from the noose and takes it again on his
shoulder, and again the whole night long the *vetala* tells him
another story while on his back. So it goes, on and on. It is
the same motif of innumerable stories, but finally, by this
trick, the *vetala* saves the King from being murdered by a
beggar monk who wanted to kill him, and who had given him
the order to get this corpse. The *vetala* not only saves the
King from being killed; he also later leads him to become one
with the god Shiva, so he leads him to the highest *unio
mystica* with the godhead.

This demon first appears to be very ambiguous, and one
does not know what its intention is. One has the feeling of a
teasing, torturing, demonic creature living in this corpse.
Only at the end of the story does it reveal its positive aspect
to the King; before that, it is really a tantalizing thing which
the King has to carry patiently. That would be a parallel
storyteller to our parrot. In the famous *Arabian Nights*, the
storyteller is the Queen, who should have been killed after
the first night, but who always tells another story to save her
own life. Here the role of the storytelling person is represented by an anima figure. In a famous twelfth-century story
by the Persian poet Nizami entitled, "The Seven Stories of
the Seven Princesses," again every night a princess tells the
King a beautiful fairy tale.

So it has become a classical motif in Oriental literature
that a mysterious storyteller is introduced. Through this
figure the many stories are brought into one and aligned
connection, as if circling around a common deeper meaning.
In his thesis, Arwind Vasavada[17] has, for instance, shown
that in *The King and the Corpse* all stories are connected by
the meaning that they teach the King how to deal with evil.
The King is a chivalrous type of hero who is clearly not up to
the problem of evil. He is the upright man who knows no

fear and does not lie, who keeps to the ethical rules of a heroic aristocratic ideal, and therefore is only up to enemies who keep the same standard. But the beggar monk who tries to kill the King is really a wicked murderer and black magician, and the King is so hopelessly naive that, had it not been for the *vetala,* he would have been destroyed right away, which shows that the ethical standards of aristocratic, heroic behavior prevalent in India at that time were utterly insufficient to cope with the problem of evil. Into this difficulty comes the figure of the *vetala* who helps the King out. The stories he tells are all of adultery and love affairs, mostly of a rather sexual character, stories of corruption and cunning and of women deceiving their husbands. The gist of it is that the *vetala* initiates the King into the world of feminine wickedness, cunning, black magic, corruption, and all those evil tricks which a noble hero of the Brahmin caste is not up to. And so, slowly, in those many nights where the *vetala* tells his stories, he cures the King of his lack of experience of life and of his incredible but well-meaning naiveté.

In the *Tuti-Nameh* a similar idea is at work, for Mâhi-Scheker, the heroine who wants to commit adultery, is an awfully naive woman. She is at first delighted with her husband, but when he is away she is just childish and cannot be without a man, so she looks out of the window and thoughtlessly would have walked into another adventure and been killed by her husband when he came back. She obviously does not realize what she is doing, but the parrot comes in and prevents such destructive nonsense. *The Arabian Nights,* those thousand-and-one-night stories, are also stories told with the intention of curing the King's misconceptions and wrong attitude toward the feminine principle. It seems, therefore, that in all those stories there is a frame in which an essential figure tells a number of apparently completely disconnected tales, just a fairytale every night. But if one looks at them more closely, one discovers a therapeutic tendency, namely curing the listener of his naiveté or lack of wisdom in some aspects of life. One is reminded also of the eighteenth sura of the Koran, in which Khidr has to cure Moses of his naiveté and conventional morality.

If we compare those stories we see that the underlying idea is that by indirect stories the storyteller matures the mind of the listener and so leads him to certain realizations which change and cure his conscious attitude, which is either ethically naive or not up to the anima problem or the problem of evil. In *The King and the Corpse*, the king is later led to mystical union with the godhead. In the *Tuti-Nameh*, the religious frame has fallen away and the parrot only prevents Mâhi-Scheker from committing adultery, but the parrot is identified with Muhammad, for Muhammad is called the parrot who speaks those pearls of wisdom.

So first a kind of worldly novel was imported with its amusing stories, but some deeper mind reading the book re-linked it with a religious background. Then in the Spanish story the parrot has lost all these aspects and has become just a precious thing to be found under great danger, which then protects the figures of our story from evil. Only two connections have survived, namely that this white parrot counteracts the effects of evil and protects very naive people; but he also still has something of his demonic nature, for if you don't get him in the right way at once, you petrify.

We now see why, in interpreting the Spanish fairy tale, I always kept a certain *reservatio mentalis,* saying that this is all right as far as it goes, but the boy does not confront the lion or the snake, and it is finally the girl who seizes the parrot when it sleeps. I felt that this was not a definite solution, though at the end of the story the quaternio owns a white parrot which is apparently a precious thing and will protect them. So in the Spanish story the motif has become more superficial, though the parrot still functions as a symbol of the Self, or of the central voice of the unconscious.

In the *Tuti-Nameh*, the religious background is confined to the introductory poem and certain descriptions of the parrot, for every time he opens his beak, pearls of wisdom come out of it; he speaks the truth and knows the hidden things of the present and the future. He certainly has supernatural and nearly divine qualities and is "the threshold of wondrous thoughts."

The parrot lends itself to the projection of being the voice of the unconscious because to hear a parrot speaking in human language for the first time is a most peculiar experience, and many people find it rather uncanny. I remember once going into an inn, when a parrot suddenly called out from the corner, *"Eine Suppe dem Herrn"*—"A soup for the gentleman." He had always heard the waiter saying this in the kitchen. I got an absolute shock! A dumb creature which is not supposed to open its beak suddenly in human language says understandable words! Further, there is one thing more to be said: birds' eyes are usually constructed so that they can see into the distance, and because they are so much at the side of their heads, they cannot focus them. A bird looks at you from the side and not straight on, as most animals do, which gives one a kind of uncanny feeling. If you try to look into a bird's eye there is this strange staring look, as though it looked through or over you objectively but did not see you in front of it. It looks into the distance. Also, because a bird lives and flies in the air, it is generally interpreted as a soul- or thought-being, something spiritual. But this fleeting soul-being, to which you cannot relate directly if it is a parrot, suddenly speaks quite clearly in human language and in very definite form.

We therefore have to interpret the parrot as a personification of the unconscious, but with a very specific aspect. In German, if somebody has a lot of odd ideas, we say that he has a bird, or sometimes even a cageful of birds, in his head. So birds mean autonomous thoughts which suddenly pop into your head and leave you again, you don't know how! They can inspire you, when it's the dove of the Holy Ghost, or they can put very devilish or odd ideas into your head, according to the different birds.

Like the parrot on the outside, the unconscious sometimes manifests itself in the same uncanny way in dreams, when either inspiring thoughts or definite voices give definite instructions. Most of our dreams contain a message in a symbolic form which we have to decipher through dream interpretation. But from time to time, there is a voice which says something definite. People come to tell you a dream, but say, "I only heard a voice saying . . . " Or the voice is included within a dream story: "but suddenly a voice said . . . ," and these dream instructions, or sayings, are always very concise and impressive and are generally more directly to the point than the more involved allusions in the symbolic dream pictures. Most people, therefore, when they have such a voice, immediately feel that it is not to be discussed, but obeyed. Generally, though we still have to use our critical mind, we can see that such voices come directly from the Self, from the innermost center of the personality, and that they convey a central and essential message. Though they can also come from other autonomous complexes, usually they are a phenomenon of the unconscious which has to be considered very seriously, since it is unusual for the unconscious to become so definite. If there is a breakthrough which even takes the form of a human voice with a human wording of facts, we can conclude that the charge behind such a message is very strong, for it represents the *non plus ultra* of clarity. In such a manifestation, whatever is constellated in the unconscious is more intensified than normal, which is why one feels that it has to be taken very seriously and cannot be discarded. Many people who do not pay attention to their dreams *do* instinctively pay attention to such messages, for they are more struck by them.

One could say that the parrot is a fitting symbol of this psychological phenomenon of the spirit of the unconscious, for, in a numinous way, it speaks in this surprisingly clear human language. When this happens, we know that it points to something essential, which accounts for the explanation that the parrot is Muhammad, the prophet of God. This, to a certain extent, also explains the parrot in the Spanish fairy tale, though not the destructive and demonic aspect of the motif of petrification, which we saved for the Persian story of the Bath Bâdgerd where it becomes clearer.

We have analyzed the structure of these stories in which the parrot originally appeared in Indian, Persian, and Turkish translations, and one could say that this composition is really a mirror image of what the unconscious does in dreams. Every night, or many nights, the unconscious tells us a story, and though they often do not seem to be immediately connected, they do accompany and promote a maturing process in the personality of the dreamer. The last sentence of the *Tuti-Nameh* says that those stories contain wise teaching and give much good advice and are gifts from which studious people can profit, for each one, even the shortest, offers great help. They are like precious pearls all strung on the same thread. Here the poet and storyteller clearly advises not only the enjoyment of the stories but that their meaning should be studied. He intimates that, though they seem to be casual and chaotic, they really have a secret connection, which strengthens the idea that the parrot must represent something similar to the inventor of dreams in us, whatever this unknown power is.

We come now to the interpretation of "The Secret of the Bath Bâdgerd." Here the hero is a grown-up young man, while in the Spanish story the seekers of the parrot were the little boy and then the little girl, pushed by the witch and helped by the wise old man. So the initial motif comes from a witch with evil intentions, and the saving advice is inspired by a wise old figure with helpful intentions, but those who carry out the orders are only children. This would mean, psychologically, that realization got stuck on an infantile level, that the secret forces of renewal subsisted in an unadulterated and unspoiled, but infantile, part of the personality. Together with this goes the fact that all the dangers which the little brother and sister encounter are not very dramatically told, as compared with the Persian story, in which one really gets a feeling of the irrationality, danger, and horrors of the spellbound garden in which the parrot lives. In the story of "The White Parrot," though, there are magic and uncanny things, such as the lion sleeping with its eyes open and the guardian snake; yet they are flattened in a manner typical for European fairy tales, which corresponds to an incomplete conscious realization. This might have to do with the fact that in the Orient grown-up people tell the stories and therefore there is much more wisdom and intuitive realization in them. Also, the fairy tale in European countries has been slowly split away from the official religious teaching and thereby relegated to the low popular and infantile realm of civilization, while in the Orient it has always remained connected with the conscious cultural life.

Throughout the story Hâtim plays the same role as many heroes of fairy tales all over the world: a rather uninteresting but well-bred Prince is interested in a Princess, but is not capable of fulfilling the deeds she asks of him, so the hero of the story steps in and acts for the Prince, but does not take the reward and walks out of the story again. There is a whole collection of stories, for instance in Russia, where the hero is always Ivan, who gets the Princess, or exorcises the bewitched Princess, or wins a Queen through great deeds, for the rather banal Czar's son. But sometimes that does not work so well, for the lady prefers to marry the man who did all the great deeds, and she rejects the Czar's son, realizing that he is not worth marrying, so that at the end of the story there is a conflict. When this happens one could say that there is a budding realization among the people that the model of the right conscious behavior is not identical with the real human being. The hero is a model figure, an ideal, a guiding factor or an image created by the unconscious to overcome certain unusual difficulties.

Generally the image of a hero appears in dreams when the dreamer is up against something unusually hard, when the person needs a heroic attitude. Let's assume, for instance, that a young man has to do such a simple thing as tell his mother that he is going to have a room somewhere out in

the need for a heroic attitude

town. One could say that that is a very simple human affair! But we know quite well what it all implies in certain cases: scenes, and regressions, and breakdowns, and tears! I even know of a mother who served herself up as a corpse to her son! She said, "Only over my dead body"—and then died (appropriately) to cure him from such impulses toward independence! In such a situation a young man would have a dream, perhaps, of a hero slaying a dragon, which would mean that the unconscious is setting the right accent on the situation. On the surface it looks like an ordinary and human affair, but actually, psychologically, an absolutely heroic attitude is required to overcome the obstacle. In such a case the archetypal image of the hero comes up in dreams and represents that right attitude which is now needed.

If we study hero figures in comparative mythology, they are characterized by a vocation which is carried through without any doubts. Now our man doubts a lot, he complains and cries a bit, and says, "Poor Hâtim, you will bury your bones in this desert," and so on, but he never considers going back. So basically, he has that typical feature of the hero: there is no discussion and the thing has to be done, and such an attitude shows an unusual oneness of the personality. We are generally divided up into twenty different complexes, and they all discuss with each other: "shall I," "shall I not," "but," "but yes," "on the other hand," and accordingly we waver around in moods of uncertainty. The young man decides to go away from home, and then Mama looks so pale at breakfast that he already gets sick to his stomach and is not quite so sure that it is really the right thing, and then his financial complex comes in and says it will be so much more expensive if he has to pay for the room himself, and so on and on and on, and then he dissolves and the heroic *élan vital* is gone once more. But the symbol of the *hero* has that oneness of the *elán vital*, the certainty that the task has to be done—even if he or everybody else dies, it has still got to be done. There is the feeling of a vocation, of obedience to an ultimate inner authority.

Medieval / modern hero

In a way, the hero personifies the Self, or what the alchemist calls the *vir unus,* the one man, the unified personality with all its strength. Now this unified personality is not what we are, but we identify with it when we listen to hero stories, to comfort and strengthen ourselves for the things we cannot do without help. In later fairy tales there is very often an opposition between such a heroic figure and an ordinary human being who does not cut a very elegant role beside the hero, and there begins a kind of doubt or difficulty as to what the hero is as compared with us as ordinary doubting human beings. The nearer you get to modern European documents— I am speaking now on a large scale, of hundreds of years— the more altered does the ideal of the hero become. Our civilization gets further and further away from the old-fashioned heroic hero, till in the Grail legend there is even an opposition of Gawain and Perceval, Gawain being the hero in the classical sense of the word and Perceval more human. Gawain is the chevalier without fear, with complete honesty and courage. He personifies the whole medieval idea of the hero: the man who fears nothing and whose shield of honor is without stain. He is opposed to his double, Perceval, who stumbles, who fails to ask the Grail question, who breaks down, who wavers all the time in the most human way, but who in the end is the one who finds the Grail, in contrast to Gawain. Gawain does all the deeds, and when finally the King wants to tell him what it is all about, he falls asleep, worn out with his great deeds. When the King says, "Now I will tell you the mystery of the Grail," and looks up, he sees Gawain and his horse, asleep! So he fails at the last minute, while Perceval fails at the beginning. Perceval is the modern man, the man who stumbles, who doubts, who is certain of nothing any longer and who has lost this primitive *élan,* the ideal of the former hero.[18]

In the Bath Bâdgerd story we still have the other situation, where the hero, though he is different from the ordinary human being, is not yet in conflict with it; he is still that type of hero who is set on his task and goes through with it.

Such a figure is compensatory to an actual setup in life, where most men are not heroes, and are weak and a bit— well, all too human—as they probably were in Persia, as well as everywhere else. After this general introduction to the structure of the story, we begin with the specific episodes.

In the service of the Queen, Hâtim has to find out the secret of the Bath Bâdgerd, and nobody even knows where that is! First there is the typical quest, the adventurous search for the previously unknown thing, like the Grail. From the beginning, Hâtim gets many warnings showing the great difficulty of the task and its mystery and unusualness, for he has to find something and does not even quite know what it is. So it is not like finding a diamond, or a precious stone, or a pearl guarded by a dragon. He has really to explore something terrible and unknown: the Castle of Nothingness, as the name says.

That the Queen has set the task would mean that the anima, Hâtim's unconscious feminine side, has put this bug into his head. Very often the anima does this to a man and in such a form that he does not even know what it is all about. Sometimes an anima creates in a man a certain searching restlessness, a constant feeling of "this isn't it," whatever I live, it is not yet *it*, there is still something not yet found, a restless longing for some kind of goal or adventure of life. If you ask him to tell you what it would be, he can't even say, but he will use a lot of words and stammer in trying to describe some idea of fulfillment, of finding out some mystery. We would say that the anima sets the goal of the process of individuation, for we know that she is the servant of this process in a man, but the goal is still absolutely indefinite.

In the final act, when Hâtim shoots at the parrot and fails for the second time, he says, "May nobody fail in the goal of his life as I did." In this exclamation he confesses that he is now trying to reach the goal of his life, though he hadn't known that when he started on his journey. On the way he has slowly realized that he was coming closer to the achievement of that thing for which he had been searching. He begins to realize that this is it, that now he has to achieve, to shoot the parrot. Then he will have reached the goal of his life, and if he fails, his whole life will have failed. So the anima figure, that exalted Queen anima, sets the unknown goal, the exploration of a mysterious bath, the name of which says that it is nothing! It is the unknown, which we might very well identify with what we call the unconscious, for the unconscious means that area of the psyche which is not known to us.

Hâtim first comes to a town which is celebrating a big festival, and he discovers that this is really the terrible day on which they have to give away a girl to the desert djin, and that this year the djin has chosen the King's daughter. But Hâtim saves her by the tricks described earlier. It is the classical hero's deed of saving a maiden in distress, as in the Greek myths of Perseus and Theseus, and so on. Everywhere the hero has to free the King's daughter from such a destructive lover, and in this Oriental setup it is naturally a dragon-like djin.

According to general belief, djins were local gods of pre-Islamic times and originated as did the nature demons of the Middle Ages with us. Usually when a new religious order is superimposed on an old one, the gods of the old order are depotentiated into demons. For instance, in European countries, the devil has a horse's hoof, which comes from Wotan. Nowhere in the Bible is it said that the devil has a horse's hoof, but old Wotan got identified with the devil and thus lent the devil his horse's hoof. In the Orient demons usually have the cloven hoof of the goat.

Generally in pagan polytheism there are local gods, gods who have certain temples and who are worshiped in certain places; but if a new religious order is superimposed the local gods continue to spook as demons and are mostly interpreted as destructive forces. Sometimes, however, they still own the treasures of the old religion, and therefore as soon as people want to use black magic they turn to the older gods; they will know better where the treasure has been hidden, for they are the older people who know more of the place itself. So those djins in the pre-Islamic times were probably also locally worshiped gods who had turned into demons, and it was generally believed that they steal girls. Even nowadays it is still said in North African countries that one should not approach a woman who lives alone too near the desert, because she is pretty sure to be possessed by a djin. We would still subscribe to that, because she would be pretty sure to be animus-possessed. These djins in their destructive aspect, therefore, would represent some (psychologically) still continuing fascination of an old archetypal figure which has a regressive character. For instance, the medieval devil still has a certain Wotan fascination by which he can possess people, as we have seen in the recent events of this century, for the old archetype revives and again takes possession of the men's animae! Nowadays a man may dream that his beloved woman is whoring about with an exceedingly nasty creature. If it is somebody the man knows, he could be interpreted as a shadow figure, but sometimes his anima is sleeping with some unknown demonic figure, and that always points to the fact that not the man himself but his anima is possessed.

What does it mean if a man's anima is possessed? The man is not possessed, but his anima is, and you could multiply such possession states through the whole unconscious. In dreams there are sometimes very complicated images of such possessions, and that means, practically, that this man's ego is completely reasonable as long as his semi-unconscious feelings and the area of his relatedness are not touched. But as soon as problems of relationship or of feeling are touched, then instead of having a normal human reaction, he suddenly blows up and acts in a kind of possessed way; not he, but his anima, his Eros function, is possessed. Possession is always characterized by the fact that every kind of human or reasonable discussion is out of the picture, that facts are no longer taken as facts, and that a kind of resentful affect bursts out. As soon as somebody behaves in such a way you know that an autonomous complex possesses this area of his personality.

So here it would mean that, as long as the problem of Eros is not touched on, the men in this town behave reasonably and everything is all right. But the problem of Eros and the women here, especially this time the King's daughter, are under the spell of this dragon demon, which means that in that area something absolutely unconscious and primitive still rules behavior.

Now Hâtim, the man in the service of the Queen, and therefore the man who has set out to differentiate his anima and his Eros function as his goal, is naturally the right person to outwit this dragon. He does it with an amulet which weakens the dragon, and afterwards by the classical trick of putting him into a barrel or bottle, or some other container, as a kind of test and then not letting him out again. There are innumerable such stories of banishing a spirit like that. One challenges him and says, for instance, "Oh, you are much too big, you will never get into this bottle." "Oh," the demon says, "I can do that," and in he goes and you put in the cork! Here it is a barrel which has the same function. Now how does man in a simple way imprison possessive affects and primitive impulses in barrels and bottles and containers? What does that mean practically? It means: rationalizing it. When you say, "Ah, I know what that is, it's nothing but . . . ," then you have put it in a bottle and you have a cork and use it and then it can't catch you any longer. Those containers are all made by human wit. The invention of how to carry about liquid, of the vessel, and of all containers, is one of the greatest original inventions of mankind, nearly as big as finding fire, and is therefore a symbol of man's capacity to imprison, by his wit and his intelligence, things which normally escape him. Generally we disapprove of rationalization, we use the word in a derogative way. We say, don't rationalize it! But like all things, there is a double aspect to it: actually, we have constantly to use our mind and intelligence to imprison djins and other demons. For instance, let's go back to the young man who wants to take a room alone. He comes to the analytical hour and says that he feels funny, he thinks he is going to have the flu, and he's feverish. Then it might be a very good thing to say, "Oh, that's just your mother complex regression tendency. Ignore it!" Then he will pull himself together and carry on. But what have you really done? You have rationalized this regressive impulse, you have called it "nothing but a mother complex regression." You have, as it were, slapped it into the container and labeled it "Mother Complex Regression" and thus cut its effectiveness.

There are demons which get very tame and beg to be let out. This motif has been elaborated in Jung's interpretation of the fairy tale "The Spirit in the Bottle."[19] There the hero has a legal arrangement with the demon and says, "All right, if you'll behave I'll let you out again," and he arranges with the spirit for it to help him and then it becomes tame. That would be a form of sublimation. But this djin is buried: that is repression. So he is not so sublimated, he is just cut off by rationalization. It is a temporary solution which mankind has very often used. Naturally it is no definite solution, that would only be so if you could convert the demon. But that doesn't happen here, so he is just rationalized away, and that is always a temporary solution. One day the djin gets off by a trick, saying, "If you'll just let me out for a minute, I'd like to stretch my legs," or something similar—and then he's off!

Let us go back to the example of the young man who has to leave his mother. If you say to him, "Oh well, your funny feeling in your stomach is just an hysterical symptom because you want to regress to Mama at the last minute," by that you squash his regressive tendency and kick him out of the nest, and that is a temporarily good solution. But what have you done that is wrong? You have taken a leading role! You've taken on the role of Mama, or Papa, of a guiding adult, and you have therefore not brought about a real solution. You have, for the moment, solved his problem, but at the cost of his now being dependent on you, for he himself has not found the courage either to rationalize the demon away or to have it out with that demon. So in this example we can be quite sure that some time later the thing will come up again. That is why certain analysts are so aware of the problem that they don't dare to do such things; they always sit there and just wait for the analysand to find the solution and never interfere with such cutting rationalizations. But I think that you have sometimes to use right or wrong means in a mixture, and know what you do, and when to do it. Sometimes you have to take on such a role and interfere, even knowing that later on you will pay for it because it is only a half-right thing. Just as you see here what would have happened if Hâtim had said to those people in the town, "Well, that's your problem, until you mature you will never get rid of the djin, so as a wise analyst I am not going to help you against him. Goodbye!" One feels, if one reads the story naively, that it was nice of him to help those people, even though they have not matured, and probably something will happen with that djin later. It would have been better if Hâtim had had an alchemical transforming liquid to transform the demon, but he cannot do that because he has not found the diamond, the Self, yet. He is still stuck with the older form of alchemy, with magic. Magic was a regressive shadow of alchemy.

That is confirmed by the historical fact that for a long time alchemy was always weighed down into unconsciousness by its magical use and magical aspect. Already in Zosimos' time it was said by some that they were seeking the religious spiritual goal and were not the people who made "metal magic." There was already a split within the alchemical effort between using it as magic and using it as a means of becoming conscious. By using the trick of the bottle, the demon is repressed and not integrated.

If you repress a complex, or rationalize it away, or cut it off from your living system because it is destructive, then there is a loss of vitality, a loss of power. You see that best, in an extreme form, in what is called clinically the regressive reconstruction of the persona after a psychotic episode. People are reasonable, they are again adapted to the outer world, but they have lost something, they have lost vitality, their *élan vital*, and sometimes, if one sees them again, one feels, "Oh God, were they not richer and nicer when they were nicely crazy!" It is an impoverishment. They have cut out the destructive autonomous complex, but they have lost its power *literally* too! It would be a *desideratum* if one could put those things nicely in a bottle, transform the destructive aspect, and keep its vitality and the dynamic aspect. But the ego cannot do that. It would be destructive if it could, for that would make it inflated—a magician ego, the master of the powers of heaven and earth. For the ego to say, "Let's take all those djins and demons, and instead of putting them in the bottle, extract their power and use it" is a dictatorship ideal. It is the ideal of certain modern men now, but they all, as far as we can see, come up against it! The unconscious will not cooperate with such a thing. So if you want really to transform them, you need the help of the Self and therefore, finally, the Self has the power, not the ego. But putting a spirit of a djin into a bottle would also imply a rejecting emotional attitude, which is what we generally understand by rationalizing in the negative sense of the word: we rationalize it *away*. Underneath there is the emotion of fear, which is why we say with a certain affect, "it is nothing but . . . ," or go even further and say, "it is *just* such and such." So I mean rationalization with the negative undercurrent, which in men generally implies that the anima is involved. If a man cannot be objective, but has this kind of "nothing but" affect underneath what he says, then you think, "Aha, the lady anima is in it!" The same applies to the animus of a woman, for if she cannot be objective and look at things quietly, if there is fear of a negative affect, that gives the "nothing but" nuance to her judgment.

This has always occurred when a new religious teaching has been superimposed upon an old religion. This kind of negativistic, rational, "nothing but" undertone is very evident in the early Christian apologetic literature against the pagan mysteries, and also in the opposition of Islamic teachers to paganism. Since the djins belonged to these older layers of religion and North African superstition, "nothing butism" was also used against such figures, and that was probably the bottle with which Hâtim imprisoned the djin. We could put a question mark after this episode by saying that the djin was not overcome, that somebody would later dig him up again. This does not happen within our story, but we can certainly say that this is never the way to overcome any demon, it is always a temporary solution, albeit one which may succeed if at the time we have something more important to do. Sometimes certain problems have to be repressed when there is no time to cope with them; one has to get on with the main task.

There is more of this on Hâtim's path towards the Bath Bâdgerd: having set his mind on his main task, he represses and casts away certain other possibilities of inner development. Clearly the djin is mainly interested in women, he gets one every year from this town, and at the end of the story Hâtim does not marry, but only finds the diamond and then goes home and does not take up any connection with the feminine element. We can assume, therefore, that whenever Hâtim in a later phase of his life takes up his anima problem, he will be up against the djin again. In our story only one part of the way is sketched, but one sees there the connection of djin-feminine, which is now cast aside to reach some other goal.

Hâtim then leaves the town which he has freed from its curse. Next comes the problem of the old man, who tells him to go to the right first; but when he comes to a bifurcation he is not to go to the right again. The way to the right is not so difficult but is full of horrors, while the left way is much more difficult but Hâtim will get on better. He tries to obey the old man but does not know whether he is on the right or wrong path. Unfortunately, the translator tells us in a footnote that the tale is confused, and that in his translation he has therefore tried to put things right, so it is hopeless for us to try to reconstruct the original text.

It is unfortunate that philologists work on texts with the idea that every sentence must have a rational meaning;

otherwise they think there is a mistake and that something went wrong in the copying of the manuscript—though in about 75 percent of the cases this would be the truth. However, sometimes texts are confused in a *meaningful* way when the unconscious of the writer interferes, and then the philologists, with their passion for rationalization, make an even worse salad, while we who can read the confusion of the unconscious could have made something out of the original. Now, unfortunately I am not an Arabist, and being unable to get at the original text, we have to give up the puzzle and say that the translator has changed the text, and what the original, meaningful confusion was, we do not know.

It looks to me as though Hâtim went on the left path and was very unhappy because it was a bad way, but that is all we can make out. In the desert he is attacked by some demonic wild animals which look like bastard foxes, jackals, and panthers—they would look something like a hyena. He is terrified and takes the talisman, or amulet, which he received from a woman during some former adventure (not described in our story). When he throws his talisman onto the ground in the midst of the animals, the earth turns first yellow, then black, then green, and then red, and as soon as the red color appears these monsters become completely wild and tear each other to pieces, so that Hâtim is able to go on. I am taking the next episode at the same time since it is parallel. In another part of the desert he is attacked by enormous scorpions as big as jackals, with claws like birds and eyes which glitter like wolves' eyes, and again he saves himself by throwing the amulet on the ground, so that the earth again changes into four colors and the demons destroy each other.

To these demonic creatures which destroy each other, there is a very clear parallel in the Greek myth of Cadmus, a hero who is himself a parallel to the ithyphallic Hermes. Cadmus' sister, Europa, had been abducted by Zeus in the form of a bull, and Cadmus was set on the quest of finding his sister. By divine order, however, he was commanded to give up this search and to follow a certain cow until it lay down to rest. At the same time he was promised Harmonia, the daughter of Ares and Aphrodite, as his wife. When the cow lay down, Cadmus, wishing to sacrifice her, sent his companions to fetch water for the sacrifice. They found it in a sacred grove belonging to Ares and guarded by a dragon, Ares' son, which killed most of Cadmus' companions. This made Cadmus so angry that he killed the dragon, and then took Harmonia as his wife. The teeth of the dragon he sowed in the ground, and from these, armed men emerged from the earth, fighting each other till only five were left alive, who then chose Cadmus as their leader. The skin of the dragon they then affixed to an oak.

In *Mysterium Coniunctionis*,[20] Jung gives an interpretation of this myth. There he writes that Cadmus has lost his sister-anima because the god—the highest instance of the unconscious—took her away; that is, she disappeared into the unconscious. He now wishes to regress into the brother-sister incest, but is forbidden to do so by the voice of God, and he has to go forward and find a new wife. His anima has now regressed into the form of a cow which guides him (she corresponds to Zeus' bull) to his new fate, namely to become a hero and a dragon killer. By killing the dragon he is able to find Harmonia, its sister. The dragon is the opposite of Harmonia, disharmony, as we can see from the fact that the teeth, the weapon of the dragon, fight each other as warriors. Cadmus clings to Harmonia, while the opposites in the unconscious eat each other up in projected form. That is the part of the interpretation which is essential for us. The image of the warriors killing each other represents the behavior of a split-off conflict which goes on and dissolves itself in itself. With this goes a certain unconsciousness about the ethical problem of opposites.

Only with Christianity did the metaphysical conflict of good and evil begin to penetrate human consciousness and create a terrific problem, which led to the theory of the *privatio boni* in Christianity. By burying the djin, Hâtim again evades an ethical conflict by magical means. By throwing his amulet among those demonic figures, he succeeds in repressing them so that they kill each other; he represses the conflict which they represent in order that he may continue on his way. The scorpion demon occurs in the ninth chapter of the Book of Revelation:

> And the fifth angel sounded, and I saw a star fall from heaven unto the earth: and to him was given the key of the bottomless pit.
>
> And he opened the bottomless pit; and there arose a smoke out of the pit, as the smoke of a great furnace; and the sun and the air were darkened by reason of the smoke of the pit.
>
> And there came out of the smoke locusts upon the earth: and unto them was given power, as the scorpions of the earth have power. . . .
>
> And the shapes of the locusts were like unto horses prepared unto battle; and on their heads were as it were crowns like gold, and their faces were as the faces of men.
>
> And they had hair as the hair of women, and their teeth were as the teeth of lions.
>
> And they had breastplates, as it were breastplates of iron; and the sound of their wings was as the sound of chariots of many horses running to battle.
>
> And they had tails like unto scorpions, and there were stings in their tails: and their power was to hurt men five months.
>
> And they had a king over them, which is the angel of the bottomless pit, whose name in the Hebrew tongue is Abaddon, but in the Greek tongue hath his name Apollyon.
>
> (King James Version, 9:1–3, 7–11.)

After this comes a different form of demons, which we might compare to those jackal bastards (though in Revelation they are mainly in the shape of lions), but they are also mixed demonic animals which can torture men.

So for demons to be represented in such mixed and bastard animal form is an old Oriental motif. In general, it can be said that if an animal appears as such in dreams, for instance a lion as a lion, and a wolf as a wolf, and a bear as a bear, without any wrong admixture, then it generally simply represents one definite instinctual drive in its positive and negative form. A bear just means a drive like a bear, not always agreeable to meet but definite in form, while such funny fantasy mixtures of beings as centaurs show that it is not an instinctive drive which wants to find expression, but an essentially *symbolic* content. By the very fact that the unconscious uses a picture which is not to be met with in reality, it says that it does not mean that specific thing, but something which *cannot* be met in reality, something completely fantastic which does not exist concretely. In an ambiguous kind of a way the unconscious tries to describe a purely psychic content which is not equivalent to an instinctive drive.

If the unconscious wants to bring up a psychological content which is still so far away from consciousness that it can only be represented by making a *mixtum compositum* of many animal drives, in their positive and destructive ways, that shows that it is a content for which consciousness has not as yet any organ of reception; it cannot be met. Therefore, it is generally experienced as something exceedingly demonic and destructive, because one would have to dissolve one's own conscious attitude and become as chaotic as such an animal to understand what is meant. Normally one could say that that is a slightly psychotic picture, something too deep down for integration and therefore very dangerous, which is why in this tale, as well as in the Cadmus story, there are magical means of coping with the problem. To cope with it one would have to go down oneself into an almost psychotic stage, thereby risking a state of inner confusion and conflict, and many people cannot take such a risk. That is why Jung says that *not* coping with the problem is equivalent to not taking up a certain aspect of moral conflict in man, and preferring some kind of guiding philosophy or other principle in order to be able to look away and to avoid going down so deeply into the conflict of good and evil.

Scorpion

In astrology, to the sign of the scorpion is ascribed the words *"Stirb und werde,"* "Die and be born again," which implies a complete and utter annihilation and resurrection. The scorpion contains the symbolism of the opposites of life and death, for it has the strange quality that when completely cornered it is supposed to commit suicide. This is said to be only folklore, but my father was once sitting at night with some friends in a temple in Japan when they saw an enormous scorpion walking along in the moonshine. They tried the thing out to see whether it was true: they made a ring of fire round it, and the scorpion actually killed itself with its own tail. It first walked around to see if there was any possibility of escape, and when it saw there was none, it committed suicide. Because there is no conscious meaningful suicide in nature (certainly not in the case of the lemmings who stupidly walk into the sea and drown), the scorpion has attracted this projection of knowing the secret of killing and renewing itself, which is why in astrology it carries the meaning of utter destruction and renewal after self-destruction.

This kind of deeper process of destruction and renewal is like the fight with the djin which Hâtim avoids. He takes the talisman, which, according to our book, he had got from some female being in a former adventure, and throws it on the ground among the wild animals. The earth on which they stand changes color and becomes first yellow, then black, then green, and then red.

These four colors are mythologically and generally the four colors from which the first man, Adam, was made. According to many legends, God took earth, which sometimes had four colors, from the four corners of the world, and with it he created the body of Adam, into whom he breathed the divine breath. We know that the Bath Bâdgerd was built by Gayomard, the Persian Adam, the first man in old Persian mythology and religion. So here we see that in this amulet Hâtim owns the *prima materia,* or something which can constellate the *prima materia* of the first man, of Adam Kadmon, who is

Gayomard. By contacting the feminine principle he got some magic device by which he could transform formless earth into that four-colored shape.

One could say, then, that first there was a chaotic world in which chaotic animals fight each other. But by throwing the amulet on the ground, Hâtim makes subdivisions, as it were, in the chaos: he creates a suprapersonal order, by throwing a pattern of colors, into this chaotic mass. When the fourth color—red—appears, the jackal bastards and later the scorpions begin to fight and destroy each other.

He therefore acts in a similar way to Cadmus, who clings to Harmonia, because that would be a pattern of harmony, and of wholeness. He too made the pattern of harmony and so shielded himself against the eruption of the chaos which destroyed itself within itself. The solution would be perfect, but for this motif of magic.

In our story Hâtim uses an old magical trick with the only justification, the same as that of Cadmus, that he is on his way to another task, and for the time being cannot cope with the problem in this form. I think, however, we might well say that that is why the dangers in the Bath Bâdgerd and with the parrot later become so bad. He simply postpones the onslaught of this conflict until he is in the center of the Bath Bâdgerd, and then he gets it. For when the barber disappears and the door closes upon him, he cannot use his amulet any more—strangely enough, he does not seem to have it with him then. But afterward the whole onslaught of the danger comes all the same, so it is only a postponing measure which, understood in that sense, might sometimes be permissible.

The justification in this sense would lie in the fact that the attacking forces are chaotic and that they have not taken on very clear shape. In such cases, if one does not do it for too long, it is justifiable to repress the onslaught of such destructive forces by telling the unconscious that if it wants something it should speak clearly, that it should come up in a form with which one can cope. Considering this fact, Hâtim is perhaps, to a certain extent, justified in repressing the attack of destructive forces by a magic trick and going on his way.

He next comes to a King who invites him to stay with him and even offers him his daughter. This King is the guardian of the Bath Bâdgerд and, knowing its dangers, has made it his task to keep everybody away from it; but the young man catches him out with a double promise so that the King has to show him the way. However, there is a long delay before he leads Hâtim to the entrance of the bath. One becomes apprehensive and feels that if so much effort is made to keep people away from the danger then there must be something terrible behind it, and we know that this corresponds to the fact that the closer one approaches the inner center of one's personality the more the repulsing forces increase. When particles of the same tension approach each other, the more you press them toward each other the stronger becomes their repulsing force, until they reach a certain point and unite.

We can say psychologically that the approach of the unconscious part of the personality to the symbol, or this inner nucleus of the Self, very often shows similar effects, namely a simultaneous reaction of attraction and terrific fear, of wanting and not wanting to get there, of being repulsed to the extreme and not being able to go away or let go. Some people even stay in that suspense of a "Yes" and a "No" for years before the releasing moment comes when they can pass the threshold of repulsion from the Self. Sometimes, not only in those central moments, one has the feeling that the unconscious is now going to bring up something, and then one thinks inwardly, "All right, I will face everything, except I hope it is not this or that",—and then you can be pretty sure it will be just that. You have already a hunch as to what it will be and that it belongs to your personality, that thing of which you say, "I'll face anything except that"; it is just what belongs to you and your life. So very often the most important steps or episodes in one's life are surrounded by a cloud of resistances and fear. If one is quite honest with oneself, one does not even know if one desired or feared it most, for desire and fear are equal. That strange feeling of "that belongs but I won't have it" seems to belong typically to the areas of realization pushed toward one by the Self.

King Sâmân, when he sees that he cannot keep Hâtim from the Bath Bâdgerd, shows him the entrance on which is the inscription "This enchanted place was built by King Gayomard and will remain as a sign for long. Whoever gives in to its magic will not escape alive. Amazement and horror will be his destiny. He will hunger and thirst, and though he will be able to eat of the fruits of the garden as long as he still lives, and will see what is to be seen in this place, yet he will have great difficulties in ever coming out again." When Hâtim read that he thought, "Well, this inscription really tells me the secret of the Bath Bâdgerd." So for a moment he feels a terrible temptation to think he knows all about it and does not need to go in. But then he realizes that this is just cheating and makes up his mind to go through with it, because as we very clearly see, this inscription only gives a general hint at the mystery which really is something quite different.

According to the oldest Persian religion, the first man created, and corresponding to our Adam of Genesis, was called Gayomard. He had a cosmic size, and when he died, all the metals (that is, the basic elements of the world) sprang from his body, and from his feet sprang two rhubarb plants, out of which came the first man and the first woman. Before mankind existed there was this one, cosmic, all-embracing figure of an Anthropos who then disintegrated, and through those plants came human beings. This is an archetypal idea to be found in many other civilizations, for instance in China.[21] The Chinese P'an Ku is an example of this idea, because he too was an enormous human being of cosmic shape. When he fell apart the different mountains of China came into being. This original man in all civilizations is generally also associated with a mandala. For instance, the two feet of P'an Ku become two mountains in the West and

his two arms become two mountains in the East and his head
is the center. So P'an Ku after his decay is shaped, or
designed, as a mandala with four corners and a face element
in the center.

In the original Persian religion Gayomard is simply the
cosmic first man whom, if we want to use an alchemical
expression, we can call the *prima materia*, the basic material
of the whole of creation. But in later legends and stories
about him he became still more amplified, and was also
looked upon as being the first priest and the first king or, to
be more accurate, the first priest-king who created all institutions of civilization. There was a tendency always to trace
back every institution to an arrangement made by the first
priest-king Gayomard. So in later Persian traditions he became amplified with other, mainly Jewish, material, and thus
became a figure not only of the first man, not only the *prima
materia* of the world, not only the father of mankind, but also
the model for every institution, the Creator of every order of
civilization. He has also been partly absorbed into the gnostic
idea of the Anthropos, a redeemer of mankind, who guides
enlightened people back to God and fights darkness and
collects the souls which belong to Him.

According to some later gnostic interpretations, the first
man fell into matter. Even about Gayomard there was specu-
lation that, having decayed into it, he was still in the visible
world, in visible creation—he had fallen into, or was scattered in it. The task was to collect and bring him together
again, to help him return to his wholeness and his origin,
though sometimes he is capable of doing that himself and
then human beings are the scattered particles which have to
be collected by him.

In Jewish mysticism this figure is called Adam Kadmon.
Sometimes he is even put in a certain opposition to the first
Adam of Genesis, though usually he is identified with him.
The name is generally used in the Midrashim when it is
meant that this Anthropos figure still exists in a secret or
hidden way in the visible cosmos, or is still looked upon as

being the psyche of the cosmic creation. As the soul is spread in the body, so is the soul substance spread in the whole cosmos in the shape of gigantic man.

This idea of a hidden Anthropos figure spread through the whole of the material cosmos is a main idea which has never died out and which always returned in some form or another in alchemy. We find it first in the writings of Zosimos of Panopolis (fourth century), which Jung has commented upon.[22] Zosimos teaches that there was an Adam figure, the man of light, who fell into matter and had to be redeemed from there. Most alchemists interpreted their opus as reextracting the Anthropos from his scattered state in matter and bringing him back to his original collected shape, thus extracting the world soul from dead matter and restoring it in its original integrity. That was the main effort of the alchemical work, and it was connected with the redemption of one's own psyche.

This mystical Adam figure is still today a living religious figure in a sect living on the borders of the Tigris and Euphrates, the so-called Mandaeans or Nasoraeans. This group was first studied by Lady E. S. Drower, who found that this kind of Adam mysticism is still completely alive.[23] Lady Drower lived with that Baptist sect for many years before she succeeded in getting access to some of their secret writings, and in her introduction she says that there is still much more which they do not want to give away. According to her theory, which is shared by most other investigators, the Mandaeans, or the Nasoraeans, as one should rather call them, probably lived originally in Jerusalem and are identical with the Essenes, who were thrown out at the time of the destruction of Jerusalem and emigrated to the upper banks of the Tigris and settled there. This is why there are such close connections with Jewish mysticism. They teach that the cosmos was first created in the form of an enormous man, and that this huge "Adam Kasia" is still the hidden soul of the existing cosmos. He is the mystic and secret Adam who preceded the human physical Adam by many myriads of years. The archetypal idea of the universe was formed in human shape.

This secret Adam is also the shape of the departed soul of every human being. He is the new spiritual body which is built up to perfection for the departed soul within the cosmic womb.[24]

As we see, the knowledge of this hidden Adam coincides with becoming conscious of what happens to the soul after death, for when a human soul departs after death from the physical body, it is then built up in a manner parallel to that of Adam Kasia. It becomes, as it were, a replica of this great spiritual original cosmic figure. So one finds in the teaching of these sects a development which is also to be found in Zosimos, namely that this cosmic Adam has to do with the individual soul, and that the process by which the individual soul becomes conscious and immortal has to follow the pattern of that cosmic man. This figure of the Anthropos is even nowadays called a *statue* among the Mandaeans, and I want you to keep that in mind when we come to the discussion of the petrification of the figures which stand around the diamond in the Bath Bâdgerd. The Anthropos, especially at the end of the days in his redeemed form, reappears as a *statue*, but is also sometimes a statue at the beginning of his existence, before God has breathed the breath of life into him. So when he is called a statue he is either the first dead body, before it has been endowed with a soul, or a resurrected body at the end of the days. I only mention this now to weave a thread ahead, and will return to it later.

Lady Drower continues:

> Adam is the All, and comprises in himself every spiritual manifestation of the Great Life as well as the universe; the mystic who tries to convey this multiple personality often becomes confused in his attempted explanation.
> Then he taught about Adam, whom all the worlds call

Adam and in all the books they call him Adam, Adam is
his name. Then he said: "I am the Adam of the mighty
Life. I am Adam of the Mighty Life for I shine in praise
of my Father. Know that, when Adam was united with
Eve, Adam was the Soul and Eve the Body, and she is the
Earth and Adam the Sky. Behold, a name was assigned to
them when they inaugurated the mysteries of kings and
put on the Body and bore children and propagated
generations."

In another text a human being says:

Then I was formed from the Wellspring and Palm Tree,
I, the King who is All Light. And a thousand thousand
years, years countless and endless, passed until I planned
to create offspring. Then spake the Father saying to me,
"O lofty King, O Tree in whose shade they will sit! Arise,
call forth sons who will be called 'kings.' "[25]

There you see he is already in those texts called the King,
which is parallel to our story where Gayomard is called a
King, and you will find a later Nasoraean text where he is
called the First Priest. He is also the date palm and the world
tree and the wellspring.

And he Adam [that is again the great Adam] ascended the
bank of the Wellspring and his glory burst forth over all
worlds. Then he arose and sat by a well of vain imaginings
and said: "I am a King without a peer! I am lord of the
whole world!"
    He travelled on into all the world until he came and
rested on a mountain; then he gazed about and perceived
a stream coming forth from beneath the mountain. Then
he prostrated himself, cast himself down on his face and
said: "Is there one loftier and mightier than I? This is a
Stream of living waters, white waters which come from
worlds without limit or count." Then his mind became
disquieted. He pondered and said: "I said that there was
no king greater than I, but now I know that there exists
That which is greater than myself. I pray that I may see
Him and take Him for my Companion."

He discovers God who is still above him. As the spring of
life he has a certain pride first, or hubris, but then humbles
himself before God. Lady Drower continues:

The First Adam is a vast shape embracing all that is to
exist in the future cosmos. As the First Priest he is
identified in one fragment with Mara-d-Rabutha, and he
sets on himself the crown of priesthood, which is the
crown of intermediation between the worlds of light and
those of matter, himself.

Every organ of this cosmic man's body is a whole world in
itself, but in harmony, so that the organs can cooperate and,
so to speak, form an enormous body.

> The head is one world, the breast one world and each leg
> a world, yea even unto liver, spleen, bowels, stomach,
> male organ, womb, skin, hair, nails, back, viscera, each
> one of them is a separate world.
>
> And when they commune together it is as between
> persons in whom there is no hatred, envy or dissension.
> And if amongst all these worlds there were one superflu-
> ous or another lacking from the structure of the Body,
> the whole Body would be harmed for they counterpoise
> one another and the Soul dwelleth in their midst as they
> with one another.[26]

Not only in the West in alchemical symbolism, but also
still in the East, the belief in this first cosmic Adam has thus
lived on. So it is not so amazing that a Persian fairy tale
should refer to it as something known in these countries.

This cosmic Anthropos, or Adam, consists generally of
four elements. I want to refer here to the detailed exposition
Jung gives concerning this theme in his *Mysterium
Coniunctionis*.[27]

The first cosmic man is generally androgynous and consists
of the *prima materia* of the whole world.

> For us the essential feature of the *prima materia* is that it
> was defined as the *"massa confusa"* and "chaos" referring
> to the original state of hostility between the elements, the
> disorder which the artifex gradually reduced to order by
> his operations. . . .
>
> The Pentateuch says, regarding the creation of the first
> being, that his body was composed of four things, which
> thereafter were transmitted by heredity: the warm, the
> cold, the moist, and the dry. He was in fact composed of

earth and water, a body and a soul. Dryness came to him from the earth, moisture from the water, heat from the spirit, and cold from the soul.

In later medieval alchemy it is also said that every star is within his body because he is a microcosm. In Jewish tradition, Rabbi Eliezer tells us that "God collected the dust from which Adam was made from the four corners of the earth," and in a text from the second century it is said that "Adam was made from dust from all over the world." In Arabic tradition it is said that "when the earth refused to provide the material for Adam's creation the angel of death came along with three kinds of earth: black, white and red," but in an Assyrian parallel text it is said that there were four elements, not only three, and the poet Rumi speaks of seven colors.

So there are three, four, or seven elements. They are generally represented as being arranged in a mandala shape. The most elaborate representation of this can be found in the Syrian *Book of the Cave of Treasures*, published by E. Wallis Budge,[28] in which it is said that Adam's body is a quaternio. He is put together with earth from the four corners of the world, namely of red, black, white, and green colors. So, except that here white replaces the yellow in our text, it is the same order as we have in the talisman. Jung continues:

> According to one Targum, God took the dust not only from the four quarters but also from the sacred spot, the "centre of the world." The four quarters reappear in the (Greek) letters of Adam's name: *anatole* (sunrise, East), *dysis* (sunset, West), *arktos* (Great Bear, North), *mesembria* (noon, South).

Adam lived and died where later the cross was erected in Jerusalem. He was buried on Golgotha, and he died on a Friday at the same hour as Christ. He had four children: Cain, Lebhûdhâ, Abel, and Kelîmath, and these afterward married each other. So he produced a marriage quaternio. Adam's burial place is in this "cave of treasures" in Golgotha, which accounts for the name of the book. All his descendants must stand in service at his corpse and never leave it, and that is why later the cross was erected at that place for, as you know, Christ was the second Adam.

We have now historical material by which to see that this idea of the Anthropos, the being at the beginning and at the end of the world, who appears in resurrected form and sometimes in different Savior figures, is, interpreted from a psychological angle, a symbol of what we call the unconscious psyche and of its totality, and is, therefore, as Jung says, an image of the Godhead.

In other words, the cosmic Anthropos represents what Jung nowadays calls the collective unconscious or the objective psyche. According to the Gnostics, this collective psyche was the soul of the universe. For us, it is still a question if the collective unconscious is a kind of psyche of the universe, but certain developments in modern physics seem to point in the direction of postulating a cosmic intelligence or psyche.

We are living now at a turning point in the attitude of the natural sciences. Until the last forty or fifty years, through our extraverted attitude, we had the naive belief that we could trust our senses and that our discoveries, when we measured and looked at outer material phenomena in physics and chemistry, were absolute, or at least statistical truths. It is only now slowly dawning on us, first in the realm of theoretical physics, but also in other natural sciences connected with it, that we cannot and never will be able to assert what the outer world is in itself. We can only cast or create mental models of outer reality on which to check; if those mental models coincide relatively frequently and well with the reactions of outer materials, then we call them true models, and if not, then we call them illusions. By this process we try to improve our models and interpretations of outer facts. In modern physics we have hitherto been stranded with the question: Where do the models and concepts, such as particle and energy, etc., come from? Where do the axiomata of mathematics come from which we use in

an elaborate form as a means by which to represent outer
energetic processes? Slowly the eyes of the theoretical physi-
cist therefore begin to turn towards the human unconscious
as the origin from which such models come.

   We know, for instance, that the famous mathematician
Henri Poincaré himself related that the "Fuchsian" equations
which made him famous had been discovered by him through
the unconscious. After having worked hard at unsuccessfully
trying to find solutions for these specific complicated equations, he dropped the problem. But then, in a relaxed state
after he had had some coffee, suddenly the solution flashed
before his inner eye. Being occupied at the time, he could
not write it down immediately, but it was so clear that he did
not even make notes; he was quite sure that he knew it and
could write it down later. It came like a sudden vision. Much
more evidence has been collected since then. One of the
famous arithmetical theorems which Gauss discovered and
which made him famous was obtained in the same way.
Gauss said he worked on it for a long time, but without
success, and then suddenly "it presented itself like a flash
before my eyes." He adds in a letter to one of his friends,
"even afterwards I could not reconstruct any thread of
thought which led to the solution."

   It seems very symptomatic that just now in the world of
natural sciences and mathematics it is realized that the
models, or mathematical hypotheses and theorems by which
we obtain our "objective" view of the outer world, come from
what we would call the unconscious and not from outer
stimuli. We could say that all our science of the outer world
is anthropomorphic and ultimately corresponds to certain
models, to inherent structures of our psychic makeup; or, to
use Jung's terminology, the basic ideas of modern mathematics and physics are archetypal representations which spring
from the collective unconscious. One sees therefore quite
clearly why in all those antique texts Adam, who from our
standpoint is a symbol of the collective unconscious, is
identified with the macrocosm. The collective unconscious

is, for those people, identical with the whole surrounding world which has this shape of an enormous psychic human being.

It is not just my intuitive jumping about to speak of Gayomard and the Nasoraeans and modern physics. This idea of the Anthropos as the underlying psychic model of the whole cosmos existed at the beginning of our development of the natural sciences. One could therefore say that the archetypal image has been the stimulus behind all that we have created through natural science. From the very beginning, this image of the Anthropos, of the divine cosmic man who has to be rediscovered by the individual and reconstructed by natural scientific effort, has been the central idea of all the greater alchemists and therefore has directly led to the development of modern sciences, first chemistry and then microphysics.

The falling apart of Adam into an all-pervading body which is the visible cosmos, and an all-pervading soul which is more invisibly hidden in it, prepares that split at which we have now arrived when we make a conceptual difference between what we call the outer material cosmic facts and the collective unconscious. Nowadays we have a complete dualism. Psychology investigates the collective unconscious by looking at the inside of human beings, and the natural sciences investigate the outer material world by looking outside. This is a split between body and soul, so to speak, of the cosmic Adam, or totality. We make a double hypothesis that there is a soul inside and a material body outside and investigate them through two different sciences. This split in which we now live and which will probably be the next step with which science has to cope, has been developing for over two thousand years. The idea of an original man consisting of a material body, sometimes called a statue, and of an invisible soul hidden therein, which is its essence, naturally also accounts for the split between the natural sciences and the humanities. That split was contained or already pre-formed by this first split in the image of the original man.

The Gnostic Anthropos figure, then, is generally slain, decays, is drowned, sinks scattered into matter, from which it has to be re-collected; and in that aspect, and in the aspect the alchemical texts gave it, it is more conceived as the *prima materia*, the initial matter of the alchemical process of transformation. We have, therefore, to specify and to say that it is the symbol of totality when it appears *first* in the unconscious, the preconscious aspect of the Self.

The first Adam figure in alchemy is not only called the *prima materia*, it is the chaos, the *prima materia* in its conflicting confused state, which in our story is banished by the talisman which makes a quaternary subdivision. This is reminiscent of alchemical ideas—of the *prima materia* as the chaos—or where the slaughtered dragon has to be subdivided in fourfold form in the sign of the cross by a sword, or into four heaps, and from then on cooked. This subdivision into four is a first attempt to bring conscious order into the chaotic material of the unconscious, for, as you know, any quaternary subdivision points to the basic structure of consciousness. Whenever we try to bring order into a chaotic situation we first draw this subdivision. We still use such a subdivision, for instance, in projective trigonometry, for most physical functions are represented as vectors on a point. Drawing four lines and then subdividing them, to represent consciously an event, or force, or movement of a particle, is a more modern "talisman," discovered by Descartes. The archetypal basic structure of our consciousness forces us to act in this way.

If we study the process of individuation as Jung understands it, we generally see that the guiding factor from the beginning is what finally turns out to be the goal, namely becoming conscious of the Self. The Self exists at the very beginning and generally in the process of individuation is what guides or regulates the process of inner growth. Thus the Self itself is the *prima materia* of the whole development. In a similar sense, therefore, this figure of Adam was conceived as that which existed at the very beginning of the world. At the same time, its reconstruction, or if scattered in light particles, its re-collection into one figure and resurrection from having been sunk or drowned in matter, is the goal of the whole alchemical process. In our story we certainly have to do with the *prima materia* aspect, for Gayomard vanished, but left this rather uncanny structure of the Bath Bâdgerd containing the diamond, which in alchemy is the symbol of the goal and therefore actually identical with Gayomard. The diamond might be said to symbolize the end aspect and Gayomard the *prima materia* aspect of one and the same thing.

The material of amplification has illustrated the fact that very often the first Adam is built up from a quaternio, whether the clay from which his body was constructed came from the four corners of the world, or the angels took earth of four different colors to form it. This helps us to understand retrospectively the trick Hâtim used when he threw the talisman on the ground to banish the jackal bastards and the scorpion beings; he used a symbolic device actually associated with the goal of his journey. This is why we interpreted it as a kind of repression, or a pushing away of the conflict or chaotic aspect, but legitimate, since he was already set on his goal. On the other hand, we can say that if he does that, if he plays the half-illegitimate trick of pushing away this chaotic aspect of the unconscious in order to set forth on his journey toward Gayomard in the Bath Bâdgerd, then he has to go through with it and face what comes afterward; for otherwise he would again meet with these dangers on the way back.

In our story we have arrived at that inscription on the door of the Bath Bâdgerd which only gives an uncanny hint at what Hâtim will be going through. The inscription says he will not return and—very similarly to Dante's *"Lasciate ogni speranza voi ch'entrate"* ("Abandon all hope, ye who enter")—he reads that whoever goes within will find amazement and horror, and will eat from the fruit of the garden as long as he still

lives, but will probably not come out again. He first gets
discouraged but then makes up his mind to go on, and when
he goes through the door he first comes into a complete desert
and says, "Ah, now I understand why this place has been
called the Bath Bâdgerd, for that means the Wind Castle or
the Castle of Nothingness."

If we compare this with Dante's descent into the Inferno,
it is very different. The unconscious here does not appear in
a series of chaotic or frightening pictures or, as in other
stories, as wild animals attacking (though we had that earlier), but as this absolutely empty, meaningless nothingness
which is also an aspect of the unconscious psyche—and
which especially drives people into utter despair. When in a
difficult situation one turns toward the unconscious and
there are either no dreams, or chaotic and bewildering
dreams which seem to have nothing to do with the actual
situation, then one wonders how one could expect anything
to come from that place of confusion. The well-known terrific
and widespread fear of the unconscious is partly due to this
aspect. People say, "Well, if I turn to the unconscious then I
shall become quite mad!" I cannot tell you how many people
have said to me, "I know I'm mad, but I also know that if I
go into analysis and dig up the unconscious, then I shall be
really mad!" There is a grain of truth there, for to them it
really appears as the castle of nothingness, and as though
there were nothing in the psyche! "Can any good thing come
out of Nazareth?" (John 1:46). It is just where nothing can
be found, but then perhaps the dreams begin to hint that one
should turn to fantasy, and you encourage people and say,
"Draw your fantasies, etc." But they say, "But this is nothing!
It's nonsense! That won't help me to get any further!"

After Hâtim has gone through this desert for a while, a
young man comes along with a mirror under his arm and
greets him and shows him the mirror. Hâtim asks him where
the bath is and if he can use it and is told that it is a little
farther on. He asks the man why he has left the bath, and
the barber replies that it is a part of his duties always to meet

strangers and lead them to it and he hopes to get a tip from Hâtim. Hâtim agrees to this and says he would like to take a bath.

The barber is an exceedingly important figure which disappears afterward. He gives Hâtim a loincloth and the bowls of warm water to pour over his head, and then the catastrophe of transformation happens and the barber is never mentioned again. He just leads him into the horrible place and then leaves him to his fate.

We find the barber in another very significant text, namely the Visions of Zosimos. Jung discusses these visions at great length in *Psychology and Religion.*[29] They are subdivided into different repetitive scenes; in one Zosimos sees a priest standing on an altar which was in the shape of a shallow bowl and sacrificing himself, eating and vomiting his own flesh, and then later this same priest is varied by the figure of a barber. So in the Visions of Zosimos, the sacrificer and the sacrificed, who are one and the same, are symbolized by a barber. Jung writes that the cutting of the hair, or shaving, has very often been associated with scalping, which also has to do with the flaying of a human being. Jung then goes into the symbolism of flaying, taking it as symbolizing the transformation of a human being, the model in support of this being that of the snake casting its skin. The idea was to cast away one's skin and renew oneself. Scalping, therefore, was a kind of partial flaying and meant mainly spiritual transformation. Jung continues:

> Since olden times shaving the head has been associated with consecration, that is, with spiritual transformation or initiation. The priests of Isis had their heads shaved quite bald, and the tonsure, as we know, is still in use at the present day. This "symptom" of transformation goes back to the old idea that the transformed one becomes like a new-born babe . . . with a hairless head. In the myth of the night sea journey, the hero loses all his hair during his incubation in the belly of the monster, because of the terrific heat. The custom of tonsure, which is derived from these primitive ideas, naturally presupposes

the presence of a ritual barber. Curiously enough, we come across the barber in that old alchemical "mystery," the *Chymical Wedding* of 1616 [by the founder of the Rosicrucian Order]. There the hero, on entering the mysterious castle, is pounced on by invisible barbers, who give him something very like a tonsure. Here again the initiation and transformation process is accompanied by a shaving.[30]

Obviously there is the influence of alchemical ideas behind our tale here, and the barber can be taken as an initiating priest. He does literally initiate, he leads people into the bath and also has the mirror. This may be rather farfetched, for it is normal for a barber in the Orient to carry a mirror; but if we want to take it symbolically, the mirror would indicate his desire to lead Hâtim to self-knowledge, to see himself in his objective form.

The barber who has gone out to meet Hâtim brings him to the bath, and Hâtim sees an enormous cupola which seems to go right up to the sky. He enters the bath, and when he looks back, the door behind has disappeared and he is walled in.

This is a real nightmare motif! You know you are in a prison and try to get out everywhere, but you get more and more hemmed in. We have probably all gone through such nocturnal agonies. This severe imprisonment is generally experienced when one feels that the Self is closing in. Jung says, therefore, that the prison is a symbol of the Self, but only as long as fear of the Self still prevails. You have probably all had all kinds of fantasies as to what should, or could, or might happen and were ready to accept anything, except something in one corner of your soul. You would say, "Anything, but not that," and then one day just that happened to you and you felt as though you had known always that it would be that one thing. It felt as though a trapdoor had shut behind you. For instance, you might think that you would never fall in love in a certain way, and then you get just that—the one situation you would have avoided at all costs, and now you are nicely fixed in it. You wanted it, and feared

it, and had an absolute kind of unconscious knowledge that
that was where you would one day land. Or there is some one
thing on which you don't want to work! At one time I had
the feeling that I should work on a theme and write about it,
and I felt that I would do anything else, but not that! I was
really afraid to go to bed at night because I knew that my
dreams would bring up just that! I could have shortened my
agony by saying, "Yes, I know I have to do it, because I fear
it so much!" But, naturally, you can't do that. You run in
circles to get away from it, you have no time, or there is
something else more important which has to be done, and all
the time the devil is behind you and whispers, "That's what
you have to do!"

Then Hâtim has water to pour over himself, that being the
normal ways of bathing in those Oriental baths, and when
he pours the third bowl of water over his head there is a
terrific thunderous noise and everything goes dark. When
the darkness has disappeared the barber and the bath in
which he was standing have disappeared and the whole place
is filled with water which is up to his calves and slowly
rising. When it reaches his knees Hâtim wades around trying
to find an exit, hunting in all directions, and he can find
neither a door nor any other way out. Soon the water is up to
his waist, and, horrified, he hunts round again but without
success. The water then reaches his neck so he has to swim,
and he thinks to himself that that is why the men who came
into this bath before never got out of it again, for they had
drowned in the water. "And you too, Hâtim, will meet death
in these floods. But when man is facing death he should turn
his thoughts toward the merciful God," and he prays, "O
God, I have given all my strength in your service. I have only
one life, but had I a thousand, I would offer them up. Thy
will be done!"

At this moment he is pressed up against the center of the
cupola, which culminates in a round stone, and, tired with
swimming and wanting to rest for a minute, Hâtim clings
with his hand to that round stone. In that moment there is a

thunderous noise and he finds himself out in the desert where, as far as the eye can see, there is nothing but endless wasteland.

Hâtim is drowning, and we could skip this interpretation easily by saying that that is how it is when one is caught in one's own being and has to face the unconscious which comes in a more and more threatening and pressing form. But there is an interesting aspect to this, inasmuch as in many alchemical texts it is the old Adam Kadmon, or in other medieval variations Adam and Eve, who are actually drowned in this way.

In the chapter on Adam and Eve in *Mysterium Coniunctionis*, Jung comments on a text written by Basilius Valentinus, which says that Adam sat in a bath in which he found Venus as his partner. The bath had been prepared by an old dragon. Adam unites with Venus, but then the water floods the couple and they are both drowned. Jung then goes on to say that the secret Arkan, or transformation substance, appears here as the inner or original man, or, to use a cabbalistic name, as Adam Kadmon. Adam, as the inner man, is deluged by Venus, the goddess of love, which is a very good description of a typical psychological situation. The higher spiritual being is here drowned in matter: bathe, immerse, flood, baptize, and drown, all alchemical synonyms, symbolize a deeply unconscious condition, and this means an *incarnation of the Self*—or rather that unconscious process whereby it, the Self, is "reborn" or changes into a state in which it can be experienced. For the Self entering into the field of awareness of the ego is like drowning, or decaying; it is a descent into unconsciousness. It is like pressing a cosmic being into a dirty little stable. We always think of the process of individuation as being a wonderful experience of the ego experiencing the Self—with spiritual exaltation, and inflation, and everything else. But from the aspect of the Self, which in the unconscious state is in a state of plenitude, it implies absolute drowning, and it is actually represented in this way in dreams.

A French poet, Gérard de Nerval, became schizophrenic and hung himself at a relatively young age after an unfortunate love affair. Shortly before his first psychotic episode, he had a terrific dream. In this he went into one of those typical courtyards at the back of Paris hotels where they have all the garbage pails and where the cats roam about, and he saw that an enormous angel had fallen there. It had wonderful wings with feathers of thousands of shining colors, but it was jammed in, all hunched up in this backyard, and if the angel made the smallest movement to free itself the entire hotel would be wrecked. That image shows the process of the "drowning" of the Self. Gérard de Nerval consciously had a Parisian-French mentality, which was too small and rationalistic and could well be compared to a hotel backyard. It was not up to the inner experience, and that brought about his schizophrenic explosion. As Jung teaches, if the conscious mind or heart is not up to a tremendous inner experience it leads to schizophrenia, for the invasion of the unconscious then explodes the conscious personality.

Gérard de Nerval was literally too narrow-minded to take this invasion of the unconscious in the right way. In his biography we read that he met a little *midinette*, of whom there are so many in the French ateliers, and fell passionately in love with her and was inspired to write poems about her, as Dante did of Beatrice. He felt that she was absolutely a goddess, but then he couldn't take that and pulled himself away with the remark, *"C'est une femme ordinaire de notre siècle"* ("she is an ordinary woman of our time"). He could not bear it that this woman should mean so much to him. That is the French hotel backyard mentality, *"C'est une femme ordinaire de notre siècle,* so I can't love her!" He therefore kicked her away and then fell into his first episode, after which he tried to have a reconciliation. But he could not get on with her because of the terrific tension of seeing clearly that she was an ordinary human being and experiencing her as a goddess and not being able to hold this paradox together. He could not see that that was the paradox of love, which is a divine mystery and at the same time a very ordinary, if not anthropoid, affair.

This dream shows the drowning of the Self, its descent into the narrowness of the human realm. In Gérard de Nerval's case, ego conception was too narrow and the Self exploded it, and de Nerval hung himself in the most horrible way. But even if the Self approaches human consciousness in a normal case there is the drowning- or falling-down process, so that it can be said that for the Self, for the greater part of the inner personality, it is agony to be imprisoned in the confines of consciousness. That is why very often, long before people realize something consciously, there are such dreams. Sometimes nowadays, due to modernization by the unconscious, a superhuman being descends from an airplane as a parachutist, or something like that. If I come across that in a dream I always watch out and say to myself that in two or three days or a week that analysand will probably have some kind of tremendous realization, for the unconscious has already shown that something hitherto unconscious is coming down from the infinite and will jump, or fall, into the realm of human realization. There are many parallels, such as the flying saucer motif, on which Jung has commented at length,[31] with all those landings by supernatural beings, and falling objects resembling airplanes. All such things represent the anticipation of a realization of the Self. That is the more modern version of this age-old motif. In Christian dogma it is said that Christ existed with God from the beginning of days as the Logos and "emptied Himself" (*ekenòsen*) to become human flesh. That is the same idea, namely that He lived in a kind of divine plenitude in the Beyond and had to "empty Himself" of his whole plenitude in order to become a human being.

Here it is Hâtim who undergoes this fate, which means that by entering the bath he has become identical with the Anthropos in which he is imprisoned, and now has to undergo the same fate, for what happens to him is now identical with what happens to the Self.

Making contact with one's inner greater personality means
a double fate for both; it is like making friends with an inner
figure, for from now on you die or go on together, your fate
is absolutely intertwined. That is why people have such a
trapdoor feeling about the process of individuation, for they
know that once that relationship is begun there is no escape,
or that you can get away only by cutting off your arms and
legs. To put it more simply and practically, I have often
noticed and been horrified to see that people who have
touched depth psychology and after a while left it again
became either devilishly evil, or terribly neurotic, or died. I
have said to Jung that sometimes it seemed to me as if Jungian
psychology were a highly dangerous poison, the poison of
truth. He agreed that to take it up and then leave it again is
absolutely destructive poison. Once one has had enough
realization of what goes on inside one and of what it is all
about, then one can only escape at the price of becoming
highly neurotic. This is why one should never encourage
people to go into a Jungian analysis if they have resistances,
because nobody can take the responsibility for such a step.
For God's sake, do not commit the beginner's enthusiastic
mistake of hinting to people that they should go into analysis,
for it means putting them in this bath, shutting the door,
and they either drown or do not come out. Only their own
inner barber can do it, but not another human being.

I once saw a mother who happily devoured her son; she
simply prevented him from marrying and was nice to him
from morning till night. He led a comfortable life, so naturally got fat and was lazy and happy at home, and at forty-
three was still unmarried. His mother sometimes said that
she did not know why he did not get married, she always told
him he should, but he always had such bad luck! The funny
thing was that she didn't seem to have a bad conscience about
it. That upset me so much that I talked to Jung about it, and
he said that she really had no idea and was honestly unconscious, so that in a way she was not guilty. But if she had one
little psychological pamphlet to read in which there was

mention of the Oedipus complex and of a mother eating her son, then see what would happen! She would be like a poisonous snake and never be the same woman again, for then she would not be able to go on doing innocently what she had hitherto done. I did not give her the pamphlet because I do not want to spray poison; but she came across somebody who thought he must let her know about the Oedipus complex, and from then on she continued to devour her son, but was nervous and restless and nasty on top of it. So you can say that wherever you have touched a psychological truth you can never get away from it again, and that is the ambiguous thing about it. That is very well represented in this part of the story which shows the water rising slowly and Hâtim drowning.

But just as much as Hâtim is drowning is the Self approaching him. It is really the Self which is drowning in or toward him, they literally approach each other; swimming on the water for a while, he is lifted up until he reaches the central stone of the cupola. He is pressed toward the Self, toward his true personality. When the masons put that stone in place the building is finished; it is the indispensable part which holds all the converging parts of the cupola in place. It is literally, from a constructive standpoint, the central regulating factor of the whole building and the one towards which the whole building converges. When this central point is touched there is a kind of magical transformation and the agonizing situation has for the moment disappeared.

In spite of this change Hâtim realizes that he is still in for more trouble, for now he is in the desert and does not know what will happen there. But he makes a very interesting remark when he says, "If I have escaped the floods then I shall probably escape the other spells and curses also!" That is a very psychological remark, for during the process of individuation again and again one gets into such issueless terrible situations and one feels as if all one had hitherto experienced were no help at all, one is again in a spot, again up against it. But having once experienced the miraculous

turns and solutions which the unconscious can effect, one
has a kind of faith. One feels, just as Hâtim does, that
previously one had been in such situations and there had
been some miraculous turn which one could not have precon-
ceived, and therefore one can hope that the same thing will
happen again. So the first crisis, the first time of being
imprisoned with one's own unconscious is generally the very
worst, because there one really feels like going off one's head
or having to commit suicide, or something like that, but
afterward, having seen that the unconscious can turn the
whole situation, one has more faith.

When Hâtim escaped from the bath and came into the
desert, he walked on and then came to a garden door; but as
soon as he had entered it the door disappeared, just as in the
bath! And he said, "What new miseries are in store for me
now? How will I ever escape this magic circle?" He walked
around in the park which was full of trees laden with fruit
and with flowers. He picked some of the fruit and ate it, but
however much he ate, he was never satisfied. He ate nearly a
thousand pounds, but remained hungry. But he took courage
and went on his way. When he came near to the castle he
saw a lot of stone statues standing like idols round the castle
square. He wondered what they meant, but there was nobody
to help him solve the puzzle.

While he was standing lost in thought he heard a parrot
from within the castle call out, "Young man, what are you
standing there for? Why did you come here, has your life
come to an end?" Hâtim looked up and then saw the inscription which we amplified before, which said that this is the
place of Gayomard, who had once found an enormous diamond and, in order to protect it, built round it the castle of
the Bath Bâdgerd. It is added that the parrot which sits in
the cage also comes under the spell, "but if you, the servant
of God, want to get away from the place, then you must take
the bow and arrow which lie on a golden chair, and shoot the
parrot. If you hit him, you will have broken the spell, but if
you miss you will become a stone statue." When Hâtim had

read that, he looked at the stone figures and said sadly, "Ah, that is how all those statues came into being and you, Hâtim, will also end your life in this confusing witches' cauldron. Yet man proposes and God disposes." With such thoughts in his mind he went into the castle and took the bow and arrow which lay on the golden chair, placed an arrow on the bowstring and shot at the parrot.

First we come to this magical garden, which naturally reminds one of the Garden of Eden and its beautiful qualities. But it also has something of the Oriental *fata morgana*, because the fruits you eat do not nourish you; they have only an illusionary quality, also in the way they appear and disappear. So we can say that this garden is the maternal aspect of the unconscious and its illusion-creating factor, and has very much to do with the capacity for imagination. Though the diamond is to be found in this garden, the garden itself belongs to the more diabolical invention; it is not the right thing. We can translate that into psychological language and say that the unconscious contains the diamond, the possibility of individuation, but it is also a kind of *fata morgana* which leads people completely astray if they do not have the right guidance. You need only listen to the delusions of mad people in hospitals to see what it means to get lost in this garden and in absolutely unreal fantasies and be unable to check them any longer.

I remember a terrific crisis in my relationship with a paranoiac case for the following reason. Being full of fantasies, this analysand always went long over the hour. I had a small dog which usually sat on my lap when I was analyzing. Once when she went over the hour and I wanted my supper but did not want to interrupt too brusquely, I shifted on my chair, and after a while, as a kind of preparation for stopping the flow (before I got up to say that it was already twenty past seven and we should stop), I put the dog down on the floor. It never got to my speaking, for when I put the dog on the floor she turned absolutely white and got up and left the room without saying goodbye! I had no idea what had happened, and for three weeks she disappeared. Later she turned up again, but she did not mention the affair until a year later, in an hour during which we had a very good contact. She suddenly broke out, "Do you know what happened at that time? I thought of never coming back to you, for I was that dog, and when you put it down off your lap I knew you would just throw me away like that." It was very understandable, for she wanted, as it were, to stay on my lap and be held there, but couldn't distinguish between the outer fact of this dog having to be put down because I wanted to have my supper, and the fantasy in which this was all involved.

You meet such delusions all the time, but the terrible thing is that when people are really caught in this garden of illusions you cannot check with them about it. Anybody might be struck by such a gesture because it is symbolic in a disagreeable way, but with a normal person you would discuss that and check the facts and then say that they did not correspond with the fantasy, that the analysand had made a projection, and the whole thing would be settled within ten minutes. But there, because she was so far away and lost in her unconscious fantasy, she took it as real. To be up against such a delusion and fantasy, which is symbolically right but where people can no longer compare it with the facts, becomes dangerous.

When people lose their emotional contact with their surroundings and become isolated in persecution ideas, they very often dream that the people they love die, which is obviously symbolic. A warning dream says that you are losing your contact with the people around you, they all die. To think that everybody around one dies is a well-known pre-psychotic symptom. The case I have just mentioned once had such a dream; she rang up the criminal police and told them that certain people had been murdered. She could not check her dream against the facts. The dream was real to her, and she naturally got in badly with the police. There you see what it means to be in this garden. The unconscious tells the plain truth but in symbolic language, and if one takes it literally, the whole truth is lost. But there is a beautiful symptom which shows that, though this is the garden of delusional fantasy, Hâtim will not go mad: he notices that the food does not nourish him. Now an illusionary beefsteak and a real one are the same thing to a mad person, but not for a normal person whose sense of reality is still alive. Hâtim, in spite of eating the food, states that he is not nourished, and with that he keeps completely sane, distinguishing the illusion and keeping his sense of reality. Then he begins to wonder about the statues and finds the inscription which tells him what it is all about and that he has to shoot the parrot in order to find his way out.

The statues are of basic importance and inextricably connected with the parrot motif, but this will be discussed later. Now we will go to the next motif, that this parrot, whatever it may stand for, has to be shot by a bow and arrow.

In Hâtim's time the bow and arrow were still weapons in use, principally in sport, though they were becoming old-fashioned and were being replaced by other weapons. The bow and arrow were among the most intelligent inventions of early mankind, and like all intelligent inventions have therefore always been understood as something numinous and miraculous, a kind of miraculous revelation. Some Australian aborigines, for instance, say that the bow and arrow came into existence when the bow ancestor and his string wife—who is always embracing him, having her arms round his neck—came to earth and revealed to mankind how to construct a bow and arrow and then disappeared again, which shows that the idea of constructing such an instrument came from an unconscious inspiration. One could not have thought it out consciously, it was the discovery of a genius, and it enabled man for the first time to avoid the body-to-body fight which animals have to go through all over the world and which at first man went through too.

After having only fought body-to-body with wild animals came the next step of throwing sticks, or spears, but it still demanded terrific courage to approach or go up to the animal. This was not only dangerous with some animals but also made bird hunting practically impossible, for one would have to go so close that the bird would be off first. So being able to hit your prey from a distance, noiselessly, was a tremendous advantage (which we have lost with the invention of the gun, for you can shoot the bow without making any noise). This was an enormous improvement in human life and a jump forward in the possibility of survival. There is also the magical quality of being able to hit from a distance. So, from the beginning, the bow and arrow was regarded as an intelligent achievement, as against brute force; it was an achievement of intuition. In addition, you can train your capacity for aiming, for, as in all those crafts, in the long run you do not only depend on a good eye and a steady hand; if you have a bad day or have just had a quarrel with your family, you will miss the target. But that belongs to all hunting, for people saw that they had not only to use craft to hit the target, but also magic to get themselves into the right psychological condition.

So, from the beginning, using the bow and arrow also meant or demanded getting into one's inner balance. That is the case even with shooting, which is why before shooting contests there are all the magical fusses which participants make as to special food and diet and all the rest of it. They talk of a good day, a lucky or unlucky day and some even, without knowing anything about psychology, watch their dreams and when they get up say, "Today I shall have an unlucky day and miss." They become involuntarily aware how much the whole thing also depends on one's inner balance. So you can say that hitting the target with bow and arrow means an exceeding concentration of intelligence and intuition out of an attitude of complete inner balance.

In Zen Buddhism in Japan, shooting with the bow and arrow has become one of those practices that have the symbolic meaning of measuring how far the novice has come into contact with the Self in himself, for according to that he will be able to shoot, and not according to his technical ability. As with all these things the original meaning has sometimes been lost and it has become a kind of technical sophisticated art in itself. When practiced with the real idea, the hitting of the target means only a symptom, and measuring from that symptom how far one has gotten into balance with oneself.

This obviously has to be done here too. It is a terribly difficult target to hit because the parrot always flies up and seems to be able to do that very quickly, so that great skill is required. But in spite of the fact that Hâtim is one of the greatest cavaliers of his age and therefore perfect in the art of shooting, he twice misses the parrot, and the third time only with a prayer and when *not* looking does he manage to hit it.

So here we have very much the Zen Buddhistic situation; it is *not* by looking at the outer target and by concentrating his skill that he hits it, but by getting into contact with the Self, and that is even literally stated in our story. Hâtim tries three times and here there is this archetypal fairy-tale rhythm that the tension is always led up to in three steps, and then comes the great change or *dénouement*. When Hâtim has missed the parrot twice and is already petrified up to his navel, he cries out and says, "May nobody miss the goal of his life as I have done!" So there he realizes that hitting the parrot really symbolically means either to get or miss the goal of his whole life. Then Hâtim aims, shuts his eyes and, shouting "God is great! [*Allah u-akbar*]," he shoots. He does not concentrate his senses in a skillful, extraverted way toward the goal, but looks inside; and with his cry "God is great," he really means, "My target is really Allah, and is what I must not miss or lose; He is great." Naturally behind this is the feeling-idea that probably he will miss again, and therefore he commits his soul to God before he is completely petrified. This is not so much a request for God's help as a declaration of his loyalty to God in what is probably the last moment of his life. In this way he turns away from the target, he gives up the attempt to shoot the parrot and concentrates entirely on keeping his loyalty to God and accepting his fate of even missing, if God has planned this for him.

One could say that that was the moment when Hâtim gave up all ego purposes, something especially difficult when one has gone through all those miseries and come to the goal of one's life, to that thing one has sought all the time and for which one has suffered so much. All that has to be given up now. One has to say, "Well, all right, if I miss it, God is great and He will know why I had to miss it." It is easy to give up one's ego obstinacy and what one wants if one has not worked for it for twenty years. It is easy to give up something which you bought yesterday, or your visit to Italy (although people even get into a childish tantrum about that), but if you have to give up your ego obstinacy about the thing which you were looking and searching for for many years, and for which you had been through all those heroic adventures, that would mean a terrific sacrifice; and it is by shutting his eyes and saying, "Allah is great" that Hâtim makes the sacrifice.

He hits the bird. Then again there is a thunderous noise and a cloud of dust, and when that subsides he sees in the place of the parrot Gayomard's beautiful diamond, and all the statues which had been petrified come alive.

We have here to amplify two motifs, namely the parrot and the diamond which replaces it. Obviously the parrot has been like a negative spell, veiling or hiding the sight of the diamond.

From the very beginning, the diamond has always been a well-known alchemical symbol of the philosopher's stone, the old alchemists having been struck by its shining splendor and its absolute hardness. One could even cut steel with a diamond, and with the means available at that time nothing could be done to cut or break it, so it was particularly suitable to carry the projection of the immortal body, that incorruptible immortal core in man which can no longer be altered by any vicissitudes of our material corruptible existence. This is why the diamond figures throughout the whole history of alchemy as one of the many synonyms for the *lapis philosophorum*. It is a symbol of the Self, as being something of indestructible matter.

We would next have to ask ourselves why in the Spanish tale the parrot functions as a symbol of the Self and here in this version veils it, and has to be removed so as to get at the Self. But it seems better first to look at the other peripeteias of our story and at the motif of petrification.

All the dangers which emanate from the Bath Bâdgerd and its central symbol are in a strange way connected with the symbolism of the Self. In the chapter on "Adam and Eve" in Jung's *Mysterium Coniunctionis*, there is a subsection entitled "The Statue."[32] In this section Jung has assembled the very complex symbolism of the statue, which boils down to the fact that already in certain Gnostic and Mandaean texts, and again in Manichaeism and parallel to this in the whole of alchemy from its very beginning, the statue has been regarded as a symbol of the resurrected body, and also, therefore, of the second Adam. Even Saint Paul's words "For as in Adam all die, even so in Christ shall all be made alive" are often quoted. The alchemists contended that we die in the first Adam, the corruptible, physical man, and that the second Adam, sometimes identified with Christ and sometimes with other savior figures, according to the religious system, is the incorruptible Adam and the immortal body which we are supposed to receive after the resurrection; this second body is a sort of statue.

It is possible that this (or at least this is my conviction) goes back to the long and complicated mummification ritual for the dead in Egypt. The very last act of the liturgy at a funeral was to erect a statue of the dead King, or in later times of any dead person, within the tomb chamber. The corpse was mummified according to the means and wealth of the person and was buried in many coffins. In all Egyptian tombs, there are several outer chambers where sacrifices for the dead are made, and then an innermost chamber where

the mummified corpse lies in its coffin. After the last liturgical prayers, and just before the High Priest shuts and seals
the door of the funeral chamber where the corpse lies, a
statue of the dead person, which has been put there before
and is lying on the floor, is slowly erected and put upright.
During the chanting of the last verses of the funeral liturgy—
"Hail, now art thou resurrected, now thou goest to the
immortal stars and art identical with the god and hast
reached immortality in the capacity of pervading the whole
world"—workmen pull cords and the statue is slowly erected
and put on its feet. This act is meant to represent, in a
symbolic form, the resurrection of the dead person. The
deceased person does not resurrect in the form of a mummy,
though all the preservation is done on the "old Adam," but
the act of resurrection is displayed by the stone statue
representing the new Adam. Possibly this has historically
influenced all later Gnostic and Manichaean ideas, support-
ing the idea that the body of the resurrection, the second
Adam, is a statue.

In certain Manichaean hymns it is said that the world will
in the end be destroyed by fire, and the good rewarded and
the bad condemned, as in our religious system, and that will
happen, the Manichaean texts say, when the statue comes.
The Greek word for "statue" in all these connections is
always *andrias*, which includes the word *anèr*, which means
"man," the word *andrias* being only used for a stone statue in
human shape. When the *andrias* comes at the end of the days
as the Savior, then the world will be partly saved and partly
destroyed. Sometimes the statue is called *eikon*, but more
frequently it is *andrias*. "On the last day the *andrias* will
resurrect, in that hour when the *andrias* rises the Evil One
will cry. The first rock in the world is this *andrias* of glory,
the complete man who has been called into the glory. He has
carried the whole world and was the one who carried every
weight." Those are excerpts from the *Kephalaia* of Mani. [33]
The motif of the statue occurs also in one of the oldest
alchemical texts, ascribed to Komarios, where it is said that

after the *prima materia* has been burned and transformed, in the end, through the glory of the fire (the text runs), the *andrias*, the statue, will appear in its full glory. These texts caused later alchemists to identify the human-shaped statue with the philosopher's stone and to imagine the latter as a statue and as the incorruptible part of the personality which survives death.

The statue, therefore, belongs to the whole symbolism of our story, for when Hâtim was nearly drowned he participated in the fate of the old Adam, who normally in alchemical symbolism *is* drowned; and when Hâtim was nearly petrified he again underwent the fate of the alchemical *prima materia*, which is petrified. But if Hâtim had been totally petrified in our story, it would have been a completely negative event. If he had been drowned or petrified, he would have been assimilated with the shape of the philosopher's stone, of the symbol of the Self, but in a negative form. Jung always points out that the process of individuation, being the strongest urge in man, always pushes its way through in every human being, but if it is not attended to consciously then it takes place in a negative form. For instance, instead of finding the philosopher's stone within oneself, one becomes petrified, i. e., transformed into the philosopher's stone in a negative form. Instead of being dissolved in the bath of the unconscious for renewal, one is dissolved in the unconscious in the form of a dissociation. One could say, therefore, that the process always takes its course, but whether it is destructive or positive depends on our conscious attitude.

We have to ask ourselves what it means if petrification takes on this negative form. An Arabic translation of a lost treatise of Zosimos runs as follows: "Take the philosopher's stone, the black, white, red, and yellow one which is a beautiful bird [here we have our parrot, the stone being in a way the bird], that bird which flies without wings in the darkness of the night and in the light of day. From the bitterness in its throat we can take the color which transforms everything. This bitterness is a coloring poison." The same bitterness in the throat of the bird in another text is later called the acid which transforms the gold into pure spirit.

Those are only a few of the many quotations I could give you which show that the bird—when the philosopher's stone still has that aspect—according to the alchemical viewpoint has an astringent bitterness in its throat, and things treated with that are first turned to salt and then are transformed into gold. I quote this parallel emphasizing the motif of astringent bitterness because I think it has to do with our petrification motif. The astringent bitterness in many other alchemical texts is similar to what we nowadays would call bitterness in a psychological sense of the word. Jung has said that bitterness in a human being seldom comes from an unhappy fate. Many people have gone through agonies and very difficult life situations without becoming bitter, but it arises in people who fight themselves, who are vaguely aware of the fact that they themselves are guilty of their own unhappiness. In other words, the people who become bitter are those who with their left hand work against their right hand, and who, due to an unconscious counterpart within themselves, are constantly in the soup, but do not notice it. Bitterness is a kind of hidden affect, or rage, but turned within, and it has a stiffening effect upon the personality. Bitter people are rarely friendly and relaxed and agreeable to deal with; they have a contracted attitude, and there we have the connection between petrification and bitterness.

In "Psychology of the Transference,"[34] dealing with a series of alchemical pictures, Jung gives what seems to me to be the explanation of this motif. He says that the human soul or psyche lives in and from relatedness. One cannot individuate sitting on the peak of Mount Everest. Being normally, naturally, and rightly related to our surrounding group is one of the necessities of the process of individuation. Now, the alchemical process, which is a symbolical representation of the process of individuation, means a fortification and a solidifcation of the individual personality. It means on one side being less identical with the group, less melted into the group through *participation mystique*, and being firmer and more independently on one's own feet; and at the same time it means being more consciously related. Now if this double process of being inwardly solidified through the process of individuation and outwardly related to surrounding people takes place unconsciously, then it has the opposite result, namely people harden and stiffen outwardly, and inwardly are like—a moldy strawberry!

Jung speaks then of the modern mass man and says that this terrible heaping up of amorphous masses in our big towns calls for a compensatory movement in those who feel that they have to protect themselves from being leveled out in the mass, and if they do not find the way of inner solidification there comes this outer hardening against one's fellow beings. We have seen it in Nazi Germany, and it is still visible in the increase of crime everywhere nowadays in the big towns, particularly in juvenile delinquents: those elegant, callous young killers who boast that they don't mind shooting, or cutting people into bits. They are driven to such acts in order to insulate and protect themselves from being crushed by mass psychology, but instead of solidifying inside they harden outside. If one gets at the inner feelings of such a person there is something like a confused mass, a sleepy bear, or something similar. There is practically nothing but a heap of sentimentality or confusion, though outwardly such people display terrible strength and hardness and are completely cut off from any kind of relatedness. This illustrates a process of petrification in contrast to inner solidification and is, so to speak, an attempt toward individuation which has gone wrong.

The urgent need of our time, because we are crushed by overpopulation and by the heaping up of masses in cities, is to separate ourselves and solidify our personalities. Weak people who cannot do this inwardly, and who do not find the process of individuation as an alchemical inner consolidation, harden instead outside and display a pseudo-superior, hard, unrelated, bitter exterior to the outer world. That is why, our story tells us, if Hâtim and all the others who tried before do not get at the diamond—*the real meaning of what lies behind this parrot mystery*—they petrify. The hard stone gets them, but in its negative and destructive form, in the form of an outer hardening. Only by hitting the target, that is, by getting at the positive meaning of the whole constellation, does Hâtim redeem them.

The process of petrification often begins with an arrogant feeling that other people are all miserable, second-rate creatures. When people think like that, it is a symptom that their feeling function is beginning to fade away, and then next all relatedness goes. One sees this also in real madness. Some years ago I read in a paper that a schizophrenic in an asylum behaved so well that he was allowed to go about freely and could work in the garden and around the house. He made friends with the director's little daughter, who was ten or twelve years old, and they would play together in the garden. He cut wood and the child talked to him, and then one day, with no kind of explanation or preparation, he took a knife and slowly cut her throat. In court he quietly said that he had to do it, the Holy Ghost had told him to cut the girl's throat. That is the same thing—in its extreme form.

By hitting the parrot Hâtim not only saves his own life but redeems all the other statues as well. This can be understood on two different levels. One could take it either on what we call the subjective or on the objective level. If you take it on the objective level, it would mean that the individual who hits the mark, or finds out what is really meant, naturally redeems a number of other people with him, because all the others wanted to find that same thing, but did not. If one can analyze a juvenile delinquent in time and show him that what he really wants is to be a personality and not to be crushed by the masses, then one can sometimes redeem him. One can take the bitterness from his bird's throat, that is, the bitterness in his soul's throat, and help him to the philosopher's stone. For there is something to that bitterness, that hatred of other people, the unhappiness and detestation of all one's miserable fellow human creatures. It comes from not wanting to be leveled out. One has the right to be oneself, but that is not attained by shooting a few people. If one could take that astringent bitterness from his soul's throat and use it rightly it would be the *prima materia* of individuation, and in that way one could say that anybody who finds it for himself naturally can help other people who are groping in the same direction.

If you take it inwardly, then those other petrified people would be complexes or parts of one's own personality. Sometimes in dreams it happens that the ego, by a heroic deed, saves a lot of other people, or rescues and helps many others. Seen on the subjective level, this would mean that one can make all the different parts of one's personality cooperate again harmoniously. If the process of individuation, the main inner life process, is blocked, then naturally all secondary instinctive processes are also disturbed. Someone who is stuck in the process of individuation will probably have trouble with a power prestige problem, a sex problem, or all sorts of other problems. In other words, all the other instinctive and secondary drives will also be disturbed, and if the life flow gets going again on the main line, then all those side channels will become normal and things will fall into place. That is why, generally, we do not pay much attention to symptoms and do not concentrate on or do much about secondary symptoms. If someone complains about frigidity, or impotence, or headaches or so on, we take it as a hint that there is a block which has to be removed, but the main thing is to find out through the dreams how the soul can flow again in its main riverbed; then generally, those side issues get reopened at the same time. They are only blocked because the main thing is not right, i.e., finding the meaning, the meaningfulness of one's own life and being on the right track.

With this we come, from another angle, to the main problem, namely: Why does the parrot, as it were, cover up the diamond? Why, in this Persian story, is there a contrast between the parrot, who has to be shot down, and the diamond, which is the goal?

In order to understand this we have to look back at the Gayomard-Adam problem. In *Mysterium Coniunctionis* Jung writes:

> The "old Adam" corresponds to the primitive man, the "shadow" of our present-day consciousness, and the primitive man has his roots in the animal man (the tailed Adam), who has long since vanished from our consciousness. Even the primitive man has become a stranger to us, so that we have to rediscover his psychology. It was therefore something of a surprise when analytical psychology discovered in the products of the unconscious of modern man so much archaic material, and not only that but the sinister darkness of the animal world of instinct. Though "instincts" or "drives" can be formulated in physiological and biological terms they cannot be pinned down in that way, for they are also psychic entities which manifest themselves in a world of fantasy peculiarly their own. They are not just physiological or consistently biological phenomena, but are at the same time, even in their content, meaningful fantasy structures with a symbolic character. An instinct does not apprehend its object blindly and at random, but brings to it a certain psychic "viewpoint" or interpretation; for every instinct is linked *a priori* with a corresponding image of the situation, as can be proved indirectly in cases of the symbiosis of plant and animal. [35]

One of the great problems of zoologists who study the behavior of animals is whether the animals function more or less as automatons or wound-up watches, or whether they have some kind of inner accompanying psychological fantasies or thoughts. In order to avoid the word *psyche*, the zoologist Adolph Portmann proposes saying that there is something like an "inwardness" in all animal behavior. With man it is very easy to see, for if someone is driven by a biological urge he can report his fantasies and the emotion he has about it; but with an animal we can only watch from the outside, and as it cannot speak, it cannot say whether it has accompanying fantasies. As an experiment, a bird was isolated for a long time in a cage, a little male bird of a species which loves to fight. Then it was given a fighting partner and they had a really good fight, which made them feel better and sleep and eat better afterward. Then the fighting partner was removed, and after that the bird, from time to time when it felt like it—not like an automaton at the same hour each day—moved toward the corner of the cage where this enemy had entered, and played the whole fight over again without any partner! And afterward, though not as much as if it had been a real fight, it was refreshed and went on busily eating and drinking, feeling better for having shoved the damned chap out of the cage!

That story is important because it shows that a certain "inwardness," as Portmann calls it, combines with every biological drive. The difficulty in investigating this field is to find a way to see it, for if the animal cannot talk, how can you prove it? With us it is simple, for we know that all our biological instinctive patterns of behavior, such as sex, fighting, domination, eating, sleeping, and so on, are surrounded by an enormous amount of meaningful fantasy material. Jung writes:

> The world of instinct, simple as it seems to the rationalist, reveals itself on the primitive level as a complicated interplay of physiological facts, taboos, rites, class-systems and tribal lore, which [and now we come to another factor] impose a restrictive form on the instinct from the beginning, preconsciously, and make it serve a higher purpose. [36]

That is one of the great problems of modern man and one of the main reasons why moderns, especially rationalistically trained people, resist the unconscious and their own instinctive nature. They assume that if they let go, it would be like a stone rolling down the mountainside to the bottom of the sea. If once they let go of their ethical or rationalistic or other inhibitions, they would absolutely lose control. Actually this is so if the instinctive basis is not sound or has been repressed for a long time. Then naturally there is an explosion. But under normal circumstances, and if one gives in with a certain elastic wisdom, not letting go all at once, one soon discovers that what one thought would lead into measureless nonsense does not do so, for there is an inner spiritual brake built into every instinctive drive, which controls it naturally from within. Jung continues:

> The primary connection between image and instinct explains the interdependence of instinct and religion in the most general sense. These two spheres are in mutually compensatory relationship, and by "instinct" we must understand not merely "eros" but everything that goes by the name of "instinct". "Religion" on the primitive level means the psychic regulatory system that is coordinated with the dynamism of instinct. On a higher level [and this touches our story and concerns it] this primary interdependence is sometimes lost, and then religion can easily become an antidote to instinct, whereupon the originally compensatory relationship degenerates into conflict, religion petrifies into formalism [the parrot], and instinct is vitiated. A split of this kind is not due to a mere accident, nor is it a meaningless catastrophe. It lies rather in the nature of the evolutionary process itself, in the increasing extension and differentiation of consciousness. For just as there is no energy without the tension of opposites, so there can be no consciousness without the perception of differences. But any stronger emphasis of differences leads to a polarity and finally to a conflict which maintains the necessary tension of opposites.

We can therefore say that Gayomard is the original unconscious, instinctive man for whom instinctive drives, purely animal existence, and spirituality, are completely one. There is no tension between the spiritual and the instinctive poles of his personality. If you want to get a feeling impression of what that means, then read Laurens van der Post's book *The Heart of the Hunter*,[37] about the Bushman tribes in the Kalahari Desert. If you look at the description of those people, keeping this question in mind, you will see that their hunting, their sex life, their fight for survival, their spiritual life, and their storytelling and dancing are absolutely one living unit. They belong together and accompany each other, and you could never see any trace of what one could call their spiritual inner life—which has some quite deep and differentiated aspects—interfering in any way with their purely natural animal life. On the other side, one of the greatest divisions of the two poles can be found in medieval Christianity, or in certain extremely ascetic movements in the East, where spirituality has become a cramped counterpole of instinctive human life. When this falls too far apart, then a neurosis develops, and one has the picture which Freud dug up and so often encountered in his practice, namely that a wrong spirituality in some form poisoned and destroyed the instinctive personality. This poisoning of the instinctive personality, according to Jung, sets up a movement in the unconscious itself to restore the original oneness of the two poles.

The diamond in our story would represent this primordial oneness. It is a symbol of totality and of the Self, in which the instinctive and animal drives of man and his spirituality are united, or are one again, as it was in the person of Gayomard. But the parrot, being a bird and therefore representing a spiritual entity, would only represent the religious spirit poisoning the natural human being, and behind it the real religious goal had to be rediscovered, namely, the diamond. It is hidden behind a spiritual teaching which, in part, still contains the symbol of totality, but because of an overemphasis on the spiritual pole, it poisons the natural human personality. We must therefore assume that at the time of our story, Shi'ite Islam was threatened, as the whole Islamic world is threatened again and again—though not only the Islamic world—by slipping into a purely formalistic religious attitude in which putting your prayer carpet down and going to Mecca, saying your prayers mechanically and reading the Koran, is supposed to effect redemption. But that, naturally, has just the opposite effect and poisons or petrifies people. The hero is the one who aims at, or finds, or whose genius of intuition hits the target of what was originally meant, namely a symbol of totality.

If we compare the different facets of the parrot figure, we get more deeply into the understanding of its meaning. We know from the oldest, the Indian version, that the parrot is a wise bird and a storyteller, and not a demon who covers up a diamond. We still find the parrot in this positive role in the *Tuti-Nameh*, where it is a mercurial spirit of wisdom. Then in our Persian story of the Bath Bâdgerd, the parrot becomes something demonic which has to be shot down because it covers up the diamond, the real symbol of the Self. In the Spanish story, the bird symbol is restored in its positive original role and is itself the precious thing which the little girl and her brother bring back home so that the family quaternio is restored. The white color is probably also added to emphasize the parrot's positive light nature. But it also petrifies people who try to seize it, if it is seized hastily and impatiently, as the little boy did. So it has kept some of its demonic features, even though it has been restored to its positive original role.

The parrot appears in the different versions of the story in ever new facets. The motif itself wanders from country to country, remaining partly the same and partly taking on new features. This has for a long time puzzled investigators of fairy tales and up till Jung's discovery and way of interpretation of the unconscious, had never been explained: namely, why motifs wander. They walk through and are borrowed from other stories and mixed up in new ones, and the motifs vary a great deal. The same symbol is sometimes described positively, sometimes half-positively, and sometimes has a demonic and negative effect in those different setups, and up till now investigators have always been stuck in trying to judge which was the best version, and which had degenerated. They always tried to give a feeling, a value judgment, and a literary judgment, about the motifs, instead of seeing that they represent the living function of a symbol and that those different variations express different compensatory unconscious processes, just as they do in the dream of an individual.

We must therefore always take the specific version and relate it to the cultural and psychological situation of the country within which it is told, applying it to each cultural unconscious situation. We can see that when it is borrowed and built into another country's fairy tale, then instinctively, without anyone noticing, those motifs which for the consciousness of that country have no compensatory meaning, are left out, while those which are important are emphasized, or even spun out and amplified by other motifs. So *all* the variations of one motif have a meaning.

This is another reason why we have to learn to amplify and circumambulate mythological motifs, amplifying through many cultural aspects, so as to get at the basic functional importance and meaning. When a motif functions destructively in one situation, in a healing form in another, and ambiguously in a third, then we acquire a kind of intuition as to what it means at bottom. So amplification is the *conditio sine qua non* which *cannot* be left out in mythological interpretation. This is why it is always helpful to examine the different cultural setups and not get stuck only in the original one in which you meet the symbol. Some investigators of fairy tales have recognized this and even praise Jungian psychology for it, saying that it is the first time that a positive explanation has been found for the fact that there are so many versions and variations of each mythological motif, something which had hitherto been looked upon as a nuisance and a formal incompleteness.

If we take the parrot as the symbol for a spiritual religious attitude, we can proceed through the different situations. In general, a bird, being a winged creature, represents a spiritual attitude, or a spiritual content of the psyche. The alchemists even literally call birds *volatilia*, or spirits. They interpret them as sublimated gaseous forms of matter and the spirit, or vapors, and evaporated substances in alchemy are symbolized by different birds. Also in most religious and mythological setups, the soul of the deceased person is represented with wings or in bird form, indicating that the body has gone and the spiritual form has survived. In this way, the parrot represents a natural spirit in the unconscious, and in the Indian story it tells the truth in a symbolic form, as the unconscious does every night in dreams. In India, however, this spirit appears in a profane setup; it is not especially linked up with any religious teaching or system. Then in the *Tuti-Nameh*, the Islamic version, the spirit of truth is identified with the wisdom of Muhammad.

In the Spanish version this link with the official religious system has again been lost, because otherwise this bird would have to be identified with the dove of the Holy Ghost. When the Spaniards took over the story, had they wanted to give it an official religious tinge, it would have had to be a white dove instead of a white parrot. That this is not possible is clear, because then you could not say such shocking things as that when you seize it at the wrong moment, you get petrified. However, we see from the instance of the madman who cut the girl's throat and said that it was the Holy Ghost who made him do it, that it is perhaps not so much off the point. He certainly seized the Holy Ghost in the wrong moment! Therefore, in the Spanish version the parrot motif again became profane, and that has its reasons in the ruling religious system, with which it is incompatible or could not be connected. In spite of this, the idea of having to find a bird which tells the truth and helps one specially in coping with the problem of evil seems to have been so fascinating, and to have encompassed such an important psychological problem, that it has been built into this Spanish fairy tale. The white parrot in the story has the specific function of protecting the Count and Countess and their children from the evil influence of the butler and the witch, for there a spirit of truth coming directly from the unconscious is needed, and has a more ambiguous and natural character than official teaching would give to the element of the spirit.

This demonstrates how fairy tales take on a function compensatory to a ruling collective attitude. In a kind of romantic, vague form, one finds in a lot of books on fairy tales the statement that they are the dreams of people and nations. I think we should take this much more literally. Fairy tales actually seem to have a similar function in the setup of a population as dreams in an individual: they confirm, heal, compensate, counterbalance, and criticize the dominating collective attitude, just as dreams heal, compensate, confirm, criticize, or complete the conscious attitude of an individual. That is their tremendous value, and is why they have never been suppressed and have never been sucked up by any official religious teaching. As an undercurrent they survived everywhere, because fairy tales functioned as a dream compensation in which those psychological needs, which for some reason were not sufficiently respected in the collective conscious attitude, could be realized.

In the Spanish setup, the parrot helps to cope with the problem of evil. In the *Tuti Nameh*, it does the same thing; it has a definitely ethical function in saving the woman from betraying her husband. Instead of helping to cope with evil, it protects the right kind of eros attitude. In the Persian story, it again has a different function, for it veils the diamond in a negative form. Here it represents spirituality which has become mechanical.

Jung's approach to religious and mythological symbolism seems to me to be so essential, because it can very often, like a key, reopen the treasures of the real original meaning of texts which, read from another standpoint, seem to us absolutely meaningless. Again and again people have told me that, thanks to the Jungian viewpoint, for the first time they could read some religious or mythological text, seeing the living meaning which it contains and being vivified by it, as if those dead parchments of the past had gained a new life. Through this key of a new understanding, analysis sometimes leads people to pick up their old religious traditions spontaneously and find life in them again. It is as though they suddenly saw the diamond behind the parrot. Having been repulsed by the parrot and turned away from it, they are now able to find the diamond behind it.

I cannot refrain from telling here an event which a young doctor wrote me about and had the kindness to let me use. He was of Jewish descent but did not practice his religion any longer; then he was asked to attend the bar mitzvah of his nephew. Shortly before the event, he picked up the sacred texts which are used for the ceremony in order to get acquainted with them. But he got bored and took up this book instead and fell upon my interpretation of the parrot. It struck home, and he felt deeply ashamed that he had wanted to "parrot" the sacred texts. At that very moment, he heard strange cackling noises outside; he went to the window, and there on a branch opposite the window sat a big white parrot! He had escaped from somewhere, because he wore a broken golden chain on his ankle. Such coincidences Jung calls synchronistic events. They show how powerfully alive this archetype behind the parrot stories still is.

3

Four Short Tales

Prince Hassan Pasha

I would now like to go into the wider theme of finding a redeeming or demonic bird, and its function within a fairy-tale quest; this will throw further light on our parrot motif. Here is a Turkestan story written by a pupil at the college of Tashkent, the capital of Uzbekistan in the U.S.S.R. It is entitled "Prince Hassan Pasha."[38]

A Sultan called Murad had three sons. The oldest was Ibrahim Pasha, the second Abdraim Pasha, and the youngest Hassan Pasha. One day the Sultan became very sad but didn't know why this terrible sadness had caught him. [Well, we could say that he had a terrific anima mood!] His eldest son, Ibrahim Pasha, went to talk to his father, but the Sultan turned away, so he approached him on the other side, but the Sultan turned away again. So the son went to the Minister and said that he should ask his father what was the matter. The Minister went to the Sultan and said, "My great Lord, we are all very grieved about your sadness. Tell us why are you so sad and why you did not want to listen to your eldest son. Is he such a bad man, or did he do something to displease you? What is the matter?" The Sultan then uttered the marvelous words [which could always be quoted of male analysands when they are in an anima mood!] "I don't know what has happened to me, but I am inexpressibly sad, and am irritated with everybody in the world."

The Minister then reminded the Sultan that he had forty of the most beautiful gardens in the world and suggested that they should go and visit them.

So the Sultan and his Minister and the Sultan's three sons

visited thirty-nine of the beautiful gardens, but the Sultan remained in his bad, irritated mood. But when they came to the fortieth garden he saw a marvelous tree and asked about it, and the gardener said, "Yes, great Lord, this tree is something very miraculous. Every day at six o'clock in the evening it has a bud at the very top of the tree and at seven o'clock the leaves come out, and at nine o'clock the flowers come out, and at midnight the fruit is ripe and at this midnight hour a strange bird comes and sits on the tree, and by three o'clock in the morning it has eaten all the fruit; it then flies away and comes again the next night and does the same thing. But the tree is so high that I have great difficulty in watching this bird and cannot say what kind of fruit the tree bears."

Scarcely had the gardener finished his tale when all the Sultan's sadness vanished and he turned to his companions saying, "Is there a man who can get the fruit from this tree?"

The Sultan's youngest son, Hassan Pasha, at once said that he would stay in the garden and pick the fruit when it was ripe. Hassan Pasha then sat at the bottom of the tree and waited, but he got sleepy and missed the bird and the next morning woke up and the fruit was eaten.

So Hassan Pasha said he would try again, and this time he stayed awake; when the bird came, he shot, but missed it. However, a big feather fell down, and when Hassan picked it up, he deciphered some holy words on it. He brought the feather to his father, who then, naturally, more than ever wanted to have the bird itself. Eventually the three brothers decided to go on a quest in search of the bird. They went into the desert, and suddenly there was a terrific storm. An enormous column of dust approached them, out of which sprang a wolf, saying in a human voice to Hassan, who had gone ahead, "Give me something to eat." It seized a large piece of bread Hassan gave it and disappeared.

Soon the two eldest brothers caught up with Hassan, and they came to an inscription on a big stone at a crossroad which said, "He who goes to the left will return happily; he who goes straight ahead will perhaps return safely, but perhaps not; but he who goes to the right will never return." They quarreled about who should take which way, and then Hassan gave in and said that they should choose what they liked and he would take what remained. Naturally, they chose the two relatively better ways and left him the bad one.

So he went the bad way, and as soon as he had gone a short distance, the wolf came and said, "Did you not read what was on the stone? Why do you go this way?" "Go away," said Hassan, "leave me in peace!" But the wolf said no, Hassan had saved him from starvation, so it was its duty to serve him.

Hassan said he didn't need the wolf, but it attached itself to him and said that without it, Hassan would not find anything. It advised Hassan to leave his horse in the woods and to sit on its back and hold on by its tail, and in twelve hours they would be in the land where the bird was.

Scarcely had Hassan sat on the wolf's back when it set off and went like the wind to the kingdom where the bird was. It was a country full of terrific devs [which are the same as djins], two at each gate, and when he had gone through the last gate the wolf said that Hassan would come to forty chambers—like the forty gardens before—which contained the treasures of the place. The rooms were in two rows, and in the twentieth row on the left he would find, in one chamber, three birds. The text says that they were the birds of Paradise, and one was the miraculous bird he was seeking. Hassan had quickly to seize the one he was looking for and not look back, but go. But something awkward happened: instead of quickly seizing the bird—there we have an amplification of our motif to seize quickly and not delay—he could not help but admire the beautiful golden stand on which the bird sat, and thought he might take it with him. But as soon as he touched it, there was a terrific noise, because from this stand were invisible threads going to a system of bells, which woke up the devs, who caught Hassan and brought him to the King of the country.

The King wanted to kill him at once, but when he heard what Hassan had to say about the purpose of his journey, he said, "All right, I see you are a hero, and I will give you all three birds if you will do me a service. Far away there is a King who has forty daughters, and if you will bring me the most beautiful one, then you can have the three birds." [Here, as so often in those Oriental stories, there is a chain quest: one quest leads to a goal, and then there is another and another to be made.]

152

So Hassan returned to the wolf feeling very depressed, and he said that they would have to find the beautiful lady for the King. The wolf was terribly annoyed that he had not done as told, and left the Prince alone, saying it wouldn't help any more; but after it had abreacted its anger, it returned and said that it would carry Hassan to the next kingdom. However, if Hassan did not obey this time, he would have to get the bird and the Princess alone.

The wolf told Hassan that he would come to a town where there was an enormous monster with many heads, and Hassan must not be afraid of it, but just walk past and he would find the forty Princesses in the palace. They would all be asleep, and he must go in and take the ninth, counting from the left, and carry her away. But when doing this, he must not look back, because otherwise everything would go wrong.

Naturally Hassan repeated the same mistake; he took the girl and carried her out, but then involuntarily looked back and saw a beautiful bowl which belonged to her. It was decorated with gold and silver and precious stones, and he thought it a pity not to take it too. But as soon as he touched it, there was again a terrific noise, a lot of servants came, and he was caught. The King wanted to execute him at once, but then the same thing happened again, and he said, "All right, I will give you my daughter and the beautiful bowl, but you must bring me the yellow horse which belongs to a dev in the mountains."

Our story is a parallel version of a German fairy story called "The Golden Bird," but there the order is bird, horse, lady, while in the Turkestan version it is bird, lady, horse! So you see what man values most in Turkestan! To those excellent riders, the horse means much more than a woman, just as a car sometimes means more to a modern man than his wife; at least he treats it better!

Crying bitterly, Hassan returned to the wolf, who was again angry and struck the Prince. But when it had abreacted its anger after a while, it said, "All right, I'll help you again, for the last time." Again the wolf took him on its back, and on the third day they arrived at the foot of a high mountain. The wolf told Hassan to go up this mountain and he would come to a

big house. In it a big dev would be sleeping, and around his
neck there would be a key which Hassan must take. He would
see many chambers: in the first there were nails, in the second
there was a long silk cord and in the third was the yellow horse.
"Go into the first chamber and take nineteen nails, and then
into the second and take thirty-eight yards of silk, and then go
to the third chamber where the yellow horse is. In the corner of
this chamber there will be a big pit, and when you come in, the
horse will neigh and wake up. Do not look around, but quickly
put the silk cord round a pillar and let yourself fall down into
the pit. The dev will wake up from the noise the horse is
making and will get on the yellow horse and look around
everywhere, and then he will go to sleep again. Then with this
silk cord, you can come out of the pit. The yellow horse will
neigh again, and the same thing will happen, several times, but
finally, naturally, the dev will get annoyed at being awakened all
the time. He will give the horse hard bones to eat instead of its
usual food consisting of raisins, and he will say it can neigh as
much as it likes, he is not going to bother any more, the
horse has deceived him so often. When the dev has said that,
you must get out of the pit, give the horse its raisins to gain its
favor, and then nail the dev to the floor while he is asleep, and
take the horse away."

Everything happened in this way, and this time Hassan
succeeded in getting the horse.

Then they decided that it would be a pity to give up the horse
for the girl; it would be much better for Hassan to keep it. So
the wolf told Hassan to shut his eyes and it turned itself into a
yellow horse which Hassan had to leave with the King, while he
rode off with the girl on the real yellow horse. But once in the
King's stall, the false horse turned itself into a wolf again and
bit the groom and ran off and met Hassan in the woods, where
they plotted not to give up the beautiful girl. The wolf played
the same trick again, transformed himself into a girl, and told
Hassan to go and get the bird and ride off with it and the
Princess.

Meanwhile the false Princess was all dressed up and in veils
at the wedding feast, and when everybody was drunk she
became a wolf again and bit and scratched the King, and
everybody was horrified and ran away. Then the two joined up

again, and the wolf took Hassan to its home for a rest. But after a time, it sent him home and warned him to be very careful of his brothers because they would be jealous. Then comes the famous episode which we know from many other fairy tales: the jealous brothers took everything Hassan had acquired, and pretended they had found the bird, the girl, and the horse. They left Hassan blinded in the desert, but Hassan prayed to Allah and in forty days was healed of his blindness. Eventually, the wolf brought him home, the brothers were executed, and Hassan married the beautiful Princess. The wolf took part in the wedding and was treated with great honor.

The end of the story is that later Sultan Murad hands the government over to his son Hassan. The last sentence of the story says that on each feather of the bird called Anka, or Anka-Kush, some sort of wisdom is inscribed in holy script, and because Hassan Pasha always went on reading this, he learned all the human virtues and became a very wise ruler.

In the German and Austrian parallel stories, the helpful animal which is here a wolf, and in the German version a fox, is redeemed and turns into a human being. In the Hassan Pasha story it is not redeemed but remains a wolf, although it is very well treated at the wedding.

We will not analyze all the peripeteias of this story, but will concentrate only on the central motif of the bird, and do as we did with the parrot, namely, chase it through several different versions.

The Bird Flower-Triller

Here is an Iranian parallel to the Hassan Pasha story, called "The Bird Flower-Triller":[39]

There was a King who had three sons: Mälik Muhammad, Mälik Dschämschîd and Mälik Ibrâhîm. Mälik Ibrâhîm was the youngest, and his father loved him most and he loved his father most. The King became sick and the doctors of the whole Empire did not know any remedy for his illness. But then one doctor said that there was a remedy if only it could be found: in

the sea there was a green fish which round its jaw had a
golden ring, and if you would catch it and cut open its belly and
put a bit of the fish's heart on the Sultan's heart, he would
certainly recover.

The three sons gave a number of divers and fishermen money
to find the fish, and finally, after some days, they succeeded in
doing so and brought it to Mälik Ibrâhîm. When the latter took
it he was tremendously impressed by its great beauty and in
looking at it he discovered that on its forehead was written:
"There is no God but Allah, and Muhammad is his prophet,
and Alî his successor." That is the Shi'ite Muslim creed. And
when Mälik Ibrâhîm read that, he was deeply moved and said,
"Even if my father could be cured by this fish, I cannot kill it,"
and he threw it back into the sea.

Meanwhile everybody was waiting for him to bring the fish
and cut it open and cure his father, and when they discovered
that he had thrown it back into the sea they bit their fingers in
astonishment and did not know how to explain this. When they
told the King he got very angry and said, "If Mälik Ibrâhîm is
really waiting for my death in order to get the throne I will
disinherit him."

Then the King became worse and worse and had no peace by
day or by night; again all the doctors surrounded his bedside and
again said, "There is still one remedy of which we know and
that is the Bird Flower-Triller. Every time it sings there drops
from its beak a beautiful flower, and if someone could get that
bird and put one of those flowers onto the King's heart, then his
disease would cease."

The King kissed his two sons and said, "Now my only hope is
that you will find the Flower-Triller." So the two elder brothers
took their horses, and went off, and after a while, Ibrâhîm
followed them. They asked him what he was doing and he told
them that he was also looking for the bird, so they decided to go
together. Then they came to crossroads where there was a tree
and a spring, and they got down from their horses for a little
rest. When his two brothers had fallen asleep, Mälik Ibrâhîm
went for a little walk and suddenly caught sight of a stone tablet
on which was written: "Those who come to these crossroads
should know that the way to the right is without danger and

very agreeable, but the way to the left is full of dangers and no
traveler may hope to return from it."

Naturally, the two brothers took the way to the right and
Ibrâhîm the one to the left. But there was another sentence on
the tablet which said that if anybody should wish to take the
road to the left then he should take the tablet with him.
Ibrâhîm did this and first, in a beautiful castle surrounded by a
lovely garden, he met a very beautiful girl and she flirted with
him and he fell in love with her and she knew his name at once.
But then he suddenly remembered his tablet and went into a
corner of the garden and read: "If you take the way to the left
you will meet a very beautiful and seductive girl, but don't fall
for her tricks because she is a shrewd old sorceress who wants
to kill you. She will propose a wrestling match and while this is
taking place you must tear off her shirt and will see on the left
side of her body a black spot. Take your knife and thrust it with
all your strength into that black spot, but watch out that you
do not miss it because otherwise you will be transformed into a
black stone." [There is the petrification motif again!]

Everything happened as foretold, and Ibrâhîm succeeded in
plunging his dagger into the black spot of the sorceress; and
then there was a hurricane and thunder and lightning and he
fainted with terror. When he recovered consciousness he
saw beside him the body of a horrible old hag; the garden and
castle and everything around her had disappeared, and he was
in the desert.

So Ibrâhîm went on and next came to a garden very like the
former one; in the middle of the garden was a lake on which
was a boat. He swam out to it and found ten men, in only one of
whom there was a sign of life. Mälik Ibrâhîm fed the man, who
was too weak and starved to speak, with small pieces of apple.
When the man had recovered a little, he told Ibrâhîm that their
boat had been caught in a whirlpool which spun it around and
that every day at midday a hand came up from the depths and
pulled one of them down, whether dead or alive, and that they
were formerly twenty, ten of whom the hand had seized, the
others having died of hunger. Ibrâhîm again pulled out his
tablet and read: "If you come to this boat, then do not be
diverted by anything you see or which happens, or which the
owner of the hand will tell you. The hand which comes up out

of the water is the hand of the first witch's sister. You must
squeeze it with all your strength so as to break the curse.
Should you be overcome in the battle you will lose your freedom
forever."

A most beautiful hand then appeared out of the water and a
voice greeted him and said, "Let us shake hands in friendship!"
Mälik Ibrâhîm said, "Yes, gladly," and gave his hand and
noticed that it was pulling him further and further into the
water, so he put himself under the protection of God and then
squeezed the hand so hard that he crushed it; again there was a
storm and again he saw the corpse of the witch beside him,
and he was again lost in the desert.

Then he came to a place where there were a tall tree and a
spring, and a lot of apes had gathered together on the tree. He
did not know how to explain the presence of these apes, but
they surrounded him and looked at him with sad eyes. So he
took out the tablet and read: "Now that you have killed the
second witch you will come to a tree with a lot of apes, and to a
spring. Follow the spring and you will come to an enormous
building and there you will find a girl, but again she is a witch
who will try to entice and deceive you, and this time you must
throw this tablet at her forehead and split her head open to
break her spell." Everything happened as said, and the moment
he threw the tablet at the witch's head she fell dead and all
the apes turned into beautiful girls. The leader of these girls
was a fairy Princess who had been hunting a gazelle with her
girls. But the gazelle had been a witch, and when they reached
a wood, suddenly it had begun to run around in a circle and had
transformed itself into a horrible woman, who in no time had
turned them all into apes. Now that Ibrâhîm had killed the
gazelle-witch, they were redeemed.

Ibrâhîm brought this fairy Princess back to her father, and
they became engaged, but then the King told Ibrâhîm that
he had not only this daughter, Maimûne, who was now redeemed, but also a son who had tried to fight the witches and
had been killed, and who was buried in the cemetery nearby.
But each night witches would come and, like the witch of
Endor in the Bible, take the body of the King's son, wrapped in
the torn remnants of his burial clothes, out of the tomb; and

each morning his corpse must be buried anew and the next
night the same thing would happen again.

So Ibrâhîm stayed near this tomb for the night and, having
again been informed as to what he had to do, he took a stick,
and when two witches appeared to begin their evil tricks again,
he beheaded them with one blow, and again there was a terrific
storm. But when everything had become calm, the dead Prince
was resurrected and said Ibrâhîm had freed him and he would
be his slave evermore.

Afterward Mälik Ibrâhîm married the fairy Princess, but still
intended to go on and find the Bird Flower-Triller. Somebody
told him it was on a big mountain which was surrounded by
thousands of devs [the story is more or less parallel to the one
we had before of the djin], and nobody can get through there.
But Ibrâhîm just went up to the thousand devs and when they
rushed at him, he stopped them and was not afraid, and so they
became quite curious and wanted to know what this naive and
nice young man was doing. They didn't kill him at once, but
gave him a chance to say what he had come for. Ibrâhîm
said that he wanted the Bird Flower-Triller! He just told the
truth quite openly, and the devs told him that it was on the
mountain and belonged to Tarfe Bânû, the daughter of the fairy
King, and that they couldn't get him the bird, but they could
carry him there and he could steal it himself; they didn't mind.
They even carried him to the castle, and in a room in this fairy
castle, led by the sound of the peeping bird, he found Tarfe
Bânû sleeping on a couch ornamented with precious stones; she
was so beautiful that no human tongue can describe her beauty.
At her head was a beautiful cage with the Bird Flower-Triller in
it, and each time it made a trill, sweet-scented flowers came
out of its beak. Ibrâhîm quickly seized the cage and sneaked
away, and asked one of the devs to carry him home. When he
was close to his home castle he put the cage onto a tree and fell
asleep, and then again, as one might imagine, the brothers
came and stole the bird and went to the King and said that they
had found it. But the bird wouldn't sing!

Eventually, Ibrâhîm succeeded in arriving at the court, and
as soon as the bird saw him, it began to sing and the flowers fell
from its beak and the King was cured. But then there suddenly
appeared an army. There were a lot of tents outside, and with

horror they discovered that it was Tarfe Bânû, who had come to
find the thief who had stolen her bird. She said that the one
who had stolen it must come to her at once; she would speak to
no one else. Everyone turned pale, but Ibrâhîm said he would
go. He dressed up and then went to her; she received him very
well and said that she had sworn on oath to marry him because
he had succeeded, in spite of all the persecutions and witches,
in finding her and the bird, and he was the only one worthy of
becoming her husband.

So Ibrâhîm married Tarfe Bânû and later let Maimûne come
as well, and they lived happily to the end of their lives till death,
as destined by fate, overtook them all.

The Nightingale Gisar

Now we will take an Albanian variation which is called "The
Nightingale Gisar." *Gisar* comes from the Turkish word
hezâr, which means "thousand," but there is no definite
explanation for this name. According to the footnote, *hezâr*
has to do with "The Thousand and One Nights," which
would again be the miraculous bird which is connected with
that; or with "The Thousand Stories"; or it has a thousand
feathers; but actually it is simply called "The Nightingale
Thousand."[40]

Here is a very nice variation of the trouble at the beginning
of the story:

There was a King who had three sons, and his desire was
always to go into the mosque and pray. He built a beautiful
mosque, and when it was finished he went to pray there. A
Dervish came and said that the mosque was very beautiful but
that the King's prayer was ineffective. When the King heard
this, he had the mosque pulled down and built an even more
beautiful one somewhere else. Again he went to pray but the
Dervish came again and said the same thing, so he pulled down
the mosque and built another, using all his money to build a
really beautiful mosque. But when this third mosque was
finished, he went there to pray and again during his prayer the
Dervish came and said the same thing.

The King got up and went to his palace and sat there very
depressed because he had no money to pull down this mosque
and build another, and he knew that all his prayers had no
effect. His sons noticed him sitting lost in thought and very
troubled. They asked him what was the matter and said that
they still had some money, that they also were kings, and
couldn't they help, and why was he so sad and thoughtful. The
King answered that he had used all his money to build the
mosque but his prayer was ineffective, and the sons asked why
this was so. The King told them that every time he prayed in the
mosque a Dervish came and said so. Then the sons said that he
must try again and that they would catch the Dervish and ask
him what could be done. And again the Dervish said to the
King that the mosque was very beautiful but his prayer was
ineffective; the sons caught him and asked why. The Dervish
replied that the mosque was more beautiful than any other
in the world, but the nightingale Gisar should sing in it, and
then it would be something not to be found anywhere else
in the world. The sons asked him where the nightingale was,
saying that they wanted to go and fetch it, but the Dervish
answered that he had heard about it but didn't know where it
was. So they let him go, and, as you can imagine, the King
wanted his sons to find this bird.

Again they went to the crossroads and found a stone on
which they read: "If you go one way you will come back and if
you go the other you are lost and will never come back." Again
the youngest took the way from which one does not return, and
he came to tigers and ogres, but always the female tiger protected him against the male tiger and he escaped. [I have to skip
a good deal because I do not wish to insist on the details of the
quest.] Finally he succeeded, for he was always shown the way
after a while, and at last, after having stayed with three eagles,
who could transform themselves into beautiful girls, for three
months, they brought him to the place of the nightingale Gisar.
The owner was a Queen called "Beautiful-of-the-Earth," and
she too was surrounded by a number of guards and wild
animals. When everybody was asleep, he went into her room,
and there he found four candles burning and four unlit candles
on the table. Those which were burning had nearly burned out,

so he blew them out and lit the new ones, and, as everyone awoke, the three eagles brought him back with the bird.

The same thing happened again. He met his brothers, who were jealous that he had the nightingale, and they took the cage and pushed him into the river, but the nightingale stopped singing.

Then Beautiful-of-the-Earth came and asked who took the nightingale; when the eldest brother went to her, she asked him where he found it and he said on a cypress tree, and she had him beaten up until he died. When the second brother heard that her cannons were set to fire on the palace and on the town and had already half destroyed it, he went to his father and told him the truth, that they had thrown the youngest son into the river. The King then sent men to search for his youngest son, who was half dead and scarcely able to breathe and couldn't speak. They hauled him out of the river and as soon as he could speak, the nightingale began to sing so beautifully that everybody was overcome.

As soon as Beautiful-of-the-Earth heard the bird sing, she had a red carpet laid from the palace to her ship, and the youngest son rode down on it with the nightingale, and Beautiful-of-the-Earth came to meet him and he told her exactly how and where he had taken the bird. So they married, and are still living and enjoying their lives, and rule as King and Queen.

The Bird Wehmus

And now a much more peasant-like variety is an Austrian fairy tale from Siebenbürgen called "The Bird Wehmus," the word "Wehmus" being a distortion of "phoenix."[41]

> There was a parson and his wife who had three sons. The two elder sons were very proud, and the youngest was modest and humble and had to stay at home and was called Aschenpuddel [the same as Cinderella; for a male, Cinderello would fit best!]. The parson became very ill and was in great pain, and all the doctors in the country were called, but no one could help. One day at eleven o'clock in the morning a wonderful bird came and sat on the roof of the parson's house and began to sing; its

singing was like faraway music, and pearls fell from its beak. The moment the bird began to sing, the parson got up and was completely cured, but at twelve o'clock the bird flew away, the pains returned, and the parson was tortured again. Day after day, the bird came and the parson would be relieved for an hour, but then his illness returned.

"Mother," said the eldest son to the parson's wife, "if Father can be cured by the song of the bird, we should catch it and put it in his room. Make me some cakes and I will go on the quest and catch it." His mother made him some cakes and gave him some wine, and he departed; toward evening he came to a hill over which he had seen the bird fly. He was tired and hungry and sat down to eat and drink, but he had scarcely done so when a fox came along and said, "Good evening, Brother, good evening, God bless your meal, couldn't you share a little with me?" "Oh yes," said the parson's son, "do you see this stick? That's what I'll give you!" And he threw the stick at him. So the fox ran off and disappeared into the wood. At last the beautiful bird appeared and flew through the bushes, and he tried to catch it but couldn't, for the bird had flown off. After looking for a long time and never finding it, he went home. The same thing happened with the second son, who was also haughty with the fox, and he saw the bird disappear into the bushes but couldn't catch it.

Then the third son went, and when the fox asked him for a bit of his meal, he gave him some, so the fox settled beside him and asked where he was going and what he wanted. He explained what he was looking for, and the fox said, "If you think it is here, you deceive yourself; it only flies through the bushes and then goes far away to a rich King to whom it belongs, and there it sits in a golden cage. If you want to take it to your father, I will show you the way, and if you ask the King he will surely give it to you."

So they set off at once and after three days and nights arrived at the King's castle. Two monsters guarded the entrance, but with some little magical poem which the fox had taught him, he put them to sleep and entered, and in the same way he overcame the two dragons.

The King had two beautiful daughters who were like the Sun and the Moon, and the son stared at them so long that he nearly forgot what he had come for. But then he saw the marvelous bird in a golden cage. When it sang it was like faraway music, and pure pearls came out of its beak. So he told the King about the trouble and the King said, "Oh yes, take the bird Wehmus to your home; but when your father is cured, you must bring it back again."

He went back and told the fox about the beautiful girls, and as they approached his home, the fox said, "Now I have to leave you, but don't stop near a trench or you'll get pushed in. If you want me at any time, just clap your hands and say 'Siweklach' [that is just a meaningless spell-word] and I will help you." Then, of course, the same thing happened; the brothers met him, and when he was inattentive for a moment they pushed him into a morass, into which he sank further and further. But just in time he remembered the magical word "Siweklach," and the fox came and lowered its tail and pulled him out. After that, the fox said, "Now wash yourself, go home, and don't be afraid of your brothers because it will come out that you found the bird; but should you get into trouble again, call 'Siweklach,' and I will help you."

The fox disappeared, Cinderello went both sadly and happily home, and the brothers mocked him, asking whether he had caught the bird. He cried and complained to his mother, telling her what his brothers had done to him; she didn't know whether to believe him or not. When he entered his sick father's room, he saw the bird sitting there with its head hanging and not singing. But as soon as the bird saw him, it flapped its wings and began to sing. Pearls fell from its beak, and the sick parson arose and was cured from that hour. Everyone realized how deceitful the two elder brothers had been, and because of their evil hearts, the parson would not put up with them any longer, but drove them away.

The bird Wehmus stayed for a week with the parson until he was completely cured, and then the youngest son wanted to take him back. When he reached the forest, he clapped his hands three times and said, "Siweklach." The fox appeared immediately, and they went on to the King's castle together. Along the way the young man again told the fox how beautiful the King's daughters were, and he asked the fox to help him win the younger one, which the fox agreed to do. He said that, upon their arrival at the palace, he would transform himself into a beautiful jeweler's shop in which the young man would be the jeweler when he emerged from the castle; thus would they lure the girls into their power. Everything else should be left to the fox. When they reached the castle, the fox took one step forward and one step backward, turning a somersault, and said, "One, two, three," immediately transforming himself into a wonderful jeweler's shop. The boy went into the castle, returning the bird, and the two girls accompanied him to the exit.

When the girls saw the wonderful shop, they went in and were delighted to see all the beautiful things in it and to hear that they belonged to Cinderello. But hardly were they inside when the fox began to race as fast as it could, and in the shortest possible time the shop stood by the King's palace. Only after they had looked at and bought a number of things did the Princesses notice that they were in a quite unknown district and they were furious at having been so deceived. The elder daughter was particularly angry and began abusing the merchant, saying, "You wretched cheat, you fox, you sorcerer," while the tears ran down her cheeks. But no sooner had she spoken than the shop had disappeared and they found themselves standing in a green wood, and instead of the fox there stood a beautiful Prince with golden hair. He knelt down before the elder Princess, saying, "Your words have redeemed me from a terrible spell. I thank you! An old wizard whose daughter I would not marry abducted me, and when I accused him of being a deceiver and a fox, he turned me into a fox, saying I should stay like that until the day when a girl freed me by using my own words. Now I am free and can return to my own kingdom."

They all returned home and, as you may guess, Cinderello married the younger Princess and the former fox married the elder girl. So there was a double wedding with two royal couples, and had we been there we also would have partaken of the wedding dinner. After the wedding, each couple withdrew to its own kingdom, and if they were humans they are still living there, if they are not already dead.

The last sentence expresses doubt as to whether they are real people or archetypes! Archetypes would not be dead, but humans would be, so that is the elegantly expressed question at the end of our story!

We now have a synopsis of this famous type of story, which in the Grimms' fairy tales is called, "The Golden Bird."[42] There the fox is redeemed at the end, in contrast to the Hassan Pasha story, where the wolf is not redeemed. But we will now concentrate on only a few general motifs.

4

The Four Tales
Considered

In the story of Hassan Pasha, the Sultan has a meaningless
depression: "I am sad, and irritated with everybody"; in "The
Bird Wehmus," the parson is ill; in "The Nightingale Gisar,"
the King cannot pray in an efficient way; and in the story of
"The Bird Flower-Triller," the King has a disease, which has
also to do with a religious problem, because it could be cured
by a fish which carries the Islamic Shi'ite creed on its
forehead. The theme is openly pointing toward a discussion
of the ruling religious principle and the bird, obviously, also
has to do with religious problems. It is not by chance that it
is a parson who has to be cured by the bird's song and that
the ruler's disease has to do with the fish carrying the Shi'ite
creed.

So we can conclude here, as Jung deduced from other
material in his chapter about the King in *Mysterium Coniunctionis*:[43] The King represents the dominant or the ruling
collective attitude, mainly the central religious representation of God. Every civilization is basically dependent in all its
features on its idea of God. If you have a central idea of God
as being good and evil, that will affect civilization differently
than if the idea is that God is only good; or, a civilization for
which God is only male will have a totally different structure
from one in which the Godhead is hermaphroditic, male and
female, as for instance in certain Hindu systems. It will
affect a civilization in every direction: its laws, its rituals, its
liturgy, its ordinary everyday life, and everything else. That

is why what Jung calls the *dominant* of collective consciousness very frequently coincides with the image of God, which
is the central religious representation in a culture.

It is well known that kings all over the world—or before
there were kings in our sense of the word, the chiefs of
primitive tribes—represent the divine principle, and that
they age and wear out. There are, practically everywhere,
rituals of killing or renewing the king, which probably on a
primitive level were first carried out literally, and later in
symbolic forms: the burning of a carnival King, or the
Egyptian Sed festival, where the King goes through a symbolic death and rebirth ritual every fifteen years. That is a
remnant of prehistoric times when, probably, the king was
killed and replaced by another king. The king is understood
in these civilizations as the earthly representative of God.
The divine spirit which a tribe or nation worships is represented or incarnated visibly in this world and therefore has
to undergo recurring processes of transformation.

Unfortunately, the conscious idea we have of the Godhead
undergoes the same fate as all other contents of our consciousness: it suffers from the tendency to wear out, and
becomes mere words which lose their emotional and feeling
substructure. It becomes an abstract formula and thereby
completely meaningless and inefficient. Just as in the my-
thologem of the king there are two possibilities, either that
of the king being killed and replaced by another king, or that
of going through a symbolic death and ritual of renewal,
there is the same possibility for dominant representations.
Either they have to be discarded and replaced by a new
concept or idea or symbol, or the symbol remains the same
but must be understood in a new form.

In interpreting fairy tales as we do here, we try to bring
out a new approach or understanding of age-old words which
have always been told and understood in some form in their
essential wisdom, but not understood in the psychological
form in which we understand and interpret them now. I feel,
with this clue of Jungian psychology, that it is possible to

renew such a story so that it again has the living meaning which people had always formerly felt in it. Nowadays fairy tales are only told to children and regarded from a literary and formal standpoint. Fairy tales, as a whole, have undergone a process of becoming mere poetical words, no one even hoping that any meaning might be conveyed by them which we could understand in an adult way. So it can be said that the Jungian interpretation acts as a renewal of the words of the fairy tale; the same thing can be done with any other representation. It can be renewed if it is linked again with its archetypal substratum, for then it becomes an emotional and feeling and intellectual total experience. One gets again the reaction of "Ah, now I understand it," with all its vivifying psychological effect.

Naturally such a thing is important for myths and fairy tales, or even minor symbolic facts. For instance, I once spoke with a young artist who had never heard about Jungian psychology. I had to discuss some technicalities, but then, by some jump in his mind, he asked me what the Christmas tree meant. And when I explained it in the symbolic Jungian form, he banged on the table so that I jumped, and actually roared like a lion in his emotion, crying, "Now I understand!" He was a Communist and had gotten into that absolutely flat materialistic rationalism of the Communist viewpoint; but the explanation of the tree got him, and he said that he must find out more about the symbolism of the Christmas tree. (I simply told him that the Christmas tree meant the supernatural inner process of the maturing of the human being, circumscribing the process of individuation; and that during this inner maturing process, again and again certain lights dawned upon one, for the process of maturing is simultaneously a process of gradual illumination, and it was that which brought about his reaction. That may not be very deep, but if someone has been brought up on stones instead of bread he will react like that.) There you see such a renewal: the Christmas tree to him, according to Communistic doctrine, was some kind of silly folk superstition, a kind of "opium for the people" affair, but it had been renewed by the psychological interpretation.

That is how a symbol which has become flat can be renewed; naturally one can say that this is all of minor importance, but it becomes much more vitally essential if it concerns the central content of a civilization, namely the symbolic idea of God. If that falls flat and no renewal is found, it is a much greater catastrophe than not understanding some minor points, and that is why so many myths circle round this theme of the renewal of the king. If the king is sick, the whole country is sick—that is primitive superstition—but, translated into our words, if the central dominant idea is deficient or not adapted to psychological needs any longer, then the whole of civilization is sick and then—as the dancing Dervish so nicely puts it—you can build the most beautiful mosques and your prayer will be ineffective.

If we make a synoptic comparison, looking at all the different stories simultaneously, one can see that in most of them (though not so intended, primarily) the bringing of the bird involves an anima experience. The motif of the bird at the King's Court together with a beautiful girl is repeated. The bird is owned by Beautiful-of-the-Earth, or by Tarfe Bânû, the most beautiful woman, and by getting or stealing the bird the hero comes into contact with this beautiful woman, and marries her at the end of the story. In our Tashkent story the horse is put above the woman, but even so there is a woman. Further, the old King is never eliminated or killed or pushed off his throne, but rather is cured, and one assumes that he continues to rule for a few years before he, in old age, leaves the throne to his successor. So there is no violent change of ruling principle, only a cure or a renewal. The ruling principle continues as before, but with the bird, which produces pearls and flowers from its beak.

The pearl is a feminine symbol. In Latin it is called *margarita*, as the name Margaret means a pearl, and in alchemy it has generally been used to characterize the silver-like feminine substance, in opposition to the golden male substance. In the earliest known alchemical texts, the pearl, because of its mysterious origin inside the shell of the oyster, is synonymous with the philosopher's stone. Since it was known in antiquity that the oyster made the pearl, it was interpreted that a very corruptible fleshly creature produced something incorruptible. It was not known at the time that the pearl is spun around a little bit of irritant, such as a speck of dust or sand.

The oyster is a fitting symbol of the corruptible, fleshly animal nature, but out of it is produced, or there exudes, this incorruptible thing. That naturally attracted the projection of the idea that within our corruptible body and bodily existence we might exude such an incorruptible substance as the body of the resurrection, the *corpus glorificationis*, the immortal body. Just as the pearl comes out when you open the oyster, so in death our fleshly existence would fall away and decay, and the immortal part of our personality, the pearl, would become visible.

Ground pearls were used as an elixir for longevity or for immortality, and continued to be sold even in the Middle Ages, when some kind of liquid containing ground pearls was given to ensure long life. The pearl has been a symbol of the innermost incorruptible center of human nature in Persian mysticism from early times. Even before, in alchemy, it was a symbol of the Self. But it is also related to the anima, the feminine quality, and if it appears in a man's material there is an anima quality about it, because of its soft, shining nature.

What we could call the anima background of our bird in some of the stories, and the fact that the bird produces flowers and pearls when singing, and that its music heals, point to the fact that the disease of the ruler, whether a sultan or a king or a parson (for the parson is the ruler of the village), must have to do with a loss of contact with the anima, the feminine psychic principle. That is beautifully represented when the Sultan says, "I am so sad and am irritated with everybody!" We know what men between forty and fifty generally are like when the anima problem becomes urgent, for then, having gone too far in developing their masculine consciousness, they easily get into such a state. Generally, if you dig up the trouble, the anima problem is seen to be right under the surface, and with it goes the whole problem of Eros, so that one could say that the ruling religious attitude lacks contact with the feeling side of life. It probably has become too Logos-like, too much on the intellectual side, or on the side of keeping to certain rules or views, so that feeling has slowly faded out.

The renewal which is intended throughout the story is thus not a change of the conscious ruling attitude or of its main content, but renewal by bringing back the feeling experience which is lacking, giving it a completely new color and dimension. After the ruler dies and the younger son brings renewal, there will be a further transformation, for he will probably rule differently. In some of the stories, it is even seen that the hero who succeeds to the throne becomes an especially wise king through reading the wisdom inscribed on the bird's feathers, and so is a different ruler from his father. By finding this new dimension of feeling experience in religious matters, wisdom and other insights are also improved.

With the exception of the parson story, where there are five people, we find the classical quaternio: the King and his three sons. The female element is lacking and is later introduced into the family as the owner of the bird. So the quaternio which first rules is not complete. In our Austrian story there is a male quaternio with the feminine element in it, and there are little indications which explain further, for Cinderello goes and complains to Mama when he is ill-treated, so he is obviously Mother's beloved son. The maternal element is completely there in the conscious ruling realm and not lacking as in the other stories. It is not a question of bringing in the feminine, but of creating the marriage quaternio. It is one of the few stories which end with not just a wedding, but a double wedding. The problem of bringing in the feminine was already solved but has now to be brought into a completely balanced fourfold structure at the end of the story, which explains why the fourfoldness is not emphasized in the beginning—the main problem is to balance out an already existing factor.

In the Siebenbürgen story, there is relatively little tension. It is short, naive, and not dramatic, which shows that it only corrects an aspect; it changes something slightly but does not have to go through all the depths and heights to bring out something completely new. We see that in certain dreams the tendency is not to change the conscious attitude but only to add some factor or give it a new shade. Such dreams are generally less dramatic in their structure than those in which the tendency is really to break the conscious attitude and give it a new direction.

It is strange that in the Islamic story of "The Nightingale Gisar" there should be such a lack of feeling in the prayer and in the mosque, because the Muslim religion contains much feeling. Jung often said that the cry of the muezzin from the minaret sounded to him like a longing love cry, a yearning, longing call toward God, and that one could not understand Islam by only looking at its intellectual content. An Islamic man's love for God is really—I must apologize for using the word—a kind of homoerotic love for God. This kind of feeling has always existed in the religious life of the Islamic world and even in Islamic mysticism, but the need to outgrow it and to bring in mature feeling by relating to the real woman has again and again been an urgent problem of this area, and continues to be so, right up to the present time. The dancing Dervish who goes into ecstasy is therefore quite rightly the man to point out to the ruler that his prayer is ineffective, for those deeper layers of religious feeling are missing.

I would like to comment briefly on a minor detail which repeatedly occurs in different ways, namely, that the third son on his quest makes a mistake, and through it he gets from the bird to the girl, to the horse, or from the bird to some other symbol and the girl, etc. The mistake is that he looks back at the golden stand on which the bird stood, or at the bowl which the Princess had; in the German story, it is even more refined. There, the golden bird he is looking for sits in a wooden cage and beside it is a golden cage; he feels that a wooden cage for a golden bird is not adequate, so he takes the golden cage, and then an alarm sounds, and he is caught. In the horse episode, which comes after the bird in the German story, he thinks that it is a pity to put a leather saddle on such a beautiful horse, so he gets the golden saddle, and everything is lost again. In the last episode, he allows the Princess to say goodbye to her parents and give them a kiss, but they wake up, and he is put in prison. He has always been warned by the helpful animal—by the wolf in the Hassan Pasha story or the fox in the bird Wehmus and in the German story—*not* to commit this mistake, and yet he does it.

If we look at the result, we can call it a *felix culpa*. In the Easter liturgy the sin of Adam and Eve in eating from the tree of knowledge has sometimes been called a *felix culpa* (fortunate guilt) because it brought redemption. Had they not eaten of the tree of knowledge, everything would have stuck in Paradise, they would have been bored to death, and the redemption and incarnation of Christ would not have taken place. One has to admit that it was fortunate that they committed the forbidden sin. A general archetypal motif, found not only in our religious system but also in fairy tales and innumerable myths everywhere, is that the hero commits a kind of mistake which, at the moment, releases a catastrophe, but, in retrospect, turns out to have been fortunate. One can thank God because, as we see here, the hero would not have found the girl, and the horse (in the Hassan Pasha story), if he had stopped short at the bird and not looked at its stand or at the girl's beautiful bowl. So, in the long run, and seen from the whole context, guilt deepens the quest or furthers it.

This occurs again and again in the individual's process of

becoming conscious, which is why we have short and long therapies: some people are quickly out of their trouble, while others take twenty years over a seemingly minor trouble without getting on with it. Then one sees how ambiguous it is to aim for a quick cure, and for people to be quickly satisfied, walking off once more into their former uncon- sciousness after having assimilated some part of their uncon- scious. In other words, there are by nature some people who are more superficial and others who have a deeper personal- ity. Some may have an interesting dream which, when they understand it, changes their conscious attitude and cures the symptom for which they started analysis. Then they just thank you and pay their bill and walk away, and never think about it any more, or very little. And there are other people to whom the same thing happens but it upsets them, because now they ask themselves *how* they got cured. What changed them? They need to understand and dig down into what has happened, and they ask a further question; and so they are led to a deeper realization.

Here it is not that our hero wants to find out the deeper thing, but he makes a naive and fatal mistake which forces him to go deeper. He has a kind of short circuit reaction, and this mistake then forces him to go involuntarily deeper, for he cannot simply obey the fox's or the wolf's orders. Here we have to understand something else: if the hero had not had the fox or the wolf to tell him not to do so, he naturally would have taken the golden bird and the golden cage. But, in spite of the fact that he has been warned by the fox and the wolf not to do this because it would lead to trouble, he disobeys.

Therefore we have to say that it is the instinctive part, the animal instinct, which advises the shorter or less deep way. If the hero does not do what the fox or the wolf tells him, he disobeys the instincts, which means, in plain words, that he prefers to stay in his neurosis rather than be cured. If you disobey your instinct, then you are split, you are two people; your instinct pulls in one direction and your conscious personality sets another direction. You have this inner conflict, a threat of tension within you which creates an energetic potential and the possibility of deeper inner experience. But when you go with your instincts, you are happy in a naive way, or living in the flow of life without inner complications. One sees this, for example, in stable people, mainly in agricultural countries. They live their lives through from beginning to end simply following their instinctive nature; and they live more or less without inner question or great trouble. Whenever some trouble comes up in life, a helpful instinct, the wolf, turns up and helps them out. If, for instance, such a man loses his wife, he will be unhappy and mourn for a time, and then his instinct will find some other possibility of life for him; it all happens without great inner question or musing over problems. It is simply the fox in him which tells him where the next possibility of life lies.

We can say that following the instincts is the "healthy" way, but also the way that does not lead to greater consciousness, and therefore sometimes it is necessary to resist the instincts. Such resistance has the advantage that it creates terrific conflict, from which alone conscious realization may spring.

We understand better now that the advice of the wolf and fox is ambiguous, for it simply means going the way of the healthy, normal instinctive life, the way in which one always solves such problems. Resisting this way means bringing in some conscious wish. The conscious idea is that the golden bird should sit in a golden cage and the beautiful horse must have a golden saddle, and it is natural for the girl one is stealing to say goodbye to her parents. That represents a higher and more human level than just taking the girl away, and to hell with it if she cries, for she will be happy later! To understand that she wants to say goodbye is the more civilized way, but such civilized behavior is an estrangement from the instinctual basis.

The cage is more difficult to understand, but it does bring the paradox that the golden bird *must* sit in a wooden cage and the beautiful horse *must* have a plain leather saddle. This probably refers to another age-old problem which has come up again and again in humanity: what does one do with a precious inner experience? If you do not ask that question, you are all right: but if you have a precious inner experience which changes your whole life, the natural thing would be to realize that you had it and never tell anybody—just as the man who found the pearl hid it again, hiding the kingdom of heaven within himself and not bragging about it in the marketplace.

We have a proverb which says, "the devil never sleeps," and with many people, when they have had an overwhelming or precious inner experience, the devil starts to bite them, saying that this must in some way appear outside as well. With introverts, naturally, the extraverted inferior shadow comes in and asks, "What is the use of being enlightened if nobody admires me because of it?" This is absolutely destructive, but so innate in human nature that anybody who has not yet assimilated his other side, the introvert who has not assimilated his extraversion completely, or vice versa, generally cannot help making this mistake.

In former times, it was a temptation to create a sect or a new movement or something like that; with us, it is a temptation to claim the ability to lead other people to the same experience and to give unwanted advice to those around us, if we have made some inner step forward, or even to make it a profession without having been pushed by an inner reason. You can take all those steps if the golden bird itself orders you to do so. If you wait until the bird says, "I want the golden cage, please get it for me," then the story is quite different, it is in accordance with that inner experience. But in our story, the Prince himself decides that the golden bird must sit in a golden cage, and there his shadow side comes in and makes him disobey the natural instinct.

Usually it is the eternal dissatisfaction and restlessness of the ego complex which brings about the catastrophe. Women generally sin in a different way; whenever they have had a happy love experience of some kind, they say, "When do we see each other again?"—which is the same kind of thing, and drives men mad. If something is positive, the devil has to spoil it in some way by bringing ego greed into it, wanting to make it a permanent thing.

Keeping an experience of the anima or of the Self intact is a tremendous problem, and has to do with this problem of the cage. The inner experience has to be preserved and to have a frame. What would be the best frame? Instinct advises the simplest thing, namely to keep it secret and inconspicuous and invisible to the outside, to hide it, so to speak, under a cheap and inconspicuous veil, which is the safest way of keeping such things unharmed. Ambition, or ego restlessness which has not been integrated, will never accept that, but, through such mistakes, will destroy the inner experience. However, one can say that it is a *felix culpa*, for it simply shows that the personality has a still bigger frame to fill out. There is a wrong desirousness of the ego because the personality has not reached its full development, and then, again and again, such catastrophes are inevitable in order to bring the whole experience into a more encompassing frame. So, after the event, we can say that the mistake was inevitable and a *felix culpa*, though it makes the person neurotic again. In our Austrian story, which doesn't have much tension, this part of the motif is lacking, so you see how everything always fits.

There is another motif which we must discuss in connection with this problem. It occurs in the Iranian story of "The Bird Flower-Triller," but not in any of the others. In that story, a Sultan who has three sons, Muhammad, Dschäm-schîd and Ibrâhîm, falls ill and the doctors say that there is only one remedy: if a green fish in the sea, which has a golden ring round its jaw, is caught and cut open and bits put on the Sultan's heart, he will be cured. A lot of money is given to fishermen who succeed in catching the fish and bring it to Ibrâhîm, but when the latter looks at it he discovers that it has the Shi'ite creed, "There is no God but

Allah and Muhammad is his Prophet and Alî his successor," written on its forehead, so he feels that he cannot kill it and has it thrown back into the sea.

This is a unique motif and therefore must refer to a specific national situation and have a less general meaning. If we hypothesize that the Sultan is the worn-out dominant of collective consciousness who needs renewal, then the doctor's idea that this fish could cure him is obviously the right thing, because the fish, in general, symbolizes a content spontaneously coming up from the unconscious. In many myths, the fish has the character of being a revealer of wisdom. For instance, the Babylonian Oannes taught all wisdom, and the priests of Oannes in Babylonia wore fish-skins. Manu as a fish saved the Vedas when they were lost in the sea. It can be said that whenever either some new wisdom is required, or an old one is lost and needs to be brought back to consciousness, the fish comes into action.

In Jung's book *Aion*, we find several chapters on the fish in alchemy,[44] where it again has the same features. The first *prima materia* is a round fish which has to be cooked and divided into four, and out of it is made the philosopher's stone. So the fish would again represent the original appearance of the central content; and if it is the dominant of collective consciousness in that civilization, it would mean that the dominant religious attitude has become obsolete, so the fish is needed to bring up a renewal.

Since the fish bears on its forehead the Shi'ite creed, that of the ruling religion in Iran, the new content which comes up from the unconscious does not carry with it a change of the ruling attitude, but probably only a new understanding of the already accepted truth. Many people rattle off their confession of faith which they learned in school or elsewhere without any thought or realization, until one day when they have an inner experience; then they can say, "Ah, *now* I understand. I never knew before what it meant!" That would mean that, in their own psyche, a revelation, a fish, has come to the surface with a message which is not different from the already existing *Weltanschauung*, but which renews it and gives it new depths.

This would be fine, but the trouble is that the doctors have said that this fish has to be cut into bits which have to be put on the Sultan's heart. Here there is another subtlety. We said before that the central content coming up from the depths of the unconscious is not a different message than the consciously accepted one; it is more probably only a new quality of experience. But the doctor's order is that the fish has to be cut up, which would mean sacrificing it, and also, psychologically analyzing it, bringing it up into consciousness. Therefore Ibrâhîm, if he has to cut up the fish—which he refused to do—would, with a knife (his thinking function), have to reanalyze its depths, and the characteristics of this revelation of the Shi'ite creed.

The Islamic religions of both confessions are book religions, which means that their basic belief is based on a past fact which is regarded as a definite revelation, not one iota of which has to be changed, but which has simply to be understood again and again in different ways and learned by heart and followed. There is to be no analysis of the basic original event. It would shock a Muslim out of his wits, for instance, if you asked such a question as: "Was Muhammad himself in a sound state of health when he received this revelation? Others have received such revelations; in what way could you, in fact, prove that the revelation Muhammad received was different from that which Moses received on Mount Sinai?" He would simply jump down your throat and say that there is absolutely no comparison, the one is true and the others are pseudo or minor revelations, and that Muhammad received the true and direct light of the Godhead, which has neither to be discussed nor analyzed. It would be absolutely sacrilegious to ask whether Muhammad's personal problems were linked with his revelation.

Therefore one can say that to question such a basic fact is in a way to destroy it, in the sense that you penetrate it with your critical mind, with the sacrificial knife, and do not let it live untouched. Of course, if there is a crisis in the dominating religious and cultural attitude of the nation, it would be the most natural thing in the world to go back to the original facts on which the whole civilization was based and to analyze them, just as, when an individual has gone off the track with a conscious attitude, we say, now let's retrace our steps and find out how this all started.

Apparently this terrific deed, which obviously would have cured the Sultan but would have led to very unsettling depths in the religious problem, is not Ibrâhîm's affair, for, from a feeling standpoint, he refuses to destroy the fish. We have to take that as a just-so story and not criticize it or say that Ibrâhîm was a coward in refusing to go into the depths of religious experience. If he had discovered some new revelation, he would have become a second Muhammad. Neither can we say that he was right to throw the fish back into the sea; we can only say that that is how the story tells it. He refused that possibility, but then took on the obligation of finding the Bird Flower-Triller, which I have already interpreted as a feeling renewal of the existing dominating religious attitude. The original revelation, which in itself is not touched or changed, acquires a new feeling aspect. All the other stories refer to this renewal, but only Hâtim at-Tai in "The Bath Bâdgerd" really goes to the bottom of the problem.

We can conclude that this is necessary from the little detail which says that if the fish had been cut up, it would have been put on the Sultan's heart, so obviously, though there is only this side reference, the old Sultan had some heart trouble—manager's disease, perhaps! It is the organ into which we project the feeling function which needs some cure; his feeling is ill, and that is why the Bird Flower-Triller, which produces flowers every time it opens its beak, cures his heart disease.

If we read the story naively, we feel rather differently about it because, in a way, this opening motif reminds one of the many, many fairy tales where a man, or the hero of the tale, catches the fish which asks to be spared, and he throws it back. Then in some later stage of the story, this fish becomes a typical helpful animal and brings something back which the hero has dropped in the water, or brings something up from the depths of the sea for the hero. If we compare the motif in this way, then it would be right for him to throw it back, because in such a situation that is what is usually done; but in our story, the fish does not reappear at all. Moreover, it would have been the pious duty of the son to sacrifice the fish for his father, if that was the only cure for him.

So this motif is strangely ambiguous; one does not know quite how to evaluate it, and it has no sequel in the story. There is no reward for its having been spared—nothing! It just appears and disappears again, and in such cases I generally try to take it as a strange dream motif, and to leave the question open without saying whether it should be this way or that way—taking it as a just-so story. The first possibility of renewal would have been to analyze the original experience from the unconscious, which probably would have led to an immediate new religious revelation. But this Ibrâhîm could not do; instead, he fulfilled the second possibility, finding the Bird Flower-Triller, and thereby effecting a renewal of the existing conscious attitude by restoring its feeling value.

Now we will proceed along the lines of the quest and compare the different stages in the five stories.

In all our versions, the hero comes to crossroads which are either trifurcate or bifurcate, and then there is a choice between two less disagreeable ways and one way to death; or a choice of only two ways, of which generally the one is relatively tolerable and not dangerous, and the other absolutely hopeless and involving death or great difficulties.

In the Iranian story, the "Bird Flower-Triller," there is an additional motif not found in the others; it is said on the tablet that the hero should take it with him if he chooses the path to death, and with it he later overcomes all the dreadful attacks of the witches. He just takes out his tablet and reads what is written on it and follows its instructions. Finally he even uses it as a weapon, throwing it at a witch's forehead and killing her. So the tablet also functions like a stone, or a sword, with which he can even kill the witches. In the other parallels the tablet simply gives an indication as to which way to take, and the hero takes it either because it is the only one left, his brothers having taken the other(s), or because he feels that it is the way he must go.

We must ask what this mysterious tablet found on the way means. It always indicates the way to the brothers after they have left home and gone into the desert, so that we can say that it appears as the threshold to the unconscious. Insofar as the tablet is never wrong and gives the complete and absolute orientation, and says clearly what will happen and what the situation is, we could compare it with what Jung called the "absolute knowledge" of the unconscious. In his paper on "Synchronicity,"[45] Jung says that a sort of "absolute knowledge" manifests in a cluster of synchronistic events which are meaningfully connected. That is, the meaningful coincidence of outer and inner facts, without any causal connection, conveys the impression of something being known in the non-ego sphere.

For those who have not gone into the problem of synchronicity, I will illustrate it with an example. Suppose a man is offered a job, and then dreams that he knocks down a child with his car. Let us assume that he is a creative person and that the new job would be lucratively advantageous but would hinder his creativeness. So if he does not accept it, he will have less money but more time for creative work; and if he takes the job, it will give him a lot of money but exclude the possibility of any private work. Then he dreams that in a very pompous car he knocks down a child, which clearly warns him that if he takes this lucrative job, he will destroy his own childlike creative nucleus. Let us assume that an accident actually occurs on the very same day, or on his way to accept the job. Now one can say that there is a coincidence of inner and outer facts; the symbolic inner situation of the person and the outer event coincide.

This is what we call a synchronistic event. We cannot say that the child acted and caused the dream, because the effect comes before the cause, and we cannot assume that the man's unconscious made the child run into his car, for probably that has some quite different causal chain behind it. But one can say that there is a meaning in this double inner and outer synchronistic event, for if we analyze the symbolism of knocking down a child, then we can say that that is the essential meaning of the event. Certainly it was not known to the man who experienced this! Had he known it he would probably have acted differently. Such a thing can only happen if there is a deep unconsciousness about the situation, but it *looks* as though *somewhere it was known*. Since the child ran into the car that very morning, it conveys the impression that the situation was objectively known, there was an absolute knowledge of it somewhere, but certainly not in the ego. That is why Jung says that behind the meaning of synchronistic events there is something like absolute knowledge.

Normally, dreams do not predict the future, or only in the sense that our future is conditioned to an extent by our psychological attitude. But this absolute knowledge appears in so-called telepathic dreams, as well as in synchronistic events. Such special dreams predict the future not only in a symbolic, but even in a completely concrete form. That would again be a hint that somewhere there is some absolute knowledge about the sequence of events, as if things were known ahead of time, outside what we identify as the source of consciousness, our ego.

Though less directly, this absolute knowledge also comes into the field of our realization when one has a definite premonition that some specific thing is going to happen, or a definite feeling that one should do a particular thing, but without any rational reason. Generally, there is a positive effect if one acts in accordance with this feeling. But it doesn't come very often and one cannot rely on getting it, even with regard to the most important questions. One tries to meditate and consult this inner knowledge, but it is screened off and it is impossible to get through to it, for its coming and going in the human psyche is absolutely irrational and we cannot bring it under our control.

Viewed from a psychological angle, the absolute knowledge is what is said in the history of religion to be a revelation. It is recorded in a sacred book and usually has been revealed by a prophet or some such person who is supposed to be nearer the Godhead. This is the historical parallel of what we would now call the experience of absolute knowledge. It is most often described in the different religions as the absolute truth, as something to be obeyed without discussion. There is the same idea in the tablet, not only in that of the law which Moses brought down from Mount Sinai, but also where it contains the absolute and indisputable basic text of the religion of the Old Testament.

Another parallel exists in alchemy, where there are innumerable legends as to its foundation. It was said that alchemy was conveyed by God to Adam's son Seth, or to one of Noah's sons (there are different versions of this); or God is said to have written down the basic rules of alchemical procedure and then given the tablet to a figure of the Old Testament. If it is Islamic alchemy, it was given to one of their prophets, or, if it is Graeco-Roman tradition, then usually the Egyptian Thoth (Hellenized as Hermes Mercurius) is supposed to have received this tablet, or even to have written it. This knowledge was then handed down through all the secret traditions of alchemy. The foundation legend of the text of the Tabula Smaragdina is an example: it is an emerald tablet on which the whole alchemical process is recorded in ten sentences of a highly symbolic character, revealed either to or by Hermes Trismegistus.[46] There is an additional variation in this alchemical version of the revealed basic law: the Tabula Smaragdina contains sentences showing how to make the philosopher's stone and at the same time it is itself also the philosopher's stone, so that actually the different sentences describing how one should produce the philosopher's stone are written on the stone itself. The stone reveals its own nature and how it is to be made, on itself and by itself. This is an important motif, because in our Iranian story the tablet is also used in this double way. It is a means of orientation at the beginning, saying, if you go that way, that and that will happen. Later, when the hero takes the tablet he can also use it as a magic weapon; it becomes its own wisdom and can be used as a means of action. There is the parallel that the tablet is more than merely an instrument of orientation; it is at the same time a supernatural amulet, or something which could be compared to the alchemical philosopher's stone.

We could interpret these revelations, which are based on the experience of what we call the absolute knowledge, in a double way. We can say that they are laws, which is why they are on stone tablets; or that there is a certain absoluteness or rigidity about them, which could be something negative. They are rigid laws or positive insights, for they represent a guiding insight which gives one an indication as to the next step. All these different tablets have a similarity, for whether symbolic or like certain ethical laws in the Old Testament, they are formulated in a specific and *lapidary* (we even say stone-like!) way.

As soon as an insight or a word is written on stone, that symbolically expresses the fact that it is now absolute, and no longer destructible—which is why, for instance, according to the Apocalypse, after the resurrection we get a new name written on a white stone and nobody knows it except the one who gets it (Rev. 2:17). Such a name is much more than only a new name; it gives an absolute identity, a consciousness of one's true personality. This sentence in the Revelation has been quoted again and again by the alchemists, the white stone being for them identical with what they meant by the philosopher's stone.

The emphasis on the necessity of having the basic truth written down on stone or some other indestructible matter is difficult for us to understand, for we are now in a civilization which suffers from too much superficial verbosity and thoughtless wordiness. We have to go into other inner conditions to understand the importance of this symbolism.

Since I personally have a certain scorn for words, I had for a long time great trouble in understanding this tablet motif. The first time it became clear to me was through the following event: An analysand who was very much of a borderline case had had some terrific inner experiences in which the "light visited her and she felt close to the God-head." She was very much overwhelmed by these inner experiences and in the asylum in which she was interned had been asked very awkward and outdated questions, whereupon she had shut herself up in mutism. At that time she had made up her mind not to talk any more about anything and to dive completely into that inner religious experience which, seen from the outside, would have amounted to a catatonic state. Under those circumstances she would have been obliged to stay in the hospital and probably would have lain in bed there for a long time without giving away anything which was happening inside her.

At this time she dreamed that she saw a series of American Indians, each of whom had received a golden ring. They had no mouths, for the skin had grown over their mouths. Then someone came with a knife and cut mouths into their faces and a voice said, "This is what has to be done." She woke up and, by herself, without any interpretation on my part, realized that she must talk to someone about her inner experience. She understood that the golden ring which the Indians had received was something similar to her experience and that the knife cutting the mouth open was important. That was the turning point, for through the fact that she could then talk over her experience with me, she did not become catatonic, and so far has not had to return to the asylum. By talking to me about it, she herself remained connected in the right way with her experience and neither became identical with it nor lost it again.

The voice here was a manifestation of absolute knowledge. Jung said that, generally, if people have a sudden voice in a dream, it settles the problem with absolute authority and removes all possible doubt. This authoritative experience would be like a telepathic dream, an invasion, a breaking-in from that sphere, for the voice told her that she needed to speak and she was completely convinced that she had to do so. What is even more interesting, though she did not find this out for herself, is that the people who had to have their mouths cut were Indians. Her religious experiences were slightly, though not absolutely, pagan; they had a certain heathen flavor about them, which was one of the reasons why she was afraid to talk about them, for they were not quite orthodox. That is why the dream said that she must cut the mouths of those Indians open. She knew nothing about American Indians; all she knew was that they were "pagans and primitives." One could say, therefore, that this religious experience had come to the primitive and religiously unprejudiced pagan layer of her personality, and that it was now absolutely essential that that part of her should open its mouth and talk about what had happened.

That gave me, for the first time in my life, more respect for the "word." I saw for the first time what it means to be overwhelmed in a primitive way by the emotional intensity of an inner experience and unable to express it, so that one disappears into the unconscious. For the first time I saw that the spoken word represents an act of remaining or becoming conscious and of keeping one's personal identity; that an insight which is formulated is on a higher level than one which has, so to speak, hit one's body but with which one has not connected on the conscious level. That is probably why, in a certain stage of the history of civilization, the sacred word recorded in all civilizations plays such an enormous role and is, as it were, the essence of the conscious cultural attitude of that human group whose whole civilized cultural life is based on a certain number of officially formulated deeper insights.

Thus we can interpret the tablet in our story as such a revelation of absolute knowledge, which has a guiding character. In certain versions it means even more—the saving factor, for example, as against the witches in our Iranian story.

I have not much trouble in formulating my own insights, and so until I analyzed this very uneducated woman, for whom it became such an achievement, I had not seen it like that. We now live in a civilization where the word is terribly misused: slogans, propaganda, blah-blah, talking all the time. People in Berlin have a marvelous expression for this: *"Hirn ausgekoppelt, Maulwerk geht im Leerlauf weiter"* ("brain de-clutched, mouth goes into automatic").

Though the voice from the unconscious has in general a positive function, it can sometimes mislead people. If one hears a misleading voice, then generally the character who speaks is described negatively within the dream. It may be this or that person, or a figure which looks like this or that person, who says with authority that this and the other thing should be done. Then you have to use your critical mind and ask, *who* says so? For the dream itself gives a hint as to who says it. It might be the animus, or a witch shadow, but normally, thank God, if it is such a misleading part of the psyche that produces the voice, then you have in the dream itself a hunch as to who is speaking. But when the voice which has this absoluteness about it comes, one does not feel that there is a being in it or behind it; it is formless, it is purely a voice which absolutely breaks into the dream event. Naturally, mad people do hear divine voices, but even then the voice is generally symbolically right—only the interpretation of the patient is wrong. The mistake in schizophrenia is that people lose their power of criticism and do not see in which dimension the orders of the voice must be realized.

I knew a woman who had a voice which sometimes was exceedingly benevolent, saving her from accidents and all sorts of things, but then sometimes it said absolutely destructive things like "Now go and throw yourself into the lake."

Once she fell in love with a very nice man and started a good relationship with him. One morning she woke up and the voice said, "Now you have to break off the relationship at once and never see this man again." Her analyst pressed her sufficiently to get her to ask the voice who it was, and the voice said, "I am Pan." Now Pan is a very ambiguous god and obviously cannot be simply obeyed, so her analyst taught her to relate to Pan as if he were an outer reality. Sometimes Pan said absolutely crazy things, telling her to behave too unconventionally, and then she had to say, "Look here, Pan, you lived two thousand years ago and we have gone through a bit more civilization since then; I can't do the things you suggest. In your goat paradise that was perfectly all right, but now things are a bit different!" Pan then generally gave in. He never kept his absoluteness, he just nodded his head and realized that perhaps he was not quite up-to-date.

So the Pan figure became, to use a primitive word, a familiar spirit of hers. One could say that that was an aspect of the animus in his double capacity; it was an animus voice and did not come from the Self. This voice had been diagnosed by a psychiatrist before as a schizophrenic symptom, and one could have said that if the woman had continued to obey it uncritically, as she was inclined to do, she would suddenly do the most crazy and destructive things.

It is one of the most frequent things in schizophrenia for a voice suddenly to say, "Do this or that." If one treats such people one can sometimes educate them by asking, for instance, whether it was a male or a female voice, or by saying, "Try to characterize who says what, in what style." Then the voices perhaps begin to have different personalities; one female will always say destructive things, and another constructive things, and they talk slightly differently. Really crazy voices generally use a different style of language: some speak in a very pompous, sacred kind of way, and there is generally somewhere a jester who makes very witty remarks in the middle of the pompous situation. I then tell the dreamer to notice that there are different people talking, that they cannot be taken only as *the voice*; for there is a witty one, a pompous one, and two females, so we have first to find out who is talking. For this reason the author of 1 John 4:1 writes, "Try the spirits whether they are from God."

But the difficulty is that as soon as you use such criticism, you put ego judgment above the voice; *you* have the last word, *you* decide whether it is the voice, if you ask what is likely to happen. Suppose the voice says, "Leave your family and go into the desert!" An inner urge told the Swiss saint Niklaus von der Flüe to leave his family—a wife with ten children, and the youngest only eighteen months old. He followed the voice, and a famous Catholic theologian wrote an article saying that he was just a misanthrope and a madman who left his family, and that the voice of God could never have ordered a married man to do such a thing! Niklaus probably asked himself the same question! To follow blindly could be quite dangerous too. The case of Saint Niklaus was a very striking example, where the voice told him to do something which, from the common sense point of view, was mad, and many people around him said so. It was only the *consensus gentium* at the end of his life, and the Pope a hundred years later, which decided that it had been right for him. Generally it seems advisable to keep a certain doubt in mind. Doubt leaves the door open so that one can return at a certain point if one feels that things become too destructive; or, a second experience might break through, correcting the first, and one would block that by taking the first too absolutely.

As an example, take Abraham, who was commanded by God to sacrifice Isaac. If he had not had terrific personal doubts and resistances, he might perhaps have missed seeing the ram. If he had gone with the attitude that he *had* to sacrifice Isaac, he would have just shut his eyes and killed the child, wanting to get it over with! But he didn't do that. He went suffering because he felt that he had to do it, but he had all his resistances to such a deed, and his natural feeling against it; and suddenly he looked up and there, at the last minute, was the ram to replace the sacrifice of his son. So I think that even if one gives in to the voice, one has to keep one's feeling, if one has some feeling against it, and one's doubts. That is essential, because those strange turns of fate can come, such as happened in what would have been the sacrifice of Isaac, where suddenly at the last moment God interfered by speaking again. Only if one doubts, then obedience becomes an ethical achievement.

The next important step in our Iranian story is that the tablet is used specifically against the witch. In the other stories the enemies are mostly devs; the Balkan story, there are tigers and lions, and in the Siebenbürgen story there are dragons to be overcome on the way. But in the Iranian story there are witches who have this specific trick of creating a *fata morgana*: first, there is the beautiful girl who, after having been exorcised, turns out to be a horrible old hag; and then, the hand which comes out of the water turns out to belong to a horrible murderous witch. In addition, they use magic and can create illusions. That is why the tablet plays the greatest role just in that story while in the others it merely gives directions and then disappears. We have to see this in connection with the context: the capacity to keep to this innermost certainty of the Self, which is specially needed when dealing with the illusionary Maya world, the illusion-creating factor, created by the negative anima power, and generally also the negative mother complex.

The ego usually is not up to such devilry, and there is nothing else but one's relationship to the Self, i.e., the tablet. But nowadays things are to a great extent reversed, for modern analysands often do not have such a tablet—which would make analysis rather superfluous—or sometimes they have it, and it makes work very easy, because instead of taking any trouble, the analyst can say, "Well, look at your tablet!" But most do not arrive with tablets in their pockets; they fall into this anima witch-work, into this web of illusions and illusionary feelings, with wrong transferences outside, or wrong enthusiasms from within. Then you can say that that is one of the factors which often forces a man to go deep enough into himself to find the voice of the Self.

In my experience, it is the anima who, for instance, likes to pull on one side. And when the man follows, she pulls on the other; and if he follows that, she pulls again on the first. So it is a "yes" and a "no." If he thinks that is how it is, and he is going to do it, then she comes in a dream which goes in the other direction. That forces the person slowly to discover that within this devil's play, there is one constant static factor underneath which can then, through all the suffering, be slowly discovered.

Here, however, we have the other situation: our hero has this tablet from the beginning, and that is what makes the story a bit flat; for every time he is confronted with a new situation, he pulls out his tablet and reads what he has to do, and acts accordingly. One can say that it works all right, and probably it mirrors a situation of civilization where men still needed certain conscious guiding principles against the play of their anima; they could not just go into the play and discover them for themselves. If we take the tablet as the absolute knowledge, one could also say that this hero has a connection with the Self which helps him every time; he has a capacity for meditating the form in which he can raise the inner voice from beneath the whole emotional, theatrical display of the witches.

The first two witches are very easy to understand because they create a kind of illusion of Paradise—of richness, beauty, beautiful women, and so on—and so they catch him, and he has only to see through it. More difficult is his last task, when he has to overcome those two witches who perform necromancy in the cemetery with the Prince, the brother of the bride he has redeemed. These witches do the same magical performance as the witch of Endor in the Bible, which, in the whole Mediterranean antique world, was one of the main features of witchcraft. They go to a churchyard and, by certain invocations and incantations, revive a corpse and then use it in one of two ways. Some witches ask the corpse questions, the answers to which were supposed to be the absolute truth; so through the corpse you could get knowledge not obtainable in any other way. Or, the corpse could be ordered to commit a murder, or to do certain other bad things which you would yourself not have done; it could be used as a puppet. That is more rare. Generally necromancy is used only, as the word *manteia* indicates, to get information which cannot be obtained in any other way. Probably the underlying idea is that the dead are close to the absolute truth; they know the hidden aspect of events. They are in the deepest layers of the unconscious and can be used as a kind of intermediary, just as in other ways a medium can be used.

In the whole of antiquity, such acts were regarded as absolutely sacrilegious, horrible, and criminal: something absolutely taboo. There is no positive necromancy, or I know no single example of it. But the use of mediums to hypnotize an adolescent boy and use him as a medium to get certain magic knowledge, was not always regarded as black magic, and certainly not at all as having this terrible criminal atmosphere around it. It used to be much practiced, and some thought it was just superstition or magic, while others approved. But to use a corpse was absolutely criminal, and something quite different from using a living medium.

We should therefore go deeper into this problem in our story. The natural feeling reaction would be to say that it means disturbing the dead, who have a right to their rest and should not be disturbed in their tombs. We even have a taboo feeling standpoint: it is absolutely criminal to disturb the last sleep of human beings. If we think about it further and take it symbolically, then it means that one regresses into modes of behavior which should no longer exist.

Different psychic complexes sometimes use a "body" for manifestation. For instance, if a man's anima is projected onto a woman, then through this projection, the anima has, so to speak, incarnated; she has embodied herself in that relationship. In this way, any psychological unconscious complex can incarnate through projection; as long as the projection works, it is a life factor, and one is even obliged to follow it up if one does not want to lose a part of one's personality. That is why, if a part of one's psyche projects itself onto a human being, or an object, or a place, it is absolutely wrong to rationally cut it off. One has to keep up a certain relationship or connection with this factor, so that the projection can come back. Many people act out symbolic things in a concrete form. For instance, they realize their feelings by painting something, or they can get at certain contents of their unconscious only by carving, and so on; through that physical activity they help to incarnate a certain part of their personality. If such an ability has died and is a corpse it would indicate that the projection had come back, or that this way in which a complex had hitherto manifested itself had worn out, and was no longer effective.

Let us assume that someone has to get at his feeling by learning to play the piano; but slowly this becomes an empty pastime and loses its numinous character. In such a case, one would see a dream insist that now the person should be able to express his feelings in a different form. But if one has once found a way to contact a part of one's unconscious personality through certain activities, then naturally one tends to slip back into that, and not make the step toward a new incarnation of the complex. Therefore, this bringing-back-to-life of the corpses really means regressively reviving such former activities when they are no longer required. Generally, that is opposed with arguments like: "but it has helped me"; "but it was the right thing"; "but it saved me in this and that way, and if I cut it out then there is no longer life," and so on. That is all true: it was life once, it was a form by which to contact the unconscious; but let the dead rest in their graves! Once something is outgrown, one cannot return to it.

I remember the case of a man who had ceased masturbating at about the age of puberty; in a certain situation when he had quarreled with his wife, he began again, instead of talking to his wife and putting the disturbance right. He then dreamed that he was trying to artificially revive the corpse of an adolescent boy, trying to bring it back to life. It was a horrible performance, because the boy tried to get up and couldn't, collapsing again. And then a voice said, "For God's sake, leave him alone, he's dead." It was a nightmare kind of dream which went on through the night, but it showed definitely what it means to revive a corpse. He had outgrown this adolescent habit, and if he revived it again, it would be regressing from the new obligation to relate to his wife. He was fighting the new step of feeling development and going back to the other thing. He had a tremendous mother complex, and that is a practical example of his inner witch trying to seduce him into reviving corpses instead of taking the next step. It is probably because of this symbolism that necromancy is looked on in all religious systems as a most criminal thing. Psychologically, it *is* in a way a criminal thing.

Strangely enough, going into the Beyond in order to revive the dead is different from disturbing the actual corpse on the surface of the earth. The dead, for instance in the Nekyia, in the *Odyssey*, do not get their bodies back by drinking blood, but only a kind of subtle body through which they can talk better. So to go down and give those people a subtle body through magic and then talk to them is not the same thing as what we have here. The illegitimate thing is to revive the corpse, which has the right to be left in peace.

The next motif we have briefly to discuss is the guiding animal, which appears in the European version as a fox, and in our Turkestan version as a wolf. The wolf and the fox are mythologically related, for the Latin word for fox is *vulpes*, which is our word for wolf.

The fox, both in our countries and in the Far East, is very frequently associated with hysterical disturbances and magical phenomena in women. In remote areas of Japan, it is still believed that hysterical women are possessed by foxes.

A German psychiatrist, Dr. E. Baelz, tells of a very interesting case he treated in Tokyo.[47] A peasant woman brought to an asylum was absolutely mute and in a strange state of complete dumbness. She would not answer anything; she would just give her name and hang around. And from time to time she would say, "Now it's coming!" Then she would put her hand on her chest and a kind of bark, like a fox's bark, would come up. She would get glittering eyes and, quite fantastically, tell off all the doctors. She even became mediumistic and told them that one doctor had had an affair outside his marriage with such and such consequences, and that someone else was troubled about something or other. In her "fox state" she proved highly intelligent and highly aggressive. After a while, she would start barking again and then that would fade away, after which she would be absolutely dumb once more. That was in 1907, but this seems to be a phenomenon which still exists.

Richard Wilhelm, the sinologist, also saw such a case. He was asked to go to a country farm where there was a case of fox possession. He could never make out if it was a hallucination or not, but as he walked toward the farm, he heard a woman utter hysterical cries in the farmhouse, and he actually saw a fox walking up and down on the mud wall which was around the farm and people pointing at it saying, "See, that's the demon!"

Not only is the fox something like the destructive animus, a nature spirit which enters women and possesses them, but it is also linked with the idea of making the elixir of life. In the Far East it sometimes is said to have the pills of the elixir of life in its possession. In Western alchemy also there is the idea that the fox guides people to the philosopher's opus, the idea being that it has something of the cunning ways of nature, the natural shrewdness which is needed to follow nature's subtle ways. Because of its red color, the fox is also associated with inflammations of the skin, and with fire. Where witch foxes turn up, there is suddenly a fire without any reason; and foxes provoke and are associated with lightning. So the fox also has to do with what we, in the words of Paracelsus, might call the *lumen naturae*, the light of nature in its positive and destructive forms. Fox possession also has to do, as this actual case of Dr. Baelz's shows, with the clairvoyance of the nature spirit in man, which is why it is often the animal in fairy tales which knows ahead of time how things will happen, and can give instructions to the hero in advance.

Strangely enough, the wolf also has to do with the *lumen naturae*, though on the whole, it is looked on as being a more uncanny and destructively demonic animal than the fox. In Greek it is called *lykos*, and the etymological root of the word is akin to our word, light: *lux*. Apollo is a *lykos*—a wolf-god. In this function the wolf has a positive meaning. Its bright eyes shine in the dark, and it howls at the moon in the dark. Certainly it is one of the animals of the sun-god Apollo in his nocturnal, winter, Boreal aspect, as a kind of luminosity like the winter sun, which, just in the darkest moment, comes up from the unconscious. Otherwise in mythology, the wolf is usually a destructive animal. One needs only to think of the Fenris wolf which gets loose at the end of the day in Germanic mythology, and of the wolf demons who, during eclipses of the sun and moon, try to devour the light of the sky and have to be chased away by noises and rattling, so that they cannot eat the sun or moon.

Just as the fox is related to the feminine principle, and a demon is related to women and witches, so does the wolf sometimes have a strange relationship to the mother principle. For instance, in Little Red Riding Hood, the grandmother, being inside the wolf, is, so to speak, replaced by the wolf. One could say that the Great Mother suddenly shows her devouring side by assuming a wolf's face. The wolf lies down in the grandmother's bed, and then, when Little Red Riding Hood says, "Grandmother, what great teeth you have," she answers, "the better to eat you with!" In some variations of the Germanic story "Frau Holle," the benevolent mother goddess, also appears with a wolf's head, and there

are many other Great Mother witches in European fairy tales
who have sometimes a wolf's, or even an iron wolf's, head.

The wolf is also associated with the god of war, Mars, or
Ares. It is his animal, and therefore it is also associated with
his metal: iron. For example, one of the mythological names
of the wolf in German mythology is *Isengrimm*—iron grim—
the wolf representing very much what one might call that
type of rage which turns cold and grim. You may all have
experienced a rage which, when it reaches a certain climax,
is suddenly replaced by a quiet, cold, murderous, grim feeling
of resentment. That is the wolf; it is that uncanny murderous
determination which springs from rage. This is not only
negative, because according to German mythology there is
such a thing as a holy rage—*ein heiliger Zorn*—which can
overcome just people when they see horrible injustice happening in this world. This holy rage takes possession of them
and makes them determined to restore order and bring light
into the situation. That is why the wolf is not only destructive. It all depends on how it is dealt with, and what the
situation is when it comes up.

In the Turkestan story of Prince Hassan Pasha, the wolf
definitely represents a positive power, for it always appears as
a helpful spirit, and at the end of the story is accepted at the
Sultan's court. It probably is to be seen here in a compensatory way, because Hassan Pasha is a bit too innocent, and not
up to the evil tricks of life. The wolf, which itself comes
from the dark side of life, is therefore the animal which can
give instruction. For instance, it says to Hassan Pasha,
"Beware of your brothers, for they will certainly harm you if
you meet them." Hassan Pasha does not listen, but that is
his funeral. In contrast to the naive Hassan Pasha, the wolf
always knows what is going to happen, has no illusions, and
sees things as they are.

In our European version, the fox is still more interesting;
although our wolf is what one would call a "helpful animal,"
it is not transformed. It remains a helpful animal to the very
end of the story. But in the naive Siebenbürgen story, the fox

has much more interesting qualities. First, it has a capacity for transformation: it makes a somersault and transforms itself into a jeweler's shop and abducts the Princess in this way. So it is really a mercurial spirit. In the very beginning it had been human; only by insulting it, and calling it an evil sorcerer and a fox, could the curse on it be broken. Then, at the end, it is redeemed, and transformed into human form.

In the German version of "The Golden Bird,"[48] which is another parallel to our five stories, there is also a transformation. At the very end of that story, the fox turns up and asks the hero to cut off its head and its paws. But the hero says he cannot do that, for it has helped him out of all his troubles; he cannot harm his best friend. The fox shakes its head sadly and says, "Then I'll never be happy," and returns to the woods. But later it comes back once more, and again begs the hero to cut off its paws and head. With a sad heart, the hero this time obeys, cutting off the paws and the head; and at this moment, a beautiful Prince stands there. He is the brother of the Princess whom the hero has married, and he is now redeemed, and marries the sister of the hero. So again, in the German version, as in our Austrian story, it ends up with a marriage quaternio.

In those two stories the fox is a pseudo-fox; it has been bewitched or cursed and is redeemed at the end. This is a frequent fairy-tale motif, so we might go into it and ask what it means, psychologically, if a helpful animal appears and remains as a helpful animal, or, if a helpful animal appears which in the end turns out to be a human being who has been cursed.

In his paper on the nature of the psyche,[49] Jung sketched the areas of psychic processes in terms of a spectrum, with its infrared and ultraviolet ends. He considered the infrared end to be the somatic area, the area of instinctual reactions and conditioned reflexes. At the ultraviolet end would be the area of the archetypes *per se*, behind the patterns or archetypal images.

If an animal is represented mythologically as a real animal, not a pseudo-animal, then it represents an instinctive impulse. Different animals characterize different styles of instinctive behavior. Obviously, the fox would represent more instinctual shrewdness and cunning, while the bull would mean more brutal impulsiveness, acting by strength. Each animal, if you amplify it in its mythological, zoological and biological contexts, represents a human pattern of behavior, but always with the accent on the instinctual, infrared area of the human psyche.

But if a spiritual impulse appears at the instinctual (infrared) end, where it does not really belong, then it has been "cursed" and forced to appear in animal, i.e., instinctive, form. Then the animal symbol represents not only an instinct, but also an archetypal or spiritual impulse, and it wants to be lived and realized on a human level. This is literally what the fox said: it had been a human being and then had been cursed by the sorcerer and so reduced to animal behavior. In such a case, we have to reckon with a process of repression in which this psychic content has been reduced to instinctive reaction, and that is all that has been left.

According to these amplifications, the fox is something like the spirit of nature, and therefore a close parallel to the god Mercurius of the alchemists, the light of nature. Up to about the seventeenth century this was a recognized concept, at least in the circles of the alchemists and of the natural sciences. Nobody thought of nature or of matter as something dead. For those people, it was animated by a spirit of its own kind, or a light which they generally called a *lumen naturae*, and which was, as it were, the living spiritual manifestation in natural phenomena. Only in about the seventeenth century was this eliminated from the scientific outlook and shouted down as a stupid superstition. From then on, therefore, the spirit of nature could no longer manifest itself or speak directly to the human being; it was relegated to the area of instinctive reactions—which is probably the curse which weighs on the fox, and from which it wants to be redeemed.

The redeeming process is very brutal. In one of our versions it consists of insulting it, and in the other in cutting off its head and paws. The hero does not want to do it, feeling that it is too brutal. To cut something apart with a knife or a sword generally stands for analytical dissection of an object, seemingly destroying it by that, but at the same time getting at the essence, or core. Also, by cutting off the head and paws of an animal, we cut off its intelligence, just that shrewdness. The paws generally stand for activity of movement and for seizing things. One could say that, in order to analyze this phenomenon, first its action must be stopped; for otherwise, it continues on the animal level and one is unable to realize the meaning.

Let us imagine that someone has such a growling wolf within—the iron grim. The natural action of that complex would always be to start an argument or to have persecution ideas, getting into an emotional row in an aggressive instinctive form. Very often, people with a paranoiac tendency have such natural activities of growling and biting. The wolf is never redeemed that way, for the libido in this complex has a tendency to realize itself in an instinctive form. They always have the tendency to project the shadow and constantly start some kind of row and quarrel. Only when they stop quarreling can they realize what is really behind these projections. The wolf also often represents a capacity which is very closely connected with people who have a wolf problem, namely, a general, all-devouring greed. The wolf and fox are very similar, but the wolf is always the victim of his hungry stomach. When that gets the better of him, he loses all his intelligence, so that you can fool or trick him by getting him into a chicken shed and slamming the door. Jung mentions this problem of greed in his paper on the transference,[50] where he says that very often such a terrific greed awakes in people that they want to eat everybody and everything—for example, to eat their analyst completely. It is not even on the level of a sexual transference, but on an even more primitive level, for it is "to have" the other: to have everything. People who are possessed in this way have to have everything: if someone has a car, they must have the same; or it might be a friendship, or any of a number of things. This desire to eat everything is very often the result of great frustration in childhood, which had built up a kind of bitter resentment on one side, combined with the greedy desire to have and eat everything. The "grim" then is a kind of sulky resentment, because one can't have the thing. Such people will always vacillate between trying to eat everything and consequently getting banged on the head, and retiring again into cold resentment and frustration. They get caught in a kind of vicious circle of cold resentment and greed, which is often fittingly symbolized by the wolf.

When someone has an unredeemed "fox" within, it appears more as the spirit which clearly evades a difficult situation by a swindle, in order to get out of some fix—as in not being completely confronted with one's own dark side and one's own being. There are many such analysands, who are deplorably clever in always avoiding the crucial moment in analysis by finding some cunning way out, starting other possibilities and never remaining cornered or up against the wall. It is the fox in them which does it, and by their evasion they never find out what is behind their inner fox, the tendency to blur over situations in a clever way. If, for instance, one presses a woman on her creative problem, she will certainly turn up stating that she is expecting another child; and in that way, for the next three years at least, she escapes the problem. During pregnancy, everything is filled out again by a life phenomenon, and escape from the inner problem is possible. Naturally, after the child becomes less dependent on her, she will again be up against the same problem. That is a famous and frequent way by which women evade their creative problem, and how a lot of unfortunate and unhappy children are born at a relatively late stage, when the mother should really do something else.

That is only one of the many, many examples of how people evade the onslaught of a problem in a natural instinctive way—through the fox, so to speak. Men, generally, are more likely to opt for some outer possibility. They suddenly find a job far away from their analyst, one which naturally they *must* take, as it is such a great opportunity, and seemingly the right solution, and so on; and so they just hop out of the hot cauldron at a crucial moment. It is a shrewd instinct in them which makes them do this, and that is why, if one wants to redeem the fox, the first thing is to cut off its paws, i.e., its possibility of action, and reduce it to inactivity, and thus force it to reveal its deeper meaning.

In both the Austrian and the German versions, a sorcerer is responsible for reducing the original human being to a fox existence, and in the Siebenbürgen story we hear that the sorcerer cursed the Prince because he would not marry his daughter. He represents the figure of the old "father of the anima," an older god-image. In the Mediterranean area that would mean an old pagan god, and in the German area a Wotan figure; in Greece it would be Kronos-Saturn, and among the Jews it would be an archaic Yahweh figure. This "father of the anima" has turned into a negative sorcerer and set a regressive trend, possessing, so to speak, the unconscious psyche underneath. One can see that it is only natural for a repressed content to regress and fall into more archaic layers of the personality and its older representations. One could say that, due to repression in consciousness, it then falls under the grip of some dark god-image in the unconscious, some dark regressive aspect of the Self.

More interesting is this motif of the fox turning into a jeweler's shop and abducting the Princess this way, because there is a parallel to this in quite a different story in the Grimm collection: it is called "Faithful John."[51] In this tale Faithful John is the servant of a Prince, and a kind of trickster figure who understands the voices of animals. He advises the Prince to have golden animals and little golden statuettes manufactured. He puts them on a ship, where there are many more such golden things, and in this way he attracts the Princess, enticing her to come aboard, and so abducting her. But it is Faithful John who has the idea, and who acts here very similarly to the fox in our story—except that he does not actually turn into a jeweler's shop himself. It seems so obvious that that is a way to catch a woman that one forgets to ask what it means symbolically. The Faithful John parallel gives us a hint, because in this case, according to the text, there are little artistic golden vessels, utensils, birds and wonderful animals in the ship; so this is a kind of magic, for products of artistic fantasy attract the anima figure.

If we take the anima as an inner figure, it would mean that the best way for a man to constellate or get hold of his anima within would be to produce images, and thereby catch his own soul. As you see from the way I formulate it, this is really what we try to do by the technique of active imagination; we produce fantasy images and so get hold of our unconscious psyche. Attracting the anima would be a variation of what we would call constellating the unconscious by active imagination. Jung first rediscovered this technique by playing with concrete materials, by painting images of his dreams, and even doing some playful building, thus releasing his unconscious fantasy and getting hold of his own unconscious. One of the royal ways for attracting and constellating one's own unconscious is by sitting down and playing, and producing the fantasy images in the way they come.

One can see, therefore, that the fox is not only the mercurial spirit in nature, but also the capacity for fantasying in the right way. The gift of fantasy creates a realm by which the anima figure, the soul, is attracted; for it is only through one's fantasies that one can actually get hold of what is going on in one's unconscious, in the dark side of one's personality. Dreams are only a passive way; we get some messages through them, but if we want to come into more intense contact and not be dependent on those single messages called dreams, which may or may not come in the night, then we can do it through the *imaginatio vera*, as the alchemists called it, in contrast to the *imaginatio fantastica*. The latter corresponded to what we would now call passive daydreams, which lead one nowhere and by which one does not get hold of one's unconscious. Most people, especially when they are tired, can go on with inner conversations or daydreams. They need only to sit down and relax, and they have an inner film rolling off before their eyes with perhaps some fantasy in it. That is the *imaginatio fantastica*, or wishful thinking. But the *imaginatio vera* is the bringing up, with great effort and truthfulness, of images constellated in the unconscious, and having an *Auseinandersetzung*, an actual ethical confrontation, with them. With the *imaginatio vera*, the alchemists say that one can literally get hold of one's own soul. Thus the jeweler's shop represents this way of getting hold of one's own unconscious through the right kind of inner images, and the fox is the spirit which can do it, or convey it to the hero. What produces the fantasy is the spirit of the unconscious (the fox), but the human being has to lend itself as a vehicle. If you don't take the brush or the pencil and give yourself as a vehicle to the fantasy, nothing happens; or it remains in the destructive stage of passive fantasy.

5

The Bird Motif: Conclusion

Now we should return to our main motif, that of the bird, because I have told all these five stories as a further amplification of the parrot problem.

In our Hassan Pasha story, the bird is called Anka, or Anka-Kush, and on its feathers are written wise sayings. The last sentence of our story says, "As Hassan always read what was written on the feathers of the mysterious bird, Anka-Kush, he became learned in all human virtues and ruled wisely over his Kingdom."

The Anka is a bird which often appears in Oriental fairy tales. *Anka* is the Arabic word for the Persian *Simurgh*, a bird which functions as does the bird called *Greif* (griffin) in German and Austrian fairy tales. It is generally a carrier bird, for it carries the hero into the land at the end of the world, or beyond the sea, or takes him back. Usually one has to climb on its back, and one always has to take a lot of food and have water to feed it. Sometimes the hero does not have enough food and has to cut some flesh off his own legs to feed the bird, so that it doesn't fall. So sometimes the bird asks for great sacrifices, but, being basically benevolent, it generally then heals the wound of the hero who has devoted himself to it with its beak.

The Arabic word *Anka* means a bird with a long neck, and the Persian word *Simurgh* means a bird of silver color. In folklore, Simurgh and Anka are enormous. When the Simurgh or the Anka spreads its wings, one does not see the sunlight any longer; it darkens the whole horizon. In many versions, it has in its feathers all the colors of all the other birds in the world, and that is why, in certain Oriental versions, it is also called the "thirty bird," from which connection we can understand why our nightingale was called "thousand." It is a bird which represents the collective soul of all birds. It is *the* super-bird which, as a totem spirit, contains all the birds of the world, or sums up the qualities of all living birds, which is why it is a thousand bird or a thirty bird, and why its feathers contain all the colors of the world. It lives two thousand years and lays enormous eggs and can even carry a camel or an elephant. According to certain Oriental versions, this bird has a human face, and there it comes close to our parrot, which has a human voice.

This bird is somehow a bit human, for either the face or voice is human, and it can speak like a human. According to certain folk tales, the birds had an assembly and elected Anka-Simurgh as the King of the Birds. This same miraculous bird reappears in our Austrian fairy tale in the form of the phoenix, the strange name "Wehmus" is a distortion of "phoenix."

The phoenix played a great role in antiquity and survived as a symbol of Christ in the Middle Ages and also in alchemical symbolism, on which Jung has elaborated in *Mysterium Coniunctionis*.[52] The phoenix, when it feels itself ageing, builds a nest out of aromatic plants, mainly myrrh, and then burns itself in it. In the ashes a little worm is born, which moves about like a caterpillar and slowly acquires feathers, and then develops into another phoenix. Thus, in Christian times the phoenix naturally became an allegory for Christ, for He, too, resurrected.

In alchemy, there is a famous *peregrinatio*, or journey, described by the seventeenth-century alchemist Michael Maier, who relates how he goes through all countries looking for an animal or a bird called Ortus. Ortus means the rising sun and is also a name for the East, the place of the rising sun; this is similar to the phoenix. He does not find this bird, which is obviously, in this connection, a symbol for Mercurius, but, at the end of the story, finds one of its feathers. Jung, commenting on this journey of Michael Maier,[53] writes that the Ortus is connected with the phoenix as a well-known allegory of the resurrection of Christ, and the resurrection of the dead. It is a symbol of transformation. It is amazing that the Erythraean Sibyl shows Maier the way to the phoenix and not the way to Christ. It shows where he can find Mercurius, which indicates very clearly that, for Maier, Christ and Mercurius were the same figure.

It is interesting that this phoenix is called by Maier a remedy against rage and suffering, *remedium irae et doloris*; for he who finds this bird is cured of all suffering and affect. It therefore shows something like a possibility of spiritual transcendence, or of getting above these most common sufferings of mankind. The phoenix, according to Jung, is a bird of the spirit, and it is important to say that here the goal of the journey is not a human figure (it would be if it were Christ or Mercurius), but a bird, which is a more impersonal symbol. This compensates the too-personal representations in the Christian religion, though the Holy Ghost also has the appearance of a bird, and that the alchemists were mainly interested in the Holy Ghost hypostasis of the Godhead.

We might say, therefore, that the likeness to a human being—it can talk like one and has a face like one, but is basically not a human being—is stressed in all these aspects of the bird. In other alchemical parallels, the bird, representing Mercurius, the substance of transformation, is also sometimes represented as an ouroboros, the snake which eats its tail—for the bird flies up and eats its own wings, and then falls down, and is, in this way, reborn. An antique eagle saga, that eagles can eat their feathers and so make themselves fall down to earth, has been transferred to all the alchemical birds. This was a symbol for the chemical precipitation of a volatile substance. Whenever a substance was sublimated into steam, into what the alchemists call a volatile form, then the precipitation, or the steam, coming back in liquid form, was very often represented as such a bird, which plucked itself of its feathers and fell to the ground. The bird thus represents a process in which the spiritual aspect, or the *prima materia*, becomes visible and returns in a purified form, in some liquid or solid form which, psychologically, would represent a process of realization. In its bird shape, it is like a spiritual hunch, or a mental realization, in a more or less ecstatic moment. It refers to an inner spiritual experience which is, or remains, transitory, if it does not come down to earth again.

Most people, sometime in their lives, have a moment in which they realize something exceedingly meaningful, or have some kind of religious insight by which they are tremendously, emotionally gripped and elated. They feel that now things are all right; but strangely enough, the damned thing does not last; slowly the misery of life ties into them again, and two or three years later this whole inner experience seems lost. That is why, according to the alchemical view, the bird is not the whole thing, but only a beginning; it is a guide toward inner experience. It is one of these first elating experiences, or realizations, which one can have, but it is still necessary for it to eat its wings and come down in some solid form again. That is, the inner experience consolidates, and instead of being a kind of emotional spiritual experience, it becomes a realization in the most literal sense of the word. We use the word "realization" rather too lightly; but if we "realize" something in its basic meaning, it becomes a real thing forever. And that, in that sense of the word, is what is still behind the bird. This is why Mercurius in the alchemical process is very often compared in its volatile form to a bird; it is called a goose, or the chicken of Hermes, or a swan, or an eagle, or a vulture, or the phoenix. There is the same parallel in the Cabala, where the *Sefira Yesod* is also called a bird.

There is more about the different bird aspects of the *prima materia* in Jung's commentary,[54] and about its not-yet-definite character: namely, that it represents a stage of development of the *prima materia*, but not yet the goal. This explains why, in the Bath Bâdgerd story, the bird had to be shot in order to find Gayomard's diamond. The diamond would be the definite realization, the inner experience of the Self having become absolutely real and no longer volatilized and capable of getting lost after a moment of elation.

The Sufi mystics in the Orient have realized much along these lines. And in Persia, naturally because of the close proximity of India, they compare their Simurgh with the Indian swan, the *hamsa*, which is a symbol of the inner Atman, or the inner immanent experience of the Godhead (we would say, of the Self). The Sufi mystic Farid ud-Din Attar actually wrote a book called *The Thirty Bird*, or *The Conference of the Birds*,[55] in which the Simurgh flies toward God in a long pilgrimage. Attar ends his book by saying that God is a mirror in which everyone only sees himself. So when the "thirty bird" approaches this mirror, it first sees itself; but then, "it disappears forever as the shadow disappears in the sun."

Here we see the same idea, that there is still something behind the bird. This time it is not the diamond, but the mirror of the Godhead, which is compared to the light of the sun; the "thirty bird" simply disappears into it like a cloud sucked up in the sunlight, or as the shadow of the night disappears in the rising sun. Seen in this light, according to Attar, the bird would still be the subjective intuitive experience of the Godhead, which only leads toward the real experience. One might compare this with Saint Paul's "For now we see through a glass darkly, but then face to face." The bird is still this mirrored experience, and in certain Persian versions there is a clear hint that it is only an intuitive hunch of something still more real, yet to be found behind it. It is the transformative substance, the process of individuation; the diamond or mirror of the Godhead would then be the goal, which would mean an absolutely concrete realization of the Self.

If we now make a survey of all the fairy tales which have been circumambulating the bird, we see an interesting phenomenon: sometimes the bird is described as the goal itself, with nothing more behind it. This is so in "The Bird Flower-Triller," in "The Nightingale Gisar," in "The Bird Wehmus," and the story of "Prince Hassan Pasha," who, till the end of his life, reads what is written on the Anka bird's feathers. In the Spanish story, "The White Parrot," the bird is the goal of the quest, and in the *Tuti-Nameh* the bird is set free, but circles our happy couple and visits them from time to time. Then there are those Persian tales with Shi'ite and Sufi influence, where the bird must be shot to find the goal behind it; or where, as in the quotation from Attar, it dissolves into the experience of the Godhead. One could say, therefore, that in wandering westward and coming across the Arab world into Europe, the bird has lost some of its deeper meaning; it has lost something of what in the Far East has been realized, but, on the other hand, we will see that it has also acquired something different.

In the beginning we counted the different figures of the Spanish tale: the Count and Countess and the two children. Afterward there is a new quaternio: the boy and the girl and the witch and the butler, the evil man; and then the restoration of the Count and Countess and the children, the overcoming of evil, and the white parrot as the new center of the quaternio. If we count the figures in our Oriental fairy tale, we can see that, in "The Bird Flower-Triller," there is an uncomplicated intermediary set of figures: at the beginning, there are the Sultan and his three sons; then comes the whole journey, and at the end there are Mälik Ibrâhîm and the two ladies, Maimûne Khatun and Tarfe Bânû. We will put the bird in the center, and then a question mark: for there are only three figures grouped around the bird. Then in "The Nightingale Gisar," there is a quaternio at the beginning (the King and his three sons), with only a couple at the end: the hero and his bride, Beautiful-of-the-Earth, and the bird. So again, as far as the number of figures is concerned, there is even an impoverishment. At the end of the Turkestan story, there is Hassan Pasha with his bride, the wolf and the bird—only two human beings. In "The Bath Bâdgerd" story, it is even more interesting, because the hero has the diamond in the end. The Queen and her lover marry, but Hâtim walks off with the diamond, so there is a complete falling apart of groups: there is a *coniunctio* in one kingdom, but Hâtim goes back home to Yemen with the diamond, inherits the throne, and nothing is said about his marrying.

In the Siebenbürgen story there is a very complicated pattern. There are the parson and his wife and three sons. One son goes on a journey and comes to a King and two beautiful daughters. On the bay he meets the fox, so that those two come together as a twin pair who always walk together. They acquire the two ladies, the fox turns into a human being, and in the end there is a double marriage, namely, the parson's son and the former fox, and the two Princesses. The King is left alone and probably dies soon. The two evil sons are chased away, for the parson is angry with them for having slandered the hero. Here the parson, and his wife in the background, and the King, are outside the border, but a double marriage is formed in the middle. The elderly figures stay around, but no longer play a role; and what happens with the bird is not said at all! Let's hope it stays with them, but we don't know. The bird in the last sentence no longer seems to be of essential interest.

If we compare these numerical constellations, we can see that it is not possible to say that one is a good tale and another a miserable variation, an impoverished re-telling. In a queer way, some stories enrich one motif, and then there is a loss on the opposite side; and others enrich a different motif, with again a loss on one side. It is as though one had a diamond and turned it so that there would always be one facet coming to light and another disappearing in the darkness.

This is an illustration of the fact that we should never try to evaluate the different stories as being good or bad versions.

Generally, if a version is alive, it has some living message to convey which has to be taken as such, and not whisked away for another version which pleases us more; that is probably also why so many versions of these tales exist. This has been a terrible cross for all folklore specialists, who ask why there are so many versions, why they are not unified. It is obvious to us that it is always the same story, but that the light is shifted onto a different problem, and personally I believe that this has to be seen in connection with the cultural conscious attitude of the people among whom the tale is told. We could say that in the Far East story of "The Nightingale Gisar," the motif of the *coniunctio* is not particularly the main theme of the story. The hero gets the most beautiful girl on earth, but there is not much problem made around that; what is emphasized in the Eastern stories is the religious mystery of the bird, for that is closer to their consciousness. For instance, unless the nightingale sings in the mosque, prayer is of no use. There it is quite consciously put forward that it is a religious problem, and in the Persian versions, there is even a realization that this bird is a kind of first intuition of an experience which guides the hero on his way to realize the Godhead. One could say, therefore, that the religious, spiritual aspect is enlarged upon and the *coniunctio* motif not very much emphasized.

In traveling to Europe, this type of tale has lost some of its religious background, but has acquired a new motif, for the bird becomes the center. The bird becomes the motif of establishing the marriage quaternio, which is a symbol of totality, of the realization of the Self.[56] The emphasis lies not so much on the motif of an elated spiritual realization, but of a human realization. It includes the problem of the human relationship between man and woman as essential to our idea for the process of individuation, but not as essential to our idea for the process of individuation in the Near East.

Whether this means progress in comparison with the Near Eastern versions remains to be subjectively judged. For our feeling, it certainly does, because it means a much greater humanization of the powers of the unconscious. It is not a highly spiritual civilized consciousness confronted with a practically inhuman and demonic unconscious; but rather, the unconscious, in the form of animus and anima, has become semi-human, or at least a human-shaped Godhead, and by that we can relate to it in a reliable form. It makes the relationship to the unconscious something like a constantly living human phenomenon, in contrast to an ecstatic one-sided spiritual experience.

Perhaps I am a bit caught in defending the European version as compared with the other; but I do not mean this in any absolute way. I only want to point out that there are different temperamental and national inclinations, and that for us, it is impossible to think of a religious society in which the feminine element is completely suppressed and excluded from spiritual experience. In Europe, this process is developing more and more, as opposed to the patriarchal tendencies of Oriental civilizations.

All the fairy tales which we have analyzed are very profound and differ from many others, which are less deep. They all circle around the process of individuation, but to my mind, if one puts many of them together, one sees much better how, in the collective form in which a fairy tale gives the pattern of the process of individuation, one can read certain of its specific aspects. The process of individuation, as understood by Jung, is essentially something which can only take place in an individual. It therefore cannot actually be mirrored in a collective tale, for it is not a collective phenomenon. Thus, *we can never say that the fairy tale represents the process of individuation, per se; for it does not, it cannot.* The process of individuation is *per definitionem* something that can only happen in *one* human being, and it always has a unique form. However, in spite of being a unique event in a unique human being, it has certain typical recurring features which repeat themselves and are similar in every process of individuation. In that way, one can say that such tales mirror typical phases in the process of individuation of many people, and these typical phases are emphasized according to the national collective conscious attitude of the people among whom they are told.

The ruling religious system of any group of human beings contains essential aspects of the process of individuation, for otherwise it would not be a religious phenomenon. But often it lacks certain accents, or it no longer responds to certain human needs which might change according to the changes in civilization. Then comes the phase where the ruling religious and social system no longer expresses the basic psychological needs of the people; so, there arise these compensatory tales, which emphasize or bring to light what is now needed. In European versions, the motif of the *coniunctio*, the marriage quaternio, seems to be one such important motif.

Also beautifully illustrated in our series is the connection between alchemical symbolism and fairy tales, which is strikingly close as an actual historical influence, going both ways between folklore and alchemical symbolism. The alchemists, in order to express their chemical processes, constantly used symbolic images taken from fairy tales; and very often they tried to describe alchemical processes by parables. Where they did not use their own dreams, like Zosimos, they very often used folklore motifs; conversely, many alchemical parables and much symbolism have been included in fairy tales, so that there is evidence of a natural affinity between the two areas. Both, as Jung pointed out, are compensatory undercurrents complementing the ruling conscious collective attitude. Alchemy has done this service to the ruling conscious Christian attitude of our European countries, and through this undercurrent, the endeavor to complement and enrich the ruling Christian symbolism and system is made. Folklore, naturally, would tie in with this, putting it at certain moments in touch with these symbolisms, which accounts for many close connections. In the Orient, such close connection is perhaps due to the fact that, in that civilization, wisdom has always been taught through the medium of parables and stories. Oriental alchemists and mystics both employed such stories, which completely influenced one another. That alchemical symbolism meant something like an individual religious experience, or rather an inner process which leads to an individual religious experience, was much nearer to the threshold of consciousness in the Orient, and occasionally even fully realized by certain individuals. In European countries, the same realization has also existed continuously, but often projected into matter. In Europe the romantic stories about God's spirit in matter have died out (except in certain Masonic and Rosicrucian circles) and given way to scientific hypotheses. However, the great physicists, such as Isaac Newton, Niels Bohr, Albert Einstein, and others, were still searching in some form or another for something like the Divine Spirit in matter. Today a surprising turn has taken place: many theoretical physicists are attracted to Eastern, mostly Hindu, philosophy and are rediscovering in that way the spiritual aspect of matter. At the same time they are seeking for a holistic interpretation of the problem. The only road, however, on which we can approach the wholeness which unites the outer and inner world is the road to our own wholeness, the process of individuation, for the psyche is the only immediate reality we can experience. Spirit and Matter, or Mind and Matter, are only abstractions of psychic experience.

The language of the psyche is myth. Ultimately, therefore, we can never reach beyond the symbolic images which the unconscious produces. In spite of all our interpretations, the parrot stories we have looked at will forever impart and forever keep to themselves their enlightening message.

Notes

1. *Spanische Märchen*, in *Die Märchen der Weltliteratur* (Jena: Diederichs Verlag, 1940), p. 155.
2. Joseph Campbell, *The Hero with a Thousand Faces* (Princeton, N.J.: Princeton University Press, 1973).
3. Helmuth Jacobsohn, "The Dialogue of a World-Weary Man with His *Ba*," in *Timeless Documents of the Soul* (Evanston, Ill.: Northwestern University Press, 1968).
4. C. G. Jung, *Collected Works* (Princeton. N.J.: Princeton University Press, 1969), vol. 9, I, para. 259ff.
5. Laurens van der Post, *The Seed and the Sower* (London: Hogarth Press, 1963).
6. Anatole France, *L'Île des pinguins* (Paris, 1908).
7. "Hansel and Gretel," in *The Complete Grimm's Fairy Tales* (New York: Pantheon Books, 1972), p. 86.
8. Cf. Marie-Louise von Franz, *Number and Time* (Evanston, Ill.: Northwestern University Press, 1974), pp. 87ff.
9. See Jung, *Collected Works*, vol. 13, para. 59ff.
10. Ibid., vol. 14, part 4, "Rex and Regina."
11. Ibid., part 2, "The Paradoxa."
12. Ibid., para. 74.
13. *Tuti-Nameh, Das Papageienbuch* (Basel: Haldimann Verlag, n.d.).
14. See Jung's interpretation in *Collected Works*, vol. 9, I, chap. 3.
15. *Persische Märchen*, in *Die Märchen der Weltliteratur* (Dusseldorf: Diederichs Verlag, 1958), p. 132.
16. Heinrich Zimmer, *The King and the Corpse* (Princeton, N.J.: Princeton University Press, 1973).
17. In an unpublished paper.
18. Emma Jung and Marie-Louise von Franz, *The Grail Legend* (London: Hodder and Stoughton, 1971).
19. Jung, *Collected Works*, vol. 13, para. 239–246.
20. Ibid., vol. 14, para. 86–87.

21. Marie-Louise von Franz, *Creation Myths* (Zurich and New York: Spring Publications, 1972).
22. See also Jung, *Collected Works*, vol. 13, para. 168; 458, n.3. Cf. also vol. 12, para. 456–461, and vol. 13, chap. 2. Cf. also vol. 14, para. 552–555.
23. E. S. Drower, *The Secret Adam* (Oxford: Clarendon Press, 1960).
24. Ibid., p. 22.
25. Ibid., pp. 22–24.
26. Ibid., pp. 24–28.
27. Jung, *Collected Works*, vol. 14, para. 552–555.
28. E. Wallis Budge, *The Book of the Cave of Treasures* (London, 1927).
29. Jung, *Collected Works*, vol. 11, para. 296–375.
30. Ibid., para. 348.
31. "Flying Saucers: A Modern Myth," in *Collected Works*, vol. 10, chap. 5.
32. Jung, *Collected Works*, vol. 14, para. 559–569.
33. Carl Schmidt, ed., *Mani: Kephalaia* (Stuttgart: Kohlhammer Verlag, 1940).
34. Jung, *Collected Works*, vol. 16, part 2, chap. 3.
35. Ibid., vol. 14, para. 602.
36. Ibid.
37. Laurens van der Post, *The Heart of the Hunter* (London: Hogarth Press, 1961).
38. *Märchen aus Turkestan*, in *Die Märchen der Weltliteratur* (Jena: Diederichs Verlag, 1923), p. 41.
39. *Persische Märchen*, p. 20.
40. *Märchen aus dem Balkan*, in *Märchen der Weltliteratur* (Jena: Diederichs Verlag, 1919), p. 228.
41. *Märchen aus dem Donaulande*, in *Märchen der Weltliteratur* (Jena: Diederichs Verlag, 1926), p. 315.
42. *The Complete Grimm's Fairy Tales*, p. 272.
43. Jung, *Collected Works*, vol. 14, chap. 4.
44. Ibid., vol. 9, II, chaps. 10, 11.
45. Ibid., vol. 8, chap. 7.
46. J. Ruska, *Tabala Smaragdina* (Heidelberg: Winters, 1926).
47. E. Baelz, *Ein Fall von Besessenheit* (Tokyo: privately printed, 1907).
48. *The Complete Grimm's Fairy Tales*, p. 272.
49. Jung, *Collected Works*, vol. 8, para. 384, 414.
50. Jung, *Collected Works*, vol. 16, para. 361.
51. *The Complete Grimm's Fairy Tales*, p. 43.

52. Jung, *Collected Works*, vol. 14, paras. 276–286.
53. Ibid., para. 285.
54. Ibid., para. 637.
55. Farid ud-Din Attar. *The Conference of the Birds*, trans. C. S. Nott (London, Melbourne & Henley: Arkana, 1985).
56. Jung, *Collected Works*, vol. 16, part II, section III.

Index

birth, 18f.
bitterness, 136f., 139
boar, 62
Bohr, Niels, 217
"Book of the Cave of the Treasures," 112
bottle, 94f.
bow and arrow, 130ff.
bowl, stone, 71f.
Brahmin, 83
brother-sister incest, 100
Buddha, 68
Buddhism, *see* Zen
bullfights, 12
Bushman tribes, 143
butler, interpretation of, 11, 13f.,
  16, 36

Cabala, 210
Cadmus, 99f., 104
cage, 48, 176f.
Campbell, Joseph, 13
castle, 127
cat, 21
Catherine of Siena, Saint, 26
Catholicism, 37, 56
Celtic folklore, 72
child, 19ff., 87
children, *see* star and star children
China: 19, 32, 106; *see also* Orient
Christ, 12, 24, 46, 112, 137, 213f.
Christianity, 12, 24, 46, 70, 97,
  100, 124, 144f., 216
Christmas tree, 169
Chymical Wedding, 120
collective consciousness, 8f., 27,
  45, 69, 168, 216
collective rules, 9
collective unconscious, 9, 113ff.,
  179
colors, 99, 103, 136
compensation, 8, 31, 56, 69f., 91
complex, 33, 86, 89, 93, 96, 194ff.

concentration, 131
conflict, 62ff., 100, 102, 175f.
coniunctio, 213f., 216
conscious behavior, 88
consciousness, 8, 46, 63, 215; *see
  also* collective consciousness
conscious personality, 17
constellation, 30f., 86, 103, 205f.
containers, 94
contamination, 33
copper, 43f.
corpse, 194f.
corruptible metal, 41
Count, interpretation of, 9ff.
cow, 100
crime, 45
crisis, 48
crystal, 15, 19
"Cuka Saptati, The Seventy Stories
  of the Parrot," 81

Dante, 117f., 123
death, 31, 43f.
delinquency, 138
delusions, 128
demons, 81f., 92ff., 101, 198
dénouement, 132
Dervish, 160f., 170, 173
desert, 92, 118, 122
destruction, 96f., 103ff.
devil, 92f., 177
devs, 152ff.
diamond, 91, 96, 98, 117, 127f.,
  133f., 144, 211ff.
dictator, 97
discrimination, 32
"Divine Child, The" (Jung), 19
divine child, *see* child
Divine Spirit, 217
djin, 73f., 92ff., 152
dog, 128
Don Juan, 50
Don Quixote, 9, 11

Index

one, 32
opposites, 54, 100
opus, 64, 197
Orient, 1, 29, 71, 88, 120, 216; *see also* China, India, Japan
Oriental motifs, 92, 101, 207f.
Ortus, 208f.
ouroboros, 64, 209
oyster, 171

paganism, 56, 92, 97, 188
Pan, 190
P'an Ku, 106f.
panther, 62, 99
parrot, 4; integration of, 11; and truth, 7f., 27
parson, 162ff., 213
participation mystique, 138
patriarchal societies, 12
Paul, Saint, 134, 211
pearl, 49, 91, 170f., 177
penguins, 25
Perceval, 90
Perseus, 13, 92
Persia, 70, 91, 106f., 211
Persian folklore, 27, 49, 56f., 64, 71f., 103, 145, 148
persona, 96
petrification, 4, 57, 66, 68f., 87, 132ff.
phallus, 64
Pharos, island of, 62
Pherecydes, 53
philosopher's stone, *see lapis philosophorum*
phoenix, 162, 208f.
physics, 33
Pilate, 16
Plato, 32
Pliny, 46
Poincaré, Henri, 114
Portmann, 141
possession, 93f., 196f.

Post, Laurens van der, 22, 143
prestige, 46
prima materia, 40, 64, 103, 107, 111, 116f., 136, 179, 210f.
"Prince Hassan Pasha," 150ff.
primitive tribes, 45
prison, 2, 6, 7, 26, 45f., 120
privatio boni, 100
projection, 194f., 202
Proteus, 62
psyche, 92, 146, 195, 204f., 217
Psychology and Religion (Jung), 119
"Psychology of the Transference" (Jung), 137
psychosis, 46, 96, 102, 123, 128f.
Pythagoreans, 32

quaternio, 6, 26f., 36, 58, 66, 112, 117, 172, 211, 214, 216
Queen, 54, 82, 91f.
quest, 182

rage, 47, 137, 199
Ramses, 13
rationalization, 94ff.
reality, 11, 102, 217
realization, 210, 214
reconciliation, 22
redemption, 150, 166, 200, 202ff.
regression, 93ff., 204
relatedness, 93, 137ff.
religious experience, 69
religious steering point, 48
renewal, 23, 45f., 54, 87, 103, 136, 169f., 172, 179, 182
repression, 14, 95ff., 104, 204f.
restoration, 7, 26
resurrection, 43, 47, 103, 134f., 209
Revelation, Book of, 101, 186
revenants, 14
ring, 187
Ripley, 45

OTHER C. G. JUNG FOUNDATION BOOKS
FROM SHAMBHALA PUBLICATIONS

The Child, by Erich Neumann. Foreword by Louis H. Stewart.

Depth Psychology and a New Ethic, by Erich Neumann. Forewords by C. G. Jung, Gerhard Adler, and James Yandell.

From Freud to Jung: a Comparative Study of the Psychology of the Unconscious, Liliane Frey-Rohn. Foreword by Robert Hinshaw.

A *Guided Tour of the* Collected Works *of C. G. Jung*, by Robert H. Hopcke. Foreword by Aryeh Maidenbaum.

Knowing Woman: A Feminine Psychology, by Irene Claremont de Castillejo.

In Her Image: The Unhealed Daughter's Search for Her Mother, by Kathie Carlson.

Power and Politics: The Psychology of Soviet-American Partnership, by Jerome S. Bernstein. Forewords by Senator Claiborne Pell and Edward C. Whitmont, M.D.

The Way of All Women, by M. Esther Harding. Introduction by C. G. Jung.

The Wisdom of the Dream: The World of C. G. Jung, by Stephen Segaller and Merrill Berger.

Woman's Mysteries: Ancient and Modern, by M. Esther Harding. Introduction by C. G. Jung.

*Published in association with Daimon Verlag, Einsiedeln, Switzerland.

Mary-Perry Miller
415-292-2261
Lucy Milburn 285-8250
re: superior